Foundation of Discovery

The Cause of Autism-Channeled

Written by Laura Hirsch

Published by Rainbow Books- 2010

Foundation of Discovery: The Cause of Autism-Channeled

ISBN: 978-0-9776653-1-0

To my sweet boy Trevor,

my love for you made this possible.

This book is dedicated to children with autism

and the families who love them.

CONTENTS

***

Foundation of Discovery

"For those who believe, no proof is necessary.

For those who do not believe, no proof is possible"

-Author Unknown

Introduction

This book that you are holding in your hands could potentially hold the keys to unlock the future for children with autism, and also prevent more children from acquiring autism. This book offers the promise of a cure. In order for that to happen, you will need to set aside everything you currently believe about the cause of autism, and possibly your spiritual beliefs as well, and look at this material objectively. All I ask is that you read the entire book with an open mind, and then decide for yourself.

After reading that the information in this book is channeled, I am sure you had a good laugh. I can assure you that this is not a joke. It is not fiction; this is a true story. Because of Publicity Rights, I cannot name certain spirits that came through in these sessions. Believe me, I applied for permission and my request was declined, and I have honored that. The reader will have to draw their own conclusions as to whom they think it is based on the information.

Even if I did choose to use names, I feel that this material should fall under the category of Informational Use, which the Right of Publicity doesn't protect. Everything else in this book falls under Fair Use. Plus, I have the Constitutional Right of a little something called Free Speech. Either way, names have been withheld to protect the innocent: me. My intention is to get this information out to help children with autism. The messages are what really matter, not who said them.

That being said, I am merely the scribe of this information. A reporter of what I've experienced. Although the story is mine, I am not the source of the information from the readings in this book. They came from spirit. I could not make this up if I tried. I am raising a child with autism, I don't have time to concoct something like this, nor would I. If your curiosity is piqued, I'm sure you're wondering how this book came to be. Let me give you a little background to help sort it all out.

First, let me assure you that I am not some gullible, naive, delusional woman with her head in the clouds. I am completely sane and have never done drugs. I am an intelligent, educated person with a BA in Speech Communications who is also very discerning and perceptive. As I will explain, I have had to deal with some very difficult situations in my life which led me to be open to new spiritual ideas and to look beyond our world for answers.

For this story to make more sense, I need to back up a bit here. I became a young widow in 1995, when I was only 27-years-old. My husband Darren and I met in college and were together for eight years. We had been married for only two years when he died in a car accident. I was devastated, but carried on. I remarried two years later and had two beautiful boys with my husband, Matt.

My older son, Trevor, now 11, was diagnosed with autism at the age of three. Regressive autism; as the majority of cases are today. He was normal, and then he wasn't. He scored a perfect ten on his APGAR test at birth and was a perfectly healthy baby. He walked and talked at nine months, and beat all of his developmental milestones. He was always in the 90th percentile or higher in height, weight and head size. He laughed and interacted, babbled and pointed; all the things he was supposed to do.

Between the ages of one and two, he began to lose skills that he had previously mastered, including speech. He began screaming a lot, not sleeping, not answering to his name, doing strange things with his hands, looking out of the corner of his eyes at things, and lining things up, among other peculiarities. I knew that something was happening but couldn't figure it out, and tried to reason away his oddities. He seemed to stall while his cousin, a year younger, surpassed him developmentally which made it more apparent that something was wrong with my baby.

I was six months pregnant with Trevor's brother, Damon, when his pediatrician suspected something was wrong at his three-year check-up. It was actually Sept. 11, 2001 when we went in for the evaluation that led to the official diagnosis. Yes, the day the World Trade Center was attacked, my own little world also crumbled down around me. Even with the diagnosis, I didn't believe it. This wasn't denial; it was an inner knowing that something happened "to" him. He was not born this way. You could see the changes in the home videos and pictures we took of him. He went from looking at the camera and smiling to not answering to his own name.

I was depressed and heartbroken, but something was driving me to find out what happened to my baby and to find a way to fix it. Eight months after the autism diagnosis, our family moved from southern California to Reno, NV. Although I survived losing a husband, as well as a divorce in 2005 from Matt, (whom I remarried four years later) nothing compared to the heartache I have endured regarding my son's condition. It is worse than death to me. Autism is chronic grief.

Before going any further, for anyone who has never had a reading with a medium or doesn't understand the process of channeling, a little "crash course" may be helpful at this point. First of all, a medium is a person who can receive messages from dead people (spirits) and pass those messages on to the living. The process of connecting to spirits and relaying the messages is known as "channeling." Think of the medium as an interpreter, getting the messages from those in spirit and relaying them back to the person getting the reading, who doesn't understand the language. The medium is either born with or has developed the skills to understand this language. We all have the ability to learn and develop this skill to different degrees.

There are many different ways in which messages from spirits can come through to the medium. "Clairvoyance" means "clear seeing." This is when the medium sees visions or images that the spirit shows them and then describes what they are seeing. "Clairaudience" means "clear hearing." This is when the medium hears the spirit talking to them and repeats what they are saying. "Clairsentience" means "clear sensing." This is when the medium senses the emotions or feelings of the spirit or even a physical sensation, such as a headache. "Physical mediumship" is when the spirit actually enters the physical body of the medium and uses their body in a physical way. Any or all of these things may happen in a reading, although physical mediumship is rare.

I became interested in channeling after my late husband Darren died. I read books written by mediums to help me understand the process of communicating with the spirit world before I was brave enough to try it myself. I was raised a Midwestern Catholic girl, we didn't talk to dead people where I grew up. But I needed to know for certain that my late husband still existed in spirit, and that he didn't just cease to exist. After my first reading with a medium, I went from skeptic to believer. The fact that a total stranger (the medium) could tell me specific, personal things that only my late husband and I knew was proof enough for me to believe that speaking to people in the spirit world was not only possible, but natural and healing.

Five years after Darren died; I wrote an autobiographical book called *Widowed Too Soon: A Young Widow's Journey through Grief, Healing, and Spiritual Transformation.* It was different than other books for young widows because much of the content was about my personal experiences with After-Death Communication, with and without the assistance of a medium. Connecting with my late husband in the spirit world was the biggest part of my healing process. Darren's death put me on a spiritual quest for answers that I probably would not have sought out otherwise. Just as having a child diagnosed with autism forced me (and many other parents) to investigate alternative ways of healing.

Once I published my book in 2004, I started to promote it at psychic fairs, mostly in California. There was an audience for my book at psychic fairs because mediums had booths at the fairs and the people who attended sought out that type of connection and information. I felt a bit like a fish out of water at first, but after a few fairs, I befriended many of the mediums, psychics, and other "weird" people, and found them to be very enlightened, and not so "weird." Some were a bit out there, but many were just normal, down to earth people who are more developed on a psychic level.

I was very connected to my loved ones in spirit and believed that they could help guide me to the help that Trevor needed. In fact, I first found out that Trevor was allergic to gluten during a reading when he was five. Once I removed it from his diet, he improved greatly. While I was at the psychic fairs, I was desperately searching for alternative methods of healing and answers from the spirit world to help my child. The fairs were a smorgasbord of tools and information for me. I was more drawn to alternative medicine anyway, so I was like a kid in a candy store at the fairs. After having an amazing energy healing session, I learned to do it myself (first Reiki and then later Reconnective Healing™) to help Trevor. I found many other methods of natural healing that helped my son improve, including essential oils, nutritional supplements and natural personal care products. I also had readings with medical intuitives for some insight on his health.

I loved to have readings from various mediums at the fairs to see how good they were for one, and second, to see who would come through and what messages they had for me to help Trevor. It was usually my late husband, but sometimes my grandparents or great grandmother who came through. I felt that they could see the "big picture" and their suggestions and guidance always helped me make better decisions.

Since I had already written a book that included After-Death Communication and planned to write another, I considered these readings "research." It was pretty amazing. I transcribed the good readings (yes, there were bad ones too) and was going to include the messages in a book. It was going to be about natural methods of healing and messages from the other side about autism.

In November 2007, I told a medium friend of mine about the book I was planning to write about autism, and asked her if she would be interested in channeling in some current information for my book. She said "yes." A few weeks later, she called me and suggested that we should do the book together, and channel in the whole book. She would channel in the information, and I would ask the questions, transcribe, and write the story. We would both do what we did best, and make it a joint effort. I immediately agreed, figuring I could always write the other book later, and we decided to get together the next day for our first session. She knew nothing about autism, but was willing to help.

She is a very gifted medium. Over the years, I had "tested" about 20 different mediums/psychics/medical intuitives in my research, and she is among the best. She had done many accurate readings for me and some of my friends and family members, including predictions that later came true. I wouldn't trust just anyone to help me with the most important thing in my life, helping my son. She had other "paranormal" gifts as well, including physical mediumship, where the spirit actually enters the medium's body and can see and speak through the medium.

She actually allowed my great-grandmother to enter her body during a reading for a short time, and she told me that she could not see very well, that everything was blurry. I told my mother about it afterward, and she said that great-grandma had cataracts and at the end of her life, couldn't see anything, couldn't make out anyone's faces, and just commented on how blue the sky was. So, that was pretty incredible to me. This medium could also do remote viewing, where she could see what was happening somewhere else. She told me some pretty crazy stories. The medium also helped police solve crimes, even some very high profile cases. Where do you think their "tips" come from? Sometimes, it is a medium. So, I was very confident in asking her to assist me in this endeavor.

The spirits that came through in this book were not summoned. They came through on their own and freely gave this information to help us. I was in that room for a reason and I was trusted with this information. However, I didn't blindly believe it without investigating it. I looked things up and the pieces fit. I didn't just blow it off. I was trusted to get it done and get it out there. I had an obligation to do it. Perhaps these spirits trusted me because I had already written a book, I had my own publishing company, I had a child with autism, and I was very open to the process of spirit communication. I could get it done.

What you are about to read is the true story of what happened when a parent of a child with regressive autism got together with a powerful medium to ask for assistance from the spirit world. Neither of us had any idea where this was going to go, or what we were about to uncover...

***

***Note to reader**: Each of the eight readings has its own chapter. The format for the chapters is that the medium's words are in all capital letters, mine are in regular text. My clarifications and some validations are within the text in bold italicized print like this. There is a section after each chapter called "Later Discoveries" that includes the discoveries that I made after the readings that validate the information given by spirit.*

CHAPTER ONE

(The medium that channeled this prefers to remain anonymous.)

MEDIUM: "TODAY IS NOVEMBER 29, 2007 AND LAURA HIRSCH AND I ARE HERE TO CHANNEL A BOOK. THIS IS OUR DAY ONE. WE WANT ANSWERS TO THE QUESTIONS

THAT ARE GOING TO GO IN THE BOOK. WE WANT THE HIGHEST AND THE BEST. WE ARE LOOKING FOR SOULS, ENTITIES, SPIRITS THAT ARE REALLY INFORMED ON THESE SUBJECTS AND WE WANT PHILOSOPHY, WE WANT FACTS, WE WANT FUTURE DEVELOPMENT, WAYS TO SOLVE THE PROBLEMS, AND WE WANT ENLIGHTENMENT AS TO WHY THE PROBLEMS EXIST. WE WANT TO COVER ALL THE AREAS THAT PEOPLE ON THE PHYSICAL LEVEL NEED ANSWERS TO. OKAY? SO YOU (LAURA) ARE GOING TO TRIGGER THOSE AS YOU GO ALONG. SPIRIT HELPED YOU FIGURE OUT WHAT QUESTIONS YOU ARE SUPPOSED TO BE ASKING, OKAY?"

(SHE SAYS A PERSONAL PRAYER) "OKAY, I HAVE MY SPIRIT CONTROL HERE, (HER SPIRIT GUIDE ON THE OTHER SIDE THAT ASSISTS HER IN READINGS) AND HE'S SAYING, THIS IS SOMETHING ENTIRELY DIFFERENT (FROM HER TYPICAL READINGS). AND HE COMES IN AND HE'S LOOKING AROUND. I ASK FOR THE HIGHEST AND THE BEST SPIRITS TO COME THROUGH NOW. I NEED THE HIGHEST AND THE BEST THAT HAVE TO DO WITH MEDICAL...THAT HAVE TO

DO WITH CHILDREN...THAT HAVE TO DO WITH PHILOSOPHY."

"NOW, LAURA, DO YOU HAVE SOME QUESTIONS?"

Laura: "Yes. First of all, what should the book focus on?"

MEDIUM: "IT SHOULD FOCUS ON HEALTH...CURRENT AND FUTURE."

Laura: "What is going on with the increase in diagnosis of all these children with autism, ADD and ADHD? What is causing these problems with our children?"

MEDIUM: "I'M PICKING UP A SPIRIT. I FEEL IT IS MALE. HE'S KIND OF WIRY. THE HAIR IS WIRY AND HE'S SAYING, DON'T YOU KNOW? YOU'RE DOING IT YOURSELVES. ALL OF YOU PEOPLE ARE DOING IT YOURSELVES. IT'S LIKE RUNNING THROUGH A RIVER AND THE MORE YOU KEEP RUNNING THROUGH IT, THE MUDDIER IT GETS. AND THEN YOU WANT TO DRINK FROM IT?"

Laura: "Are you talking about pollution in general? Poisoning our kids in different ways?"

MEDIUM: "AND THEN DUMPING...YOU DUMP STUFF IN THAT SAME WATER, AND THEN SHAKE IT ALL ABOUT! AND IT'S NOT THE WATERS OF THE OCEAN THAT I'M TALKING ABOUT; IT'S THE WATER FROM THE RIVERS. THE WATERS YOU DRINK. THE WATERS THAT ARE SUPPOSED TO BE CLEANSING YOU ARE BACKFIRING AND FAILING YOU."

"EVEN THE BOTTLED WATER THAT YOU THINK IS SO CRYSTAL CLEAR...YOU NEED TO WATCH THAT AS WELL BECAUSE THERE IS A LOT OF MONEY INVOLVED IN ALL OF THAT. MANY TIMES YOU ARE JUST RECEIVING THE VERY WATER THAT YOU'RE TRYING TO KEEP FROM DRINKING. SO, MANY OF THOSE COMPANIES ARE NOT FOLLOWING THE RULES. THEY SAY THEY ARE, BUT HOW DO YOU CHECK SO MANY BOTTLES?"

(U.S. consumers spend $15 billion annually on bottled water. Pepsi's Aquafina and Coca-Cola's Dasani are both made from purified water sources from public reservoirs.[1] About one-

---

[1]http://www.cnn.com/2007/HEALTH/07/27/pepsico.aquafina.reut/

fourth of bottled water is bottled tap water, and by some accounts, as much as 40 percent is derived from tap water, sometimes with additional treatment, sometimes not.[2])

"SO IT'S A LOT OF TAKING RESPONSIBILITY AND PEOPLE UNDERSTANDING WHAT THEY ARE DOING TO THEMSELVES AND THOSE AROUND THEM. BECAUSE IT WILL COME BACK TO BITE THEM. THOSE VERY PEOPLE THAT ARE HARMING OTHER PEOPLE AND THINKING THAT THEY'RE STAYING SAFE WIND UP INVITING AND MARRYING THE VERY PEOPLE THAT ARE SICKLY AND THEY BRING IT INTO THEIR OWN ENVIRONMENT. AND THEY WILL PAY...IT WILL COME BACK AROUND."

Laura: "Besides the water, what else? What about the vaccine connection?"

MEDIUM: "YOUR GOVERNMENT IS A BIG MONSTER! THERE IS A LOT OF SECRET AGENDAS, A LOT OF HIDDEN THINGS IN THAT AREA. TOP SECRET! TOP SECRET! BOY, THAT STAMP KEEPS STAMPING AND STAMPING AND STAMPING. THEY

[2]http://www.money.cnn.com/2007/07/27/news/companies/pepsi_coke/

SAY IT GIVES THEM MORE FREEDOM. THE PEOPLE ARE SUPPOSED TO HAVE THE FREEDOM, BUT IT IS THE GOVERNMENT TAKING OVER. THEY'RE THE ONES WITH THE FREEDOM. THE MONEY KEEPS GOING IN ONE DIRECTION."

"YOUR PRESIDENT (BUSH) GETS PAID A LOT MORE THAN WHAT IS PUBLICISED. BECAUSE EVERY PRESIDENT...THIS IS WHAT YOU SEEK, AND THIS WILL BE WHERE YOU CAN DIG UP YOUR ANSWERS...WHEN A PRESIDENT BECOMES THE PRESIDENT AND TAKES OFFICE, HE WINDS UP WITH SOME SHARES. AND EACH PRESIDENT IN THE PAST, AND THOSE THAT ARE COMING, SINCE WATERGATE, ALL HAS SHARES IN THAT SAME COMPANY. AND THAT WILL GIVE YOU YOUR ANSWER."

"IT IS AN AUTOMATIC THING THAT HAPPENS. IT IS LIKE PART OF A PACKAGE. THEY GET SHARES IN THIS COMPANY. SO IT IS NOT ONLY GOING TO BE THE CURRENT PRESIDENT, BUT THE PRESIDENTS FOLLOWING BACK TO WATERGATE."

<u>Laura:</u> "Eli Lilly? Lillygate?"

(Eli Lilly is a drug company/vaccine manufacturer that has ties to the Bush family. Former President George Herbert Walker Bush was once a member of the Eli Lilly board of directors; as was former CEO of Enron, Ken Lay. George W. Bush's Homeland Security Advisory Council member Sidney Taurel is the current CEO of Eli Lilly. George W. Bush's former director of Management and Budget Mitch Daniels is a former Eli Lilly vice president. There was a provision snuck into the Homeland Security Act, which was later removed, to protect Eli Lilly and a few other big pharmaceutical companies from lawsuits by parents who believe their children were harmed by thimerosal, a preservative containing mercury used by Eli Lilly and others in vaccines.[3] Note: this is not necessarily the company that was being referred to in the reading, but I had heard about Lillygate previously.)

<u>MEDIUM:</u> "PEOPLE KNEW SOMETHING WAS WRONG BACK IN THOSE YEARS, BUT THEY WEREN'T PINPOINTING IT. WHAT WAS GOING ON WITH WATERGATE AND ALL OF THAT WAS JUST THE TIP OF THE WRONG. BUT THE PEOPLE HAD A KNOWING, A PSYCHIC KNOWING, AND THEY WEREN'T

---

[3]http://psychright.org/articles/LevineLillyandBush.htm

REALIZING THAT THEY WERE GOING TO BE CAUGHT IN THE WHIRLWIND OF WHAT WAS GOING ON THEN. THAT WAS THE BEGINNING."

Laura: "The government mandates that our children receive all these vaccines, and then they make money off of it…is that what you're saying? Because they are financially tied to the company that makes vaccines?"

MEDIUM: "THEY DON'T HAVE AS MUCH CONTROL AS THEY USED TO, BUT THAT WAS WHAT WAS IN PLACE FOR A LOT OF YEARS. AND NOW, PEOPLE ARE FIGHTING IF THEY WANT GOD IN THE CONSTITUTION AND ALL THE OTHER AREAS. BUT THEY ARE FIGHTING THE WRONG THING. HUMANITY NEEDS TO GO BACK AND LOOK AT WHEN THINGS GOT INTO PLACE. THE WHOLE THING ABOUT GOD AND ALL OF THAT WAS IN PLACE WAY IN THE BEGINNING. THEY NEED TO LOOK FROM WATERGATE FORWARD. THAT IS THE TIME FRAME WHERE THE MISTAKES STARTED."

"THAT IS THE TIMEFRAME WHEN THE ILLNESSES WERE PUT INTO THE PEOPLE. BUT THERE IS MORE THAT IS GOING ON THAN THAT."

Laura: "I've heard that the government is actually releasing viruses and bacteria into people through vaccines and other ways to make us sick. Experimenting on us."

MEDIUM: "THAT'S BEEN GOING ON FOR YEARS AND YEARS. BUT IT DOESN'T GO BEYOND WATERGATE. THAT IS WHEN THE CORRUPTION STARTED. AND IT'S HARD TO CLEAN IT UP, BECAUSE IT IS LIKE ONE COMES IN, AND ANOTHER, AND ANOTHER. AND IT'S JUST REPLACING SOMEBODY. WHAT DO YOU DO? FIRE EVERYBODY AND START ALL OVER? A LOT OF CHANGES HAVE HAPPENED."

"IN THE BACKGROUND, OUR CURRENT PRESIDENT (GEORGE BUSH) HAS BEEN FIGHTING AGAINST THIS, BUT HE'S ONE PERSON. EVEN BEING THE PRESIDENT IS STILL NOT GOOD ENOUGH TO MAKE THE CHANGES THAT NEED TO BE CHANGING BECAUSE THE WHOLE CABINET OF PEOPLE HE HAS TO WORK WITH. SO, IT WILL GET BETTER GOING

FORWARD, BUT IT IS BECAUSE THE PEOPLE ARE SENDING OUT THEIR CRY."

"OUR SOIL IS VERY CONTAMINATED IN THE NEVADA AREA. IT IS VERY, VERY CONTAMINATED, AND IT IS COMING FROM THE DESERTS."

Laura: "Is it the mercury coming from the mines?"
(They use mercury to extract gold and silver, and Nevada is a big mining state.)

MEDIUM: "NO, IT'S MORE THAN THAT. IT'S COMING FROM... THE CREATION OF MILITARY WEAPONS. AND IT'S COMING FROM THE DESERTS. IT'S COMING FROM THE AREAS WHERE IT'S NOT POPULATED. BUT IT'S BLOWING THROUGH AND GETTING IN OUR SOILS."

"AND WE ARE TALKING TOPSOIL AND THAT'S HOW WE GROW THINGS. NEVADA NEEDS TO STOP GROWING FOOD!"

Laura: "Nuclear-type weapons? What weapon is it?"

<u>MEDIUM:</u> "THERE IS A WHOLE POPULATION OF MILITARY LIVING UNDERGROUND, AND THEY ARE WORKING ON TECHNIQUES... (HEAVY SIGH). THEY ARE WORKING ON TECHNIQUES TO KILL PEOPLE AND WHEN THEY DIE, THEY THINK IT WAS NATURAL CAUSES. AND THEY ARE GOING TO USE THIS ON THE ENEMIES OF THE WORLD."

"BUT THEN PRODUCING THAT HERE IS AFFECTING THE NEVADANS. IT SHOULD BE ALERTED IF THEY ARE GOING TO BE DOING THIS KIND OF WORK! THEY SHOULD BE ALERTING NEVADA SO THEY DON'T GROW FOOD BECAUSE THE FOOD GROWS ON TOPSOIL, AND THE TOPSOIL IS WHAT IS BEING CONTAMINATED."

"AND SINCE THIS IS A NEW THING THAT'S GOING ON, IT IS LIKE WE DON'T SEE IT AS CONTAMINATION BECAUSE WE DON'T HAVE RECOGNITION OF IT. IT IS NEW TECHNIQUE; NEW TECHNOLOGY IS WHAT'S GOING ON."

"THE UNITED STATES SHOULD NOT HAVE CONTROL OVER THE WORLD IN THAT MANNER. THEY SHOULD NOT BE ABLE TO SNEAK IN AND DROP SOMETHING, AND THE WHOLE

ENTIRE PLACE GETS SICK AND WIPE OUT CIVILIZATIONS THAT THEY DON'T AGREE WITH. THAT'S NOT HOW GOD INTENDED. THIS IS NOT A GOOD THING. ESPECIALLY IN THE SNEAK WAY THAT IT IS HAPPENING. IT'S ONE THING TO HAVE AN ARGUMENT AND TRY TO SETTLE IT, AND COME TO A CONCLUSION ABOUT WHAT NEEDS TO BE DONE, BECAUSE ALL LIFE IS PRECIOUS. YOU KNOW, WANTING THE UPPERHAND IS GOOD WITH A COLLECTIVE OF GOOD-MINDED PEOPLE WHO ARE PULLING IN THE SAME DIRECTION, BUT THIS IS NOT WHAT'S COMING UP."

"WHAT'S COMING UP IS...THIS IS MURDER...THIS IS MASS MURDER. THIS IS MASS MURDER BECAUSE THERE IS NOT COMPROMISE; THERE IS NOT LOOKING FOR A SOLUTION, LOOKING FOR SOLVING THE PROBLEM, OR CHANGING PEOPLE, OR HELPING THEM. THIS IS SAYING 'YOU'RE BAD' AND PLAYING A PART OF GOD. AND WE'RE NOT GOD. NONE OF US ARE GOD. AND ALL LIFE IS PRECIOUS."

"I'M GETTING SIX YEARS. SIX YEARS AND MORE OF THIS IS GOING TO COME TO A HEAD. THE HIGHER PEOPLE FEEL THAT THIS IS WHAT GOD WANTS, AND IT'S NOT. IT'S NOT

WHAT GOD WANTS. GOD DOES NOT WANT THEM TO BE HIM."

"I'M SEEING EARTHQUAKES AND I'M SEEING EVERYTHING FALL UPON THEM. I'M SEEING EVERYTHING FALL UPON THE VERY PEOPLE THAT ARE IN THE WORKS OF THIS."
(Nevada is the 4th highest state in the country for number of earthquakes with a magnitude of 3.5 or higher.[4])

"BUT AGAIN, THERE'S A LOT OF INNOCENCE BECAUSE THEY'RE WORKING UNDER INSTRUCTION. THE MILITARY HAS NO CHOICE. THEY HAVE TO DO WHAT THEY'RE TOLD AND THAT COMES FROM THE COMMANDER, AND THEIR COMMANDER, AND THEIR COMMANDER, WHICH GOES BACK ALL THROUGH. SOME OF THE PRESIDENTS HAVE WANTED TO CHANGE SOME THINGS, BUT THEY CAN'T BECAUSE OF THE CABINET."

"ARNOLD SCHWARZENNEGER IN CALIFORNIA, AS NAIVE AS HE IS...AND HE IS VERY NAIVE, CLEANED UP BEFORE HE STARTED. HE SAW THE CORRUPTION, SO HE GOT RID OF

---

[4]http://earthquake.usgs.gov/regional/states/top_states.php

EVERYBODY. THE ONLY THING IS, NOW WHAT DOES HE DO? BECAUSE THE EXPERIENCE IS ALL GONE. SO HE'S WINGING IT, BUT HE'S DOING THE BEST HE CAN. AND HE'S DOING BETTER THAN IF THE CORRUPTION WAS THERE. AND THAT'S WHAT NEEDS TO HAPPEN ON A HIGHER LEVEL."

Laura: "So what about our children?"

MEDIUM: "THE RESEARCH THAT NEEDS TO BE DONE SO THAT THE PROBLEMS CAN BE PINPOINTED IS... WHERE ARE THESE KIDS? BECAUSE THE NUMBERS, THE PERCENTAGES, ARE GETTING HIGH, BUT IT'S CONCENTRATED. IT'S NOT HAPPENING ALL OVER THE UNITED STATES. IT'S NOT HAPPENING ALL OVER THE WORLD. IT'S CONCENTRATED. IN CONCENTRATED AREAS, AND IT HAS TO DO WITH SOIL CONTAMINATION. THE FOOD AND THE WATER AND WHAT THEY ARE BEING FED."

"IF YOU TAKE THE VACCINE, AND YOU DO RESEARCH ON EVERYTHING THAT'S IN IT, IT WILL TURN UP AS SOMETHING MINOR THAT COULD HAPPEN. IT'S NOT DEATH. IT COULDN'T CAUSE AUTISM."

"BUT IF YOU TAKE THE CONTAMINATION IN THE SOIL OF THE PRODUCT THAT THEY'RE USING THAT'S GOING TO BE A FUTURE WEAPON, AND YOU PUT A DROP OF THAT INTO THE VACCINE, AND YOU COMBINE THOSE TWO, THEN YOU HAVE THE REACTION THAT WE'RE HAVING NOW. SO, AUTISM IS NOT COMING FROM THE VACCINE ALONE. IT IS AN INGREDIENT ADDED TO SOMETHING ELSE. AND THE THING IS, NOT ALL KIDS HAVE THE TWO INGREDIENTS, SO SOME DON'T HAVE THE REACTION AND SOME DO."

"BUT IT'S LIKE COMET. YOU PUT THE COMET DOWN AND IT'S POWDER, THE POWDER COMET. AND THEY'RE SHOWING ME IT'S PUT DOWN IN THE SINK AND IT'S NOT CLEANING, IT'S NOT DOING ANYTHING. YOU ADD THE WATER, AND THEN IT BLEACHES, AND YOU HAVE A CLEAN SINK. BECAUSE THEN IT TRIGGERS THE PRODUCT TO GO TO WORK."

"THAT'S WHAT'S GOING ON WITH WHAT'S CAUSING THESE KIDS TO GET SICK. AND THEN YOU'RE GOING TO SEE KIDS THROWING THEMSELVES AROUND, YOU'RE GOING TO SEE

KIDS SCREAMING BECAUSE THEY DON'T UNDERSTAND WHAT'S GOING ON IN THEIR HEADS. THESE ARE THE EFFECTS THAT THEY ARE HAVING ON THEIR SYSTEM. IT IS A NEURAL ATTACK ON THE SYSTEM."

<u>Laura:</u> "What are the ingredients that are combining to cause this? Is it thimerosal? It is the mercury preservative."

<u>MEDIUM:</u> "THE INGREDIENT THAT'S DOING IT, I DON'T KNOW THE NAME OF IT, ALL I DO KNOW IS THAT THE WHOLE BATCH OF WHAT THEY ARE GOING TO PUT IN THESE NEEDLES...THE WHOLE BATCH IS COMPLETE, AND THEN THEY JUST PUT A LITTLE BIT OF THAT IN IT, IT'S VERY LOW. IT'S NOT A MAIN INGREDIENT; IT WOULD BE LISTED AT THE END. SO, IT'S NOT A LOT IN THERE, BUT IT'S ENOUGH TO ADD THE WATER AND IT TURNS TO BLEACH."

<u>Laura:</u> "So are the two ingredients that are mixing together both in the vaccines, or is it part vaccine ingredient and part environment?"

<u>MEDIUM:</u> "PART ENVIRONMENT, PART VACCINE. IT IS NOT THE VACCINE ALONE."

<u>Laura:</u> "So they are getting exposure from the environment, and the trigger is the vaccine?"

<u>MEDIUM:</u> "THE SECOND INGREDIENT TO MAKE IT GO. LIKE THE WATER ADDED TO THE COMET, AND THEN THE BLEACH GOES TO WORK AND THEN IT WHITENS EVERYTHING. AND THEN THERE'S CONFUSION IN THE BODY."

<u>Laura:</u> "So what is it in the environment that needs to be cleaned up?"

<u>MEDIUM:</u> "THE MUDDY WATERS."

<u>Laura:</u> "Specifically, what?"

<u>MEDIUM:</u> "I'M SEEING POTATOES...AND THEY ARE A ROOT PRODUCT. I JUST SEE STUFF UNDERGROUND, ROOT VEGETABLES."

Laura: "So, the root vegetables are pulling in the contamination from the soil, and they are eating that, and the vaccine triggers a reaction?"

MEDIUM: "BUT I SAW POTATOES."

Laura: "What kid doesn't eat French fries?"

MEDIUM: "I SHUT MY EYES TO SEE IF I SAW SOMETHING ELSE....POTATOES, THEY HAVE A STARCH, HAVE A SUGAR, IT CHANGES IN THE BODY. POTATOES ARE ROUGH ON THE BODY IN THOSE CIRCUMSTANCES."

"YOUR CHILD WAS NOT BORN THAT WAY. YOUR CHILD WAS ***NOT*** BORN THAT WAY. HE WAS OKAY WHEN HE WAS BORN."

Laura: (choked up) "Yes."

MEDIUM: "YOUR CHILD HAS WHAT'S GOING ON WITH HIM NOW BECAUSE OF THOSE TWO INGREDIENTS. YOUR CHILD WAS HEALTHY."

Laura: (fighting tears) "Uh-huh."

MEDIUM: "AND NOW, AS WERE MANY, MANY CHILDREN...THE GOVERNMENT NEEDS TO STOP AND SEE WHAT THEY ARE DOING BECAUSE THESE PEOPLE ARE OUR FUTURE. AND YOU'RE TALKING...ARE THEY GOING TO GET IT TO 1 IN 10 BEFORE THEY STOP AND TAKE A LOOK?"

Laura: "How do we fix it? How do we heal them?"

MEDIUM: "HEALING IS GOING TO COME FROM A MAN THAT IS TAKING THE RESPONSIBILITY TO HAVE AN ANDTIDOTE TO THE PROBLEM THAT'S BEING CREATED, BECAUSE THE GOVERNMENT IS NOT GOING TO LET THIS GO. THIS IS A WEAPON THAT THEY ARE GOING TO BE USING; THIS IS A WEAPON THAT IS WRONG! BECAUSE WE ARE NOT GOD, WE ARE A NATION ***UNDER*** GOD."

"AND THE WAY THAT THIS IS GOING, THEY ARE GOING TO WORK ON ANOTHER VACCINE THAT IS GOING TO NEUTRALIZE IT. IT'S NOT GOING TO MAKE THE PROBLEM

GO AWAY; IT'S JUST GOING TO FREEZE IT, OR NEUTRALIZE IT. IT IS GOING TO BE THERE, BUT IT'S NOT GOING TO BE ACTIVE. LIKE HERPES...SOME PEOPLE HAVE HERPES AND THEY BREAK OUT; AND OTHER PEOPLE HAVE IT AND THEY NEVER HAVE THE SYMPTOMS. AND THAT IS HOW THIS IS GOING TO TURN OUT TO BE. IT WILL BE NEUTRALIZED, BUT IN SOME PEOPLE IT WILL SHOW AND SOME PEOPLE IT WON'T. THEY'LL START TURNING THIS AROUND."

"AND THERE IS RESEARCH GOING ON RIGHT NOW, BECAUSE THEY KNOW THE PROBLEM. THE GOVERNMENT KNOWS THE PROBLEM AND THERE IS A MAN THAT IS WORKING ON THE RESEARCH NOW BECAUSE HE'S TOP NOTCH. THERE ARE MANY PEOPLE WORKING ON IT. IT HAS BEEN ADDRESSED. THE GOVERNMENT KNOWS WHAT'S GOING ON. BUT THE BREAKTHROUGH THAT THIS MAN NEEDS...HE NEEDS THE INGREDIENTS."

"AND IT'S COMING FROM...IT HAS TO DO WITH WAR. IT HAS TO DO WITH MASSIVE...IT'S LIKE WIPING OUT CIVILIZATIONS AND THEY DON'T EVEN KNOW WHY OR WHO DID IT TO ATTACK BACK."

<u>Laura:</u> "It's like stealth biological warfare where the people get sick and they think it is something else. It is biological weapons." ***(Biological warfare (BW), also known as germ warfare, is the use of pathogens: bacteria, viruses, or other disease-causing agents as biological weapons.[5])***

<u>MEDIUM:</u> "THEY THINK IT'S NATURAL OR NORMAL AND THEY DON'T FIGHT BACK."

<u>Laura:</u> "What is the treatment, the cure?"

<u>MEDIUM:</u> "WE NEED TO EAT MORE OUT OF THE WATERS BECAUSE THEY ARE NOT CONTAMINATED LIKE THE LAND. TO BE HEALTHIER, WE NEED TO EAT MORE OUT OF THE WATERS. WHATEVER IT IS THAT YOU CAN GROW IN THE WATERS, FROM MEATS TO VEGETABLES...BECAUSE THE OCEANS ARE NOT CONTAMINATED."

<u>Laura:</u> "What about organic farming?"

---

[5]http://www.wikipedia.org/wiki/biological_warfare

MEDIUM: "YOU'RE STILL USING THE SOIL. YOU HAVE THE TOPSOIL, YOU'RE BUYING THE SOIL, IT'S STILL THE SOIL."

Laura: "They're just not adding more poisons to it, it is already poisoned."

MEDIUM: "IT'S ALREADY THERE."

Laura: "So organic is not good because it already has this stuff in it?"

MEDIUM: "YES, IT'S ALREADY CONTAMINATED. THE PROBLEM IS THE SOIL IN THE FIRST PLACE. SO ALL THE MONEY THAT IS BEING SPENT ON THE ORGANIC STUFF, IT'S NOT ANY BETTER THAN THE OTHER. ONE WAY TO SEEK OUT WHOSE PRODUCTS TO USE IS TO SEE WHERE THE CHILDREN ARE NOT SICK. BECAUSE THEY ARE EATING THE FRUITS OF THAT LAND, PERCENTAGE-WISE, BECAUSE A LOT OF IT GETS IMPORTED AND SO FORTH."

Laura: "So what do we do in the mean time for the kids until this man develops the antidote? How do we heal them?"

<u>MEDIUM:</u> "IT'S NOT SO MUCH ABOUT HEALING THEM; IT'S MORE ABOUT UNDERSTANDING AND CONTROLLING THEM, AND THEN TEACHING THEM TO CONTROL THEMSELVES. BECAUSE WHEN YOU CONTROL THEM, THEY KNOW HOW IT FEELS AND THEN THEY'LL GET IN TOUCH WITH THAT FEELING, AND THEN THEY'LL KNOW THAT THEY ARE ACCEPTABLE TO SOCIETY. BECAUSE IN THEIR MINDS, IN THEIR EYES, IT IS IMPORTANT TO THEM. THESE CHILDREN WILL SAY, 'I JUST WANT TO BE THE SAME, I JUST WANT TO BE LIKE EVERYBODY ELSE. I DON'T WANT TO BE DIFFERENT. I KNOW I HAVE THIS PROBLEM, AND I JUST WANT TO BE THE SAME. AND I DON'T WANT YOU TO TELL ME THAT I'M DIFFERENT.'"

"SO THE PARENTS ARE INSTILLING THE CONTROL, AND THEN FEELING BAD ABOUT IT, THEY SHOULDN'T BECAUSE THEY ARE BRINGING THEM UNDER CONTROL. AND THEN THEY NEED TO TELL THEM, 'FEEL THAT FEELING, SEE HOW THAT FEELS.' AND THEN WHEN THEY GET OUT OF CONTROL, YOU NEED TO TELL THEM, 'BRING THE FEELING BACK.' BECAUSE WHEN THEY GET IN TOUCH WITH THEIR

FEELINGS THEN THEY KNOW WHERE THEY'RE AT IN A SITUATION. THEY VERY MUCH WANT TO BE A PART OF SOCIETY. THEY VERY MUCH NEED LOVE, THEY VERY MUCH NEED TO BE HUGGED."

Laura: "Yes, they do."

MEDIUM: "A LOT OF PARENTS ARE TURNING AWAY FROM THEM. A LOT OF PARENTS ARE NOT BEING RESPONSIBLE AND UNDERSTANDING THAT SOMETHING IS WRONG. AND SOME PEOPLE AREN'T TAKING THE RESPONSIBILITY AND THEY ARE RUNNING AWAY BECAUSE INSTEAD OF TAKING THE RESPOSIBILITY THEY ARE SEEING IT AS A FAULT. THINKING SOMETHING IS WRONG WITH ME AND I HAVE THIS KID. WHAT IS WRONG WITH ME? I NEED TO GET THIS KID AWAY FROM ME BECAUSE PEOPLE ARE GOING TO LOOK AT ME AND THINK THERE IS SOMETHING WRONG WITH ME. AND IT'S NOT SOMETHING WRONG WITH ME; IT'S THAT KID...SO GET HIM AWAY FROM ME."

"AND THAT IS ANOTHER THING THAT IS HARMING THE CHILDREN IS THAT PARENTS THINKING THAT THEY HAVE

PRODUCED A CHILD THAT IS NOT PERFECT, AND IT IS PART OF THEM, AND IT IS THEIR FAULT. SO INSTEAD OF HELPING THE CHILD, THEY RUN AWAY. AND THEN IT CAUSES ABANDONMENT AND IT CAUSES FAMILIES TO BREAK UP AND THEN IT CAUSES A LOT OF THESE CHILDREN TO WIND UP IN FOSTER HOMES AND DIFFERENT PLACES, EVEN THOUGH THE REST OF THE CHILDREN THAT DON'T HAVE THIS HAPPEN TO THEM, THEY SEEM TO HOUSE THEM PRETTY WELL. SO HOW CAN THEY DO THAT TO THEIR VERY OWN? BUT, THE REASON THAT THEY DO THAT TO THEIR VERY OWN IS BECAUSE IT SCARES THEM THAT SOMETHING IS WRONG WITH THEM, AND THAT IS WHAT THEY PRODUCED. THAT IT'S THEIR OFFSPRING."

Laura: "Mmm-hmm."

MEDIUM: "PEOPLE NEED TO TAKE A LOOK AND STEP BACK AND REMEMBER THE CHILD THAT THEY DID HAVE. IT'S NOT THE ONE THEY HAVE NOW. IT WAS AFTER THE CHILD WAS CONTAMINATED. THE LITTLE BODIES DON'T HAVE THE IMMUNE SYSTEM THAT THEY NEED TO POWER THROUGH THIS."

<u>Laura</u>: "No, they don't."

<u>MEDIUM</u>: "AND SEE, THEY'RE SEEING IT AT A VERY YOUNG AGE, AND PEOPLE ARE THINKING THAT THEY JUST MISSED IT. AND THEY FORGET HOW INTELLIGENT AND HOW WONDERFUL THIS CHILD WAS BEFORE THAT TURNING POINT WAS."

<u>Laura</u>: "So it's not genetic. They're barking up the wrong tree trying to pin it on genetics, is that what you're saying?"

<u>MEDIUM</u>: "THIS IS NOT GENETIC."

<u>Laura</u>: "The government is spending millions of dollars looking for the 'genetic cause' of autism. There can't be a genetic epidemic. It is impossible. Going from one in 10,000 to one in 150?"
(Shortly before this book was published, the statistics rose to one in 91. Roughly one percent of American children are on the autism spectrum, one in 58 boys.[6])

---

[6]http://talkaboutcuringautism.org/resources/1-in-91-children-has-autism.htm

<u>MEDIUM:</u> (MEDIUM'S THOUGHTS) "LET'S GET MORE, BECAUSE ALL OF THAT, YOU NEED TO INCORPORATE INTO WHAT'S COMING THROUGH. I DON'T KNOW ANYTHING ABOUT ANY OF THIS. MY YOUNGEST CHILD IS GOING ON 20. SO THAT WAS BEFORE THE PROBLEM GOT TO THE POINT IT IS NOW."

"NO, THIS IS NOT GENETIC. THAT'S WHAT JUST CAME THROUGH. THE GUILT AND THE PEOPLE RUNNING AWAY FROM THEIR OWN CHILDREN BECAUSE THEY THINK THAT SOMETHING IS WRONG WITH THEM; AND THAT IT HAS TO DO WITH GENETICS. NO, THAT'S NOT THE PROBLEM."

"THE CHILD WAS HEALTHY WHEN IT CAME INTO THE WORLD, THE PROBLEM CAME AFTERWARD. THIS IS NOT CONTAGIOUS. THIS IS NOT SOMETHING THAT CAME FROM OTHER PEOPLE'S GENES. THIS IS NOT SOMETHING THAT WAS BREATHED IN A SOLO INSTANCE. THIS IS A COMBINATION OF ONE THING, ADDING AN INGREDIENT, AND MAKING IT TRIGGER. SO, IT'S NOT THE SHOT, THEY ARE NOT GOING TO SAY IT'S THE SHOT AND LET'S STOP. IT'S THE INGREDIENT THAT GOES WITH IT, AND IT

TRIGGERS IT, AND THAT'S WHEN THE CHILD HAS A PROBLEM."

"AND THE NUMBERS ARE IN SECTIONS, THEY ARE IN AREAS... HIGHER NUMBERS... AND IT IS ALL AROUND THE STATE OF NEVADA BECAUSE THIS IS WHERE THEY ARE CREATING IT."

(MEDIUM'S WORDS) "AND I KEEP SEEING THOSE UNDERGROUND MILITARY AREAS. THE ONES THAT WE WERE SENSING WHEN WE DROVE THROUGH THERE."
(In 2006, while on a trip to a convention, the medium and I drove through a remote military town. We were driving from Reno to Las Vegas. She told me that she sensed military people working underground, and asked me if I could pick up on it too. I did. I got a chill up my spine, and the hair on my arms stood up. I felt scared.)

(MEDIUM'S WORDS) "THEN WE STARTED EXPLORING (PSYCHICALLY) AND I WAS PICKING UP ON THEM. THEN WHEN I DROVE THROUGH THERE LAST YEAR (2005) WITH ANOTHER MEDIUM WE BOTH SENSED THEM

UNDERGROUND, AND WE STOPPED AT A GROCERY STORE, AND THOUGHT, 'OKAY, WE'RE OUT HERE IN THE MIDDLE OF NOWHERE, WE ARE GOING TO HAVE A ROTTEN APPLE, BECAUSE WHO IS EATING THEM IF THEY ARE NOT FRESH?' WE GO IN THE STORE AND IT LOOKS 100 YEARS OLD, THE PAINT IS UGLY, AND YOU GO IN, AND IT LOOKS LIKE RALEY'S GROCERY STORE. THEY HAVE FRESH FRUITS AND VEGETABLES GALORE. TONS AND TONS, AND I SAID, 'SEE, THEY ARE DOING UNDERGROUND WORK HERE. PEOPLE ARE LIVING UNDERGROUND AND THEY ARE EATING ALL OF THOSE FRUITS AND VEGETABLES OR THEY WOULD NOT BE FRESH.' THERE IS MILITARY STUFF GOING ON. I WAS THERE, I CHECKED IT OUT. SO ALL OF THAT IS THERE."

Laura: "Yeah, I know."

MEDIUM: "AND THAT MARKS AN 'X.' THAT IS WHERE IT IS GOING ON. I JUST SAW IT. I JUST SAW AN 'X' AS TO WHERE ALL THIS IS COMING FROM."

(The town we drove through where she sensed military people living underground is where they are creating the biological warfare causing autism.)

"YOU KNOW, THE GOVERNMENT INTENTIONALLY DID IT UNDERGROUND BECAUSE THEY WANTED TO NOT ALLOW WHAT IS HAPPENING TO HAPPEN. BECAUSE THE TOPSOIL IS BEING CONTAMINATED, AND THEY FIGURED IF THEY WERE DIGGING AND WORKING FROM WITHIN, THAT IT WOULDN'T COME OUT, BUT OUR PEOPLE HAVE TO BREATHE. AND IT IS OUR PEOPLE DOING IT. IT IS OUR SOLDIERS, BUT THEY ARE UNDER COMMAND."

"IT'S NOT LIKE IT'S THEIR FAULT. WHAT? ARE THEY GOING TO DISMISS THEM? SHOOT THEM? WHAT ARE THEY GOING TO DO TO THEM IF THEY REFUSE TO DO THEIR JOB? AND BESIDES THAT, EACH ONE IS DOING A LITTLE PIECE THAT CONNECTS TO THE OTHER, AND THEY HAVE NO IDEA WHAT THE WHOLE PICTURE LOOKS LIKE. IT'S LIKE SAYING, 'OKAY, YOU'RE GOING TO WASH THIS CUP. THE OTHER PERSON IS GOING TO PUT SOMETHING IN THE CUP, AND THE NEXT PERSON IS GOING TO PUT SOME COLOR IN THE CUP. ALL HE'S DOING IS PUTTING COLOR IN THE CUP ALL DAY LONG; HE DOES NOT KNOW HOW IT'S WASHED, AND WHAT THE NEXT PERSON PUTS IN IT. SO IT'S LIKE A CHAIN OF

COMMAND AND THE FINAL PRODUCT IS IN THE HANDS OF ONE PERSON. AND THEY ARE JUST DOING THEIR PART, AND THEY HAVE NO IDEA."

"BUT IT'S COMING OUT THROUGH THE AIR THAT THEY HAVE TO BREATHE. IT'S COMING OUT AND GOING ALL AROUND."

Laura: "So they are coming out after being exposed to it and it's getting into the winds and blowing around?"

MEDIUM: "IT'S COMING ALL AROUND AND CONTAMINATING ALL AROUND THERE. SO THE PEOPLE IN WINNEMUCCA, THEY ARE PROBABLY GOING TO BE RETARDED BY THE TIME IT'S ALL DONE."

Laura: "Is that the city that we were in? Where was that?"

MEDIUM: "I DON'T KNOW, BUT I'M PICKING UP WINNEMUCCA, AND CLOSE TO LAS VEGAS, ALL UP IN THERE. THAT AREA, THOSE PEOPLE, IT'S LIKE THEY'RE IN A FOG. AND IT'S TAKING LONGER, IT'S A LONGER PROCESS,

BECAUSE PEOPLE COME AND GO THERE, AND IT'S JUST A LITTLE DOSE OF SOMETHING THAT THEY GET."

(Winnemucca is northeast of this military area, the way the wind typically blows. Las Vegas is southeast.)

"BUT THE MAIN PROBLEM IS THE POTATOES, THE ROOT VEGETABLES, AND THINKING THAT YOU CAN GROW THEM ON YOUR OWN...THAT'S NOT THE SOLUTION. YOU NEED TO BE EATING OUT OF THE WATER. THINGS THAT GROW FROM THE WATER. IF YOU COULD PUT A POTATO IN WATER, AND LET IT ROOT IN THE WATER, AND GROW IN THE WATER, THAT WOULD BE CLEANER THAN THE ONES IN THE GROUND."

Laura: "Like sea kelp and dulce, that type of sea vegetable?"

MEDIUM: "THAT'S WHAT YOU NEED TO TURN TO. IN ORDER FOR YOUR MONEY TO BE WELL SPENT, THAT'S WHERE THE FOOD NEEDS TO COME FROM, IS THE SEA. THE SEA IS REALLY HARD TO CONTAMINATE BECAUSE OF THE SALT. YOU CAN CONTAMINATE THE OCEANS WITH OIL, AND YOU CAN CONTAMINATE IT WITH WHATEVER YOU WANT, BUT

IT CLEANSES ITSELF BECAUSE OF ALL THE SALT. THE RIVERS AND LAKES CAN'T CLEANSE THEMSELVES, IT JUST STAGNATES. BUT THE OCEANS HAVE ALL THE SALTS. AND WHEN YOU GET A CUT AND YOU PUT SALT ON IT, OR YOU HAVE CANKER SORES IN YOUR MOUTH AND YOU NEED TO ALLEVIATE THE PAIN, YOU USE WARM SALT WATER. AND THAT'S WHERE YOUR FOOD NEEDS TO COME FROM, THE OCEANS. AND THEN YOU'RE SPENDING YOUR MONEY CORRECTLY INSTEAD OF WASTING IT."

"ALL THE PRODUCTS IN THE ORGANIC SECTION, IT'S A RIP-OFF. IN THEIR HEARTS, THEY ARE SELLING IT AND THINKING THEY ARE DOING THE RIGHT THING, BUT, YOU START WITH MUD...YOU HAVE MUD. AND YOU HAVE CONTAMINATION."

"AND THIS IS NOT GOING TO BE ABLE TO BE CLEANED UP, IT NEEDS TO BE REMOVED OR REPLACED."

Laura: "How would you explain these kids (with autism) being called 'Crystal Children'? Are they coming in more susceptible?

Are they a higher spiritual vibration already that makes them more susceptible than other kids?"

<u>MEDIUM:</u> "WHAT'S HAPPENING IS THAT THEY ARE CALLING THEM 'CRYSTAL CHILDREN' AND ALL THESE OTHER THINGS BECAUSE...IT'S NOT REALLY THAT THEY'RE BORN AS A 'CRYSTAL CHILD,' OR THEY'RE SPECIAL IN ANY WAY, IT'S THAT THEY'RE WITHIN THEMSELVES AND THEY ARE SCREAMING. THEY ARE WITHIN THEMSELVES, AND THEY ARE NOT ABLE TO RELATE TO YOU."

"SO, IT'S LIKE A BLIND PERSON THAT CAN WALK, AND SENSE, AND SMELL YOUR PERSONALITY. THEY CAN WALK AND KNOW WHICH WAY TO GO BECAUSE THEY'VE LEARNED WHERE ALL THE FURNITURE IS. BECAUSE WHAT THEY DO IS THEY GO FOR ANOTHER SENSE. ONE SENSE DOESN'T WORK, SO THEY USE ANOTHER."

"THESE CHILDREN ARE USING THEIR PSYCHIC, BECAUSE THEY ARE INSIDE OF THEMSELVES AND THEY CAN'T RELATE TO YOU, THEY CAN'T RELATE TO THE PEOPLE AROUND THEM, SO THEY ARE REACHING WITHIN

THEMSELVES. THEY ARE TRAINING THEMSELVES TO USE ANOTHER SENSE, WHICH IS THEIR PSYCHIC, BECAUSE THEY ARE BEING FORCED TO."

"THE CHILDREN WHO DON'T HAVE THIS PROBLEM, THEY'RE USING THEIR PHYSICAL; THEY ARE RELATING AND LEARNING AND ALL THIS. SO, THEY DON'T HAVE TIME FOR THE PSYCHIC. AND SEE, THESE CHILDREN AREN'T HAVING THAT CHOICE, SO THEY HAVE TO DEVELOP THE ALTERNATIVE, LIKE A BLIND PERSON HAS A KEEN SENSE OF HEARING. THEY WILL KNOW WHEN SOMEONE IS COMING UP BEFORE THE PERSON WHO CAN SEE AND HEAR. BECAUSE THAT PERSON HAS DEVELOPED OTHER WAYS TO TAKE CARE OF WHAT THE EYES CAN'T SEE."

"AND THIS IS WHAT THESE CHILDREN ARE DOING; THEY ARE DEVELOPING THEIR PSYCHIC BECAUSE THEY HAVE TO HAVE SOMETHING ELSE TO HELP THEM. AND THEN WE'VE LABELED THEM AS 'CRYSTAL CHILDREN.' WE'VE LABELED THEM AS DIFFERENT. BUT THE FACT IS...YES, THEY ARE PSYCHICALLY MORE DEVELOPED, BECAUSE THAT'S WHAT

THEY HAD TO TURN TO. THEIR INNER SELF; THEIR CONSCIOUSNESS."

"BECAUSE THEY'RE SCREAMING, THERE IS MORE THAT THESE CHILDREN WANT TO SAY TO YOU, THAN THEY ARE SAYING BECAUSE THEY ARE LOCKED IN THERE. IT IS LIKE A SOUL TRAPPED IN A BODY THAT'S NOT FUNCTIONING LIKE IT SHOULD. IT IS LIKE A SHELL THAT'S NOT DOING SERVICE. IT'S LIKE THIS BODY THAT WE LEAVE BEHIND, AND THE SOUL KEEPS GOING."

"BUT THEY'VE ENTERED A BODY, AND IT'S GOTTEN HARD. IT'S SOMEWHAT MUMMIFIED. SO, THEY HAVE TO LOOK WITHIN THEMSELVES. AND MUMMIFIED IS WHAT CAME THROUGH, BECAUSE WHEN YOU MUMMIFY, YOU USE A SOLUTION. AND THEN IT PUTS AN OUTER PROTECTIVE LAYER. AND THAT'S WHAT'S HAPPENING TO THEM. AND BECAUSE MUMMIFIED CAME THROUGH, THIS WILL BE UNWRAPPED ONE DAY! BUT THESE KIDS ARE GOING TO BE IN THEIR 40'S. I HEARD ACTUALLY, THE NUMBER 45."

Laura: "Before what?"

<u>MEDIUM:</u> "BEFORE THEY ARE UNWRAPPED. BECAUSE IT IS LIKE A MUMMIFICATION THAT THEY HAVE. THAT IS ANOTHER WAY YOU CAN DESCRIBE WHAT IS GOING ON WITH YOUR CHILD. WHEN YOU LOOK AT THEM, AND THEY ARE NOT TELLING YOU EVERYTHING, IT'S BECAUSE THEY'VE GOT SOME KIND OF...IT'S LIKE THEY ARE WRAPPED IN SOME KIND OF SOLUTION. THEIR BODY IS NOT PROPERLY WORKING."

"THIS IS NOT THE FAULT OF ANY PARENT. AND THEY NEED TO QUIT RUNNING AWAY FROM THEIR CHILDREN. THEY NEED TO QUIT RUNNING AWAY FROM IT THINKING THAT IT IS A PRODUCTION OF THEM. THIS IS SOMETHING THAT HAPPENED AFTERWARDS."

<u>Laura:</u> "Okay."

<u>MEDIUM:</u> "AND THE CHILDREN ARE VERY PSYCHIC BECAUSE THAT'S ALL THEY HAVE TO STUDY, AND THEY ARE BEING FORCED TO. SO, YOU COULD CALL THEM A CRYSTAL CHILD

BECAUSE THEY DEVELOP INTO THAT. THEY ARE NOT BORN THAT WAY."

Laura: "So, until that healing happens when they are 45, when they are 'unmummified', what is the best protocol, what are the best things to do for them?"

MEDIUM: "DON'T GIVE THEM ANY MORE OF WHAT TRIGGERED IT IN THE FIRST PLACE."

Laura: "Vaccines?"

MEDIUM: "AND EAT OUT OF THE SEA. OR THINGS THAT HAVE GROWN IN SALT WATER. YOU CAN EVEN MIMIC THAT YOURSELF BY GROWING THINGS IN WATER, IN SALT WATER."

"THIS IS THE TYPE OF GARDEN OF THE FUTURE. THINGS LIKE RICE, AND OTHER PRODUCTS LIKE THAT, YOU USE WITHOUT THE SOIL. IF YOU KEEP SOIL IN SALT...BUT IT HAS TO BE ENOUGH OF IT, IT WILL RAISE THE GOOD TO THE TOP. BUT IT HAS TO BE ENOUGH OF IT. YOU CAN'T

TAKE A SMALL LAYER OF SOIL AND PUT THE SALT IN IT. BECAUSE WHAT HAPPENS IS THE CONTAMINATED NEEDS TO DROP TO THE BOTTOM AND THE OTHER FLOATS TO THE TOP, AND THE SALT KEEPS IT BOUYANT."

"SO THERE WILL BE WATER GARDENS. AND I SEE IT REALLY PRETTY, BUT I DO SEE THEM LINED. THEY ARE NOT ON THE GROUND; IT'S NOT LIKE A POND. I SAW IT LINED, IT'S KEEPING THE DIRT OFF. AND I SEE IT IS GOOD. IT IS A GOOD THING TO DO."

"BECAUSE THEN YOU ARE NOT LIMITED TO WHAT GROWS THERE. YOU CAN TAKE THE PRODUCTS THAT YOU ENJOY NOW, AND SEE WHAT WILL GROW IN THOSE WATERS. BECAUSE THERE HAVE NOT BEEN A LOT OF EXPERIMENTS DONE ON ALL OF THIS, AND IT'S BECAUSE THERE HASN'T BEEN A NEED FOR IT. SO, THERE ARE THINGS THAT WILL GROW IN WATER THAT YOU WOULD ONLY THINK WOULD GROW IN SOIL. YOU KNOW WHETHER YOU HAVE TO PROP THEM UP, AND PART OF IT BE IN THERE SO THAT THE ROOT CAN BE IN THERE, AND THE OTHER PART BE OUT OF THE WATER. DIFFERENT TECHNIQUES LIKE THAT. AND I'M

SEEING THE ROOT IN THE WATER AND THE PLANT UP ON TOP, BUT IT'S NOURISHED BY THE WATER, AND WHAT YOU HAVE IN THERE; AND NOT THE DIRT. AND THOSE ARE THE WATER GARDENS THAT I AM SEEING. BUT THEY'LL BE MASSIVE. AND THE MASSIVENESS...THEY'RE NOT ON THE GROUND. THEY HAVE LIKE A LINER. THEY'RE NOT DIRECTLY ON THE GROUND."

Laura: "Okay. Going back to the whole metaphysical part of this...Did the kids choose this for themselves before they came here?"

MEDIUM: "NO...NO."

Laura: "It just happened to them? What are we supposed to learn from this? What is this supposed to teach us?"

MEDIUM: "IT'S SURVIVAL...IT'S SURVIVAL. AND THE GOVERNMENT WON'T TAKE RESPONSIBILITY. THEY'LL HAVE A SOLUTION, AND I JUST SEE IT ALL SWEPT UNDER THE RUG. AND IT'S A WITCH'S BROOM. THEY WILL GET INVOLVED WITH THE SOLUTION BECAUSE THEY KNOW

OUR PEOPLE ARE THE FUTURE, AND THE NUMBERS ARE JUST TOO HIGH NOW."

Laura: "So what percentage of these kids is going to heal and get well, and function in society?"

MEDIUM: "THE ONES THAT DON'T HARM THEMSELVES."

Laura: "With what?"

MEDIUM: "I JUST HEARD THE ONES THAT DON'T HURT THEMSELVES."

Laura: "How can we fix the damage to their brain now? What about homeopathy, and the things I'm doing now? Am I wasting my time?"

MEDIUM: "RIGHT NOW, WHAT YOU ARE DOING IS TRYING TO POTTY TRAIN A CHILD THAT'S NOT READY...YOU'RE POTTY TRAINING YOURSELF, IF YOU CAN RELATE TO THAT. IT'S LIKE IF A CHILD IS NOT READY, AND THEY CAN'T CONTROL THEIR BLADDER, YOU'RE GOING THROUGH THE

MOTIONS. YOU ARE FIGURING OUT WHEN THEY NEED TO GO TO THE BATHROOM, AND YOU'RE TAKING THEM ON A TIMELY BASIS. YOU'VE NOT TRAINED THE CHILD, YOU'VE TRAINED YOURSELF. ASK YOUR QUESTION AGAIN."

Laura: "What about homeopathic remedies I'm giving him to detoxify the junk in his body? Is that a waste of time, or should I continue?"

MEDIUM: "RIGHT NOW, YOU DO NEED TO CONTINUE, BECAUSE YOU'RE CONTINUING TO CONTAMINATE HIM. SO, UNTIL YOU CHANGE HIS FOODS, THEN YOU'LL SEE SOME CHANGES IN HIM. BECAUSE THEN YOU'LL THIN IT OUT."

Laura: "Is it the potatoes, is that the main problem?"

MEDIUM: "THINGS THAT GROW IN THE GROUND ARE VERY BAD."

Laura: "Like all the carrots he eats?"

MEDIUM: "ALL THE ROOTS."

Laura: "He eats a lot of vegetables like cucumbers and tomatoes."

MEDIUM: "SEE, THOSE GROW ON TOP, BUT THEY ARE STILL GETTING NUTRIENTS FROM THAT SOIL. YOU NEED WATER VEGETABLES."

Laura: "What else am I doing that's contaminating him?"

MEDIUM: "THEY ARE TALKING ABOUT THIS WHOLE THING BEING MUMMIFIED; THAT IT CAUSES A MUMMIFICATION. SO, YOU NEED TO DO A LITTLE RESEARCH ON THAT. SO THAT YOU CAN SEE WHAT WILL HAPPEN TO THESE PEOPLE AS THE YEARS GO BY, AND WE MAKE OUR CHANGES IN OUR WORLD. SO IF YOU UNWRAP A MUMMY, WHAT HAPPENS? SO, THERE'S A LOT OF ANSWERS IN THAT. THAT IS A BIG, HUGE, GIGANTIC CLUE IN THE FUTURE."

"I'M BEING TOLD THAT I'M NOT BEING GIVEN SPECIFIC ANSWERS ON THAT AREA, AND IT'S BECAUSE THERE ARE THINGS THAT ARE TO COME THAT WE DON'T UNDERSTAND RIGHT NOW. BUT, IT WILL BE VERY SIMPLE WHEN WE TAKE

A LOOK AT IT THEN...BUT IT HAS TO DO WITH MUMMIFICATION. WHAT'S HAPPENING TO PART OF THEIR BODIES."

(TIMER GOES OFF. WE HAD SET IT FOR AN HOUR SESSION).

"OKAY, LET ME TELL YOU THE LAST THING THAT CAME THROUGH BEFORE THAT WENT OFF. HIS PSYCHIC ABILITIES ARE GOING TO TRAIN HIM TO BE ABLE TO EXIST IN SOCIETY. AND THAT'S HOW THE FUTURE OF THE UNITED STATES IS GOING TO BE ABLE TO GO ON WITH THE PERCENTAGE OF PEOPLE WITH THIS THING GOING ON WITH THEM."

<u>Laura:</u> "By tapping into their psychic abilities?"

<u>MEDIUM:</u> "BECAUSE THAT'S ALL THEY ARE GOING TO HAVE TO RUN ON. AND SO, PART OF WHAT WE ARE SUPPOSED TO BE DOING, AS PARENTS, IS TEACHING THEM ABOUT THE FEELING WE TALKED ABOUT IN THE BEGINNING."

"OKAY, I'M GOING TO TURN THIS OFF."

<u>Laura:</u> "Wow!"

(CD ends)

***

Later Discoveries

We chatted for a bit about what had just transpired while the medium made a copy of the CD for me to take home to transcribe. We decided to call the book "The Mummy" as a working title because of the comparison made to children with autism being mummified. The medium doesn't recall everything that comes through during a reading, as she goes into a trance-state at times to channel the spirit's words. The spirit basically takes over. I had a much different experience, soaking in every word. This was not the information I was expecting at all. It was like pulling teeth to get answers, and the answers I got didn't make sense to me. I was completely dumbfounded by what was revealed.

I was in shock and denial. Could all of this be true? Is our military creating biological weapons just two hours from where I live in NV in an underground city? Could biological warfare in the environment be combining with an ingredient in a vaccine in children's bodies causing regressive autism? It seemed unbelievable. But what if it wasn't? How could I prove it? Who would believe me? Especially when I had to reveal the source of the information. I knew from having years of readings with this medium that she was very accurate and that her predictions came true, so why would this time be different?

I listened to the CD again as I drove home, and I couldn't shake the horror I was feeling. I felt so sad for my sweet boy. I needed to use this information to help my son if it was true. I went home and threw out all of the potato chips and told my mom that he was not to eat them or French fries either. If I was continuing to contaminate him with the foods he was eating, I needed to remove it immediately.

We already used reverse-osmosis or distilled water as drinking water, maybe I needed to get a whole house filter after the information came through about the "muddy waters." What if the

BW is in tap water and gets absorbed into the skin when bathing? Maybe I needed to grow my own vegetables for him in uncontaminated water. I certainly didn't want to have my family eat anything grown in Nevada. I didn't care if it sounded crazy. I had already changed his whole diet to gluten-free and dairy-free, and it helped a lot. Maybe this would help more?

Discovering the Town

I was so torn up about this information from the readings that I had to talk to someone about this that might understand. I wasn't sure if I even believed all of this at this point, but if it was true, I had to do something. The information given went against everything I had previously believed about the cause of autism. I kept asking myself, "But, what if it is true?" It could change everything. I had to try to find out more.

I called a good friend of mine, who also has a son with regressive autism, who had also had a reading with this medium before, and I shared some of this with her to see what she thought. I told her about the combination of the biological warfare and the vaccine causing autism. When I described the place that was supposedly making the biological warfare underground in Nevada, she said, "Oh, yeah, **Hawthorne**, my parents live there."

Now I had a town! She told me what little she knew about the military base in Hawthorne. Most of the town is employed there, including her father, and a private contractor operates it. I don't know if she believed what I was suggesting, but she was intrigued and didn't dismiss it or think I was losing my mind. I don't know if this is related or not, but her mom has breast cancer. Just saying. She asked her dad, who is a security guard at the base, if he knew anything about an underground base. He replied, "What are you talking about?" Not surprising. He's not on the "need to know" list.

I decided to do some more research. I looked up Hawthorne, NV on Google Earth, and it was definitely the place the medium and I had driven through. Then I searched the internet for more information and found an archived article from a Las Vegas newspaper from 2005, when the base was being considered for shut-down. The article said that Hawthorne Army Depot is the largest ammunition storage facility in the nation and that it holds about 300,000 tons of military bombs and other ammunition. It encompasses 147,000 acres of mostly barren desert 130 miles southeast of Reno and 300 miles north of Las Vegas.

There are 2,900 buildings, about 80 percent of them steel-reinforced concrete bunkers covered in a couple feet of dirt. The bunkers, which surround Hawthorne, look like oblong brown igloos with bushes sprouting out the top. (As far as the eye can see, there are row after row of these mounds.) Hawthorne has more than 7 million square feet of storage space, roughly 56 percent in use to store ammunition.

The depot was opened in 1930 as a U.S. Navy facility and employed 13,000 military personnel and civilian employees during World War II. The Army took over operation of the depot in 1977 and transferred it to a private contractor, Day and Zimmerman, in 1980. The Army retains command of the site now, but it's a privately run operation. The article said that it would take at least 4 ½ years to destroy all the ammunition on base that's scheduled for destruction, and that it would cost an estimated $400 million to get the land clean enough for public use, if they closed the site.[7] Apparently, they burn old ammunition there and have had complaints from local Native American Indian tribes and others who are attributing high incidents of cancer with the burning of ammunition at the base.

Then I found another article from the local Las Vegas newspaper about the same potential closure, (which was voted down,) and there was a quote that caught my eye. Nevada Senator Harry Reid was quoted as saying, "Hawthorne Army Depot has unique qualities that are vital to our national security. They do work in Hawthorne that can't be done at any other base."[8] Although vague, I was shocked by this discovery. Not exactly proof, but the potential was definitely there.

I was beginning to realize that the scenario described in the readings could actually happen! I felt sick to my stomach when I thought about it. I felt the need to flee, move away and save my family.

---

[7]Lake, Richard, "Hawthorne faces losing its identity", *Las Vegas Review-Journal* (May 29, 2005).

[8]Werner, Erica, "Base closing commission votes to save Hawthorne Army Depot", *Las Vegas Sun* (Aug 24, 2005).

Mummification

I didn't do that much research after this reading. It was a lot to absorb, much less believe wholeheartedly. I was curious about all the "mummy" references however. I did some research online and found that the Egyptians used Natron in the mummification process; which is a naturally occurring salt and a dehydrating agent. I watched a program on National Geographic about mummification of the Pharaohs. It said that once the body dries out, it is covered in oils and resins containing frankincense and myrrh and wrapped in linens. The body is essentially carbonized. I didn't see the connection to what happened to my son, but maybe it would make sense someday.

There was another program on National Geographic called *Egypt Unwrapped- Secrets of the Valley of the Kings* in which they showed an underground burial site in Egypt, with many intricate underground tunnels and rooms with the tombs where they buried their pharaohs. They even had a 3D layout of the site; it was huge and they were still discovering more. I asked myself, if technology has existed to excavate underground tunnels and rooms centuries ago, then isn't it possible that there could currently be underground military bases? This discovery made it seem more probable.

Part of me wasn't sure if I believed the information given in the reading and I almost wanted to forget about finishing it. I thought about all of the ramifications of putting this information out there for people to read. I felt fearful. There were a lot of sacred cows being implicated in some serious wrong-doing. I didn't want to mess with the government, the military, or the medical community. I thought, maybe I needed to write this as fiction, because who would believe it was a true story? I am sure it would be ridiculed. Or maybe I should not write it at all...

***

CHAPTER TWO

MEDIUM: "OKAY, TODAY IS DECEMBER 4, 2007, AND THIS IS SESSION TWO OF 'THE MUMMY,' THE BOOK THAT LAURA AND I ARE DOING. HERE WE GO LAURA. (SHE SAYS A PERSONAL PRAYER) I ASK FOR THE HIGHEST AND BEST SPIRITS TO COME THROUGH THAT CAN GET INFORMATION ABOUT HEALTH, ABOUT WHAT'S GOING ON WITH THE WORLD, ABOUT WHAT THIS BOOK IS SUPPOSED TO CONTAIN. THE HIGHEST AND BEST WHO CAN BRING ALL THE ANSWERS THAT ARE NEEDED TO HELP HUMANITY IN THE HIGHEST WAY. IT DOESN'T MATTER WHO IT EXPLOITS OR WHAT HAPPENS, WE JUST NEED THE HIGHEST AND BEST INFORMATION, THE HIGHEST AND BEST INFORMERS, THE HIGHEST AND BEST PHILOSOPHERS OF HEALTH AND WELL-BEING."

"OKAY, I'M STARTING TO SEE THEM LINE UP. I SEE THE WIRY HAIRED..."

(This spirit identifies himself here, but due to possible legal ramifications, I cannot reveal his identity. He will be referred to as "The Wiry One.")

<u>MEDIUM:</u> "YEAH, I THINK THAT'S WHO WE WERE GETTING BEFORE BECAUSE I REMEMBER A WIRY ONE, AND SO I SEE HIM FIRST."

"AND I SEE A CLEAN-CUT, SLICKED, HE'S GOT THAT OLD-FASHIONED HAIRCUT, YOU KNOW, IT'S JUST A PART ON THE SIDE, CUT SHORT, AND GOT THE WET LOOK GOING ON, LIKE A LOT OF GREASE, YOU KNOW HOW THEY WORE THAT. HE HAS A REAL THIN MUSTACHE, JUST A LINE, AND BROWN EYES. AND THEN HE SHOWS HIMSELF IN BLACK AND WHITE. BECAUSE HE'S SHOWING ME A PHOTOGRAPH. THIS IS A MEDIUM. HE'S SAYING THAT HE CAN HELP IN THIS SITUATION."

"THEN I'M PICKING UP A...I FEEL THIS WAS A PRESIDENT. 'WE ARE GOING TO TALK IN YOUR EAR TODAY AND WE'VE GOT AN EARFUL FOR YOU' IS WHAT I'M HEARING."

(The President's identity is also revealed, but again, because of possible legal ramifications, his name is not given. He will be referred to as the President.)

<u>Laura:</u> "Bring it on!"

<u>MEDIUM:</u> "OKAY...THE WIRY ONE...AND I MEAN HE'S GOT HIS HAIR ALL OVER THE PLACE. AND HIS INFORMATION SORT OF DOESN'T MAKE SENSE, BUT IT DOES, BECAUSE THAT'S HOW HE WORKS, HE SAYS. EVEN WHEN HE'S THINKING, BECAUSE HE'S A GREAT PHILOSOPHER, HE SAYS THAT HE FORESAW A LOT OF THINGS AND HE WOULD THROW HIMSELF INTO THE FUTURE IN ORDER TO GET WHAT HE WAS GETTING TO HELP THE WORLD AT THAT TIME. BUT HE DIDN'T UNDERSTAND A LOT OF IT. EVEN UNTIL IT STARTED GETTING PUT TOGETHER BY OTHER PEOPLE. SO IF YOU READ MY STUFF, IT'S LIKE YOU HAVE TO READ IT BACKWARDS IN ORDER TO MAKE SENSE OF IT BECAUSE WHEN HE WAS GETTING THE INFORMATION AND

HE JOTTED THINGS DOWN, IT DIDN'T MAKE ANY SENSE TO HIM EITHER."

"AND HE SAYS THAT THIS IS GOING TO BE A GOOD BOOK BECAUSE IT DOESN'T MAKE A LOT OF SENSE TO US. AND HE'S SAYING THAT IT IS A GOOD IDEA TO PICK UP INFORMATION THAT HAS TO DO WITH FUTURE, BECAUSE THAT'S HOW WE CAN HELP OURSELVES. IF WE DON'T KNOW FUTURE, HOW ARE WE SUPPOSED TO INVENT OR HAVE A REMEDY FOR ANYTHING? I'M SEEING THE KITE, ELECTRICITY, AND ALL OF THAT. THAT HAS TO DO WITH SOMEONE ELSE; OTHER INVENTIONS."

"AND ALL OF THIS IS REALLY GOING TO HELP OUT IN THE FOOD SITUATION. THAT IS OUR BIGGEST THING THAT'S COMING UP THAT'S GOING TO BE A DILEMMA. BECAUSE WE AREN'T GOING TO WANT TO RESORT TO AN ALL LIQUID DIET. WE LIKE THE SOLIDS. AND IT'S JUST GOING TO BE VERY DIFFICULT. SOME PEOPLE WOULD RATHER DIE THAN GIVE UP A SOLID INGREDIENT OF FOOD. AND IF WE DON'T DO SOMETHING ABOUT IT QUICK, WE ARE GOING TO WIND UP ON LIQUIDS."

"A LOT OF WHAT THEY ARE SHOWING ME IS A LOT OF POLITICAL ARGUMENT IN THE NEXT FEW YEARS. THE YEARS OF 10, 11, 12....EVEN IN 2008, THAT'S ALL GOING TO COME TO A HEAD. BUT IT IS GOING TO HEAT UP MORE, AND MORE, AND MORE. YOU KNOW WHEN THEY SAY 'FOR THE PEOPLE,' THOSE WORDS DON'T HAVE A LOT OF CLOUT OR MEANING BEHIND WHAT THEY ARE TALKING ABOUT. YOU KNOW IT'S GOING TO TAKE THE GOVERNMENT TO TAKE THE BULL BY THE HORNS BECAUSE WE HAVE A LOT OF TROUBLES COMING."

"YOU HAVE SOME QUESTIONS?"

<u>Laura:</u> "Yeah...I wanted to ask about the ingredients that were discussed in our last reading. About the biological warfare that is contaminating the soil. Does it have anything to do with Mycoplasma or Lyme? Is that what we are talking about?"
(Mycoplasma has been implicated as a biological agent used in the Gulf War, causing Gulf War Syndrome. Lyme (Borellia burgdorferi) is a spirochete which causes Lyme disease. Both have allegedly been weaponized.)

<u>MEDIUM</u>: "SAY ONE AT A TIME."

<u>Laura</u>: "Mycoplasma."

<u>MEDIUM</u>: "OKAY. THAT INGREDIENT IS TO HOLD THINGS TOGETHER. IT'S LIKE A GLUE. IT'S NOT AN ACTIVATOR; IT'S MORE OF A GLUE. IT'S MORE FOR STICKING TOGETHER ALL OF THE ITEMS YOU'RE STICKING TOGETHER."

<u>Laura</u>: "Are they combining things with it?"

<u>MEDIUM</u>: "OKAY, I'M SEEING HIM, THE WIRY ONE, HE'S LOOKING AT THAT, AND POKING AT IT WITH SOME SORT OF GADGET. HE'S SEPARATING IT, AND LOOKING AT IT AND HE SAYS, 'HMMMM.' YOU KNOW, THIS INGREDIENT IS SUPPOSED TO BE USED FOR OTHER THINGS BUT IT'S A SUBSTITUTE FOR SOMETHING ELSE. AND IT HOLDS THINGS TOGETHER SO THE PROPERTIES CAN TAKE PLACE. SAY IT AGAIN."

<u>Laura</u>: "Mycoplasma."

<u>MEDIUM:</u> "AND YOU WANT TO KNOW IF THEY ARE USING THIS?"

<u>Laura:</u> "Where they are creating these biological weapons, is this what they are weaponizing?"

<u>MEDIUM:</u> "YOU KNOW, SOME OF THE THINGS THAT I'M SEEING GOING INTO ALL OF THIS IS NATURAL BACTERIA. LIKE WHEN YOU LEAVE A COW LYING OUT THERE AND IT JUST STARTS ROTTING, AND WHAT YOU GET FROM THAT. A LOT OF IT IS NATURAL. THE ONLY THING IS THAT THEY ARE USING THINGS TO BRING IT UP SEVERAL NOTCHES. TO MAKE IT VERY, VERY FINE, SOMETHING THAT YOU BREATHE IN, LIKE A DUST. IT IS VERY SMALL PARTICLES. THEY ARE NOT GOING TO MAKE IT LIKE A RAIN, IT'S MORE LIKE A DUST, AND PEOPLE ARE BREATHING IT. AND THAT'S WHY IT HURTS THE TOP LAYER OF THE SOILS IS BECAUSE THIS DUST IS NOT EASY TO CONTAIN. IT'S NOT EASY TO KEEP IT ALL IN ONE PLACE."

(The dead body of an animal that died of anthrax can be a source of anthrax spores. Anthrax is from the bacteria Bacillus anthracis.)

"YOU KNOW, AS THEY'RE WORKING WITH IT, THEY HAVE TO BREATHE. THE PEOPLE THAT ARE WORKING WITH THIS, THEY LOOK LIKE THEY ARE WORKING WITH BEES TO ME. THEY HAVE ALL THAT STUFF ON LIKE THEY WERE WORKING WITH BEES. BUT THEY'RE NOT, IT'S PROTECTION. THERE IS A LOT OF PROTECTION THAT THEY ARE USING."

"BUT IT'S SO THIN AND POWDERY, IT'S LIKE DUST. IT'S A BUNCH OF DUST. SO, IN PLACES LIKE INDIA AND PAKISTAN, WHEN YOU HAVE THIS FORM OF A SUBSTANCE COMING DOWN ON YOU, YOU DON'T THINK ABOUT IT, BECAUSE THERE IS A LOT OF IT ALREADY. BUT THAT IS SAND, AND THIS IS MORE LIKE A DUST. IT'S GOT COLOR, IT IS A DARKER COLOR. IT'S NOT LIKE SOME KIND OF CLEAR SOMETHING THAT YOU WOULDN'T BE ABLE TO SEE. YOU WOULD NOTICE THAT IT IS A DIFFERENT KIND OF DUST AROUND HERE, AND IT SURE HAS BEEN DUSTY. SO,

IT'S NOT A WHITE COLOR, IT IS MORE OF A VERY LIGHT GRAY."

"THIS THING THAT YOU'RE TALKING ABOUT (MYCOPLASMA), THAT RIGHT THERE IS TEN TIMES SAFER THAN WHAT THEY ARE USING. THIS STUFF THAT YOU ARE TALKING ABOUT, YOU WOULD ALMOST FEEL SAFE HANDLING IT WITH YOUR HANDS IN COMPARISSON TO WHAT THEY ARE WORKING WITH."

"BECAUSE THEY HAVE ONE-SHOT TO GO ACROSS, AND THIS WILL BE SPREAD IN THE SKIES. AND IT HAS TO BE THIN ENOUGH TO WHERE IT SCATTERS WITH THE WIND. SO, IT CAN'T GO STRAIGHT DOWN. THAT STUFF YOU'RE TALKING ABOUT IS TOO HEAVY. THAT'S WHY THEY COULDN'T USE IT. THEY HAD TO USE SOMETHING LIGHTER, BUT THEY FOUND THAT IT'S MORE POTENT."

<u>Laura</u>: "What is it?"

<u>MEDIUM</u>: "ALSO, THEY DIDN'T WANT TO USE SOMETHING THAT STRONG. SO THE CONTROLLING IS NOT GOING TO BE

AS GOOD AS THEY WANTED. IT IS GOING TO SPREAD. BUT THEY ARE THINKING IF THEY SPREAD A CERTAIN AMOUNT AND THEY CAN MONITOR IT AND HAVE SOME SORT OF CONTROL. BUT I DON'T SEE IT...THE WIRY ONE DOESN'T SEE IT."

Laura: "How do you control the wind?"

MEDIUM: "THAT'S JUST IT. THEY CAN'T EVEN CONTROL THE MAKINGS OF IT, MUCH LESS THE SPREADING OF IT. AND IT IS LIKE A VERY, VERY THIN DUST. BUT IT DOES HAVE COLOR."

Laura: "So, which vaccine is it specifically that is combing with this ingredient in the children? I can tell you which one I think it is." (I was still asking the question as she began...)

MEDIUM: "I HEARD SMALLPOX."

Laura: "Which vaccine in the children?"
(They don't get the smallpox vaccine.)

MEDIUM: "LET'S GO THROUGH THEM."

Laura: "In the kids, is it the MMR? The Measles, Mumps, Rubella vaccine?"

MEDIUM: "WHAT WAS THE SHOT THAT THE PRESIDENT COULD HAVE GOTTEN THAT HE WOULDN'T HAVE WOUND UP IN THE WHEELCHAIR?"

Laura: "Oh, Polio."

MEDIUM: "POLIO. I THINK THAT'S WHY HE SHOWED HIMSELF."

Laura: "Is it because it is a live virus?"

MEDIUM: "YOU KNOW, THEY HANDLE THAT SUBSTANCE LIKE CANDY. IT IS TAKEN TOO MUCH FOR GRANTED. I JUST SEE SOMEONE SHAKING IT UP, AND LOOKING AT IT IN A VIAL, AND SAYING 'OH, THAT'S GOOD ENOUGH.' SO THEY ARE NOT PAYING ATTENTION LIKE THEY SHOULD BE.

SOMETHING ELSE IS GOING ON WITH THAT PARTICULAR SERUM. IT'S NOT LIKE IT USED TO BE. THEY ARE THINKING WE ARE MORE IMMUNE, WE'RE MORE THIS, WE'RE MORE THAT. THEY ARE LETTING THEIR GUARD DOWN. AND BY THEM LETTING THEIR GUARD DOWN, SOME OTHER DISEASES HAVE COME INTO PLAY."

"OKAY, THERE'S A DISEASE THAT IS GOING AROUND IN WOMEN, YOUNGER WOMEN, THAT MAKES THEM LOSE CONTROL OF THEIR ABILITY TO BE MOBILE. AND THEY ARE CALLING IT SOME SORT OF RADICAL SOMETHING. THEY DON'T HAVE A CURE FOR IT BECAUSE IT IS RADICAL, IT MOVES AROUND, MOVES AROUND. BUT IT HAS TO DO WITH NOT COVERING THE POLIO SHOT CORRECTLY. AND SO THIS IS HITTING WOMEN THAT ARE IN THEIR TWENTIES AND THIRITES."

Laura: "Is it MS? Multiple Sclerosis?"

MEDIUM: "I JUST HEAR A BELL. LIKE ONE OF THOSE BELLS WHEN THE FIGHTER IS GOING TO COME OUT?"

<u>Laura:</u> "Ding, ding, ding."

<u>MEDIUM:</u> "AND I SEE IT, WHEN YOU SAID THAT."

<u>Laura:</u> "They (doctors) are trying to tell my sister that she has MS."

<u>MEDIUM:</u> "DOES THIS DISEASE STOP WHEN YOU GET PREGNANT, AND WHEN YOU'RE NOT PREGNANT, IT CONTINUES ON? PREGNANCY FREEZES IT."

<u>Laura:</u> "Oh, I don't know."

<u>MEDIUM:</u> "SO THAT DISEASE RIGHT THERE (MS) HAS TO DO WITH THE TOYING OF VACCINATIONS. BECAUSE IT HAPPENED 20, 30 YEARS AGO."

(MEDIUM'S WORDS) "HOW OLD IS YOUR SISTER?"

<u>Laura:</u> "38. She started to get blurry vision, and they did some tests, and say she has lesions in her brain, and can't figure out why. They're calling it MS, which is just based on symptoms. But

it can cripple you, or immobilize you. And I think MS symptoms do get lighter during pregnancy."

<u>MEDIUM:</u> "IT PUTS THEM INTO A REMISSION, IT STOPS THEM."

(Pregnancy does put MS into remission.[9])

(MEDIUM'S WORDS) "AND HOW WOULD YOUR SISTER BE GOING THROUGH THIS, AND NOW THAT'S COMING THROUGH?"

<u>Laura:</u> "Because it is about vaccines. We all got them. Now look, all these years later, we are still feeling the effects from them. What's going to happen to all the little kids who got 30 plus vaccines, plus biological warfare?"

<u>MEDIUM:</u> "THERE ARE ONLY TWO THAT ARE REALLY MESSED UP. OF ALL THE VACCINES, THERE ARE ONLY TWO THAT ARE REALLY MESSED UP."

---

[9] http://www.thisisms.com/articl-151-thread-0-0.html

"ONE, IS THAT ONE THAT WE JUST TALKED ABOUT (POLIO), AND I SEE THAT PRESIDENT AGAIN. REMEMBER WHEN I TOLD YOU THAT THE PRESIDENT CAME THROUGH. I THOUGHT, 'WHY IS HE HERE?,' I THOUGHT MAYBE HE WAS GOING TO TELL US ABOUT POLITICS OR SOMETHING, BECAUSE WE HAD PICKED UP THAT THEY GET A SHARE OF SOMETHING, MORE COMPENSATION THAN WE SEE. BUT IT WASN'T THAT. HE WAS SHOWING HIMSELF BECAUSE OF HIM BEING IN THE WHEELCHAIR, AND IT IS THE VACCINE THAT HAS TO DO WITH ALL OF THIS."

"AND THERE IS ANOTHER ONE. THERE ARE TWO OF THEM THAT ARE AFFECTING HUMANITY, BUT YOU SEE, WE ARE DOWNING ALL OF THE VACCINES. THE DOCTORS WERE GOOD, THERE'S A LOT OF THINGS THAT ARE GOOD FOR US, THAT HAVE HELPED US."

"BECAUSE LOOK AT HIM, MAYBE HE WOULDN'T HAVE BEEN IN THAT WHEELCHAIR. BUT THEN, HE SAYS, MAYBE I WOULDN'T HAVE BEEN AS STRONG IF I WASN'T IN THE WHEELCHAIR. BECAUSE IT MADE HIM THAT MUCH STRONGER, ALTHOUGH HE WAS VERY ANGRY AT HIMSELF."

Laura: "What is the other vaccine, is it the MMR?"

MEDIUM: "THE OTHER ONE IS SOMETHING THAT THEY ADDED. IT WASN'T AROUND WHEN YOU AND I WERE LITTLE."
(They added the MMR vaccine in the 1980'S.)

(MEDIUM'S WORDS) "SO THE MMR? WHAT IS THAT?"

Laura: "Measles, Mumps, Rubella."

MEDIUM: "ASK IT LIKE A QUESTION."

Laura: "Is the second vaccine that is affecting humanity the Measles, Mumps, Rubella vaccine?"

MEDIUM: "SEE THE MEASLES, AND MUMPS...I DON'T GET ANYTHING. BUT THE RUBELLA... SOMETHING."

Laura: "Is that the one vaccine that is combining with the biological agent to create that reaction in the children (autism)."

<u>MEDIUM:</u> (ASKING OUTLOUD) "OKAY, WHAT IS IT THAT THIS DUST, OR WHATEVER IT IS, THAT'S COMING OUT, THAT THEY ARE NOT ABLE TO CONTAIN BECAUSE IT'S TOO POWDERY, AND THEY ARE WORKING WITH IT, SO IT'S SPREADING ACROSS NEVADA..."

"THIS CRAP CAN SPREAD OVER THE NATION! IT IS SO THIN AND IT IS SO POTENT, THAT IT CAN SPREAD ACROSS THE NATION IF THEY ARE NOT CAREFUL. BUT THEY ARE SPREADING IT THROUGHOUT NEVADA."

"AND IT HAS TO DO WITH THE WINDS. AND THEY THINK THAT THERE IS A LOT OF DESERT, BECAUSE THEY ARE WORKING IN A DESERT AREA, BUT THEY ARE NOT CONTAINING IT. THEY ARE NOT CONTAINING WHAT THEY ARE MAKING TO DO HARM TO SOMEONE ELSE, THEY ARE ACTUALLY HARMING HERE...THE VERY PEOPLE THAT THEY ARE SUPPOSED TO BE PROTECTING."

<u>Laura:</u> "Is it an ingredient in some vaccines? Or is it one specific vaccine that is the culprit?"

<u>MEDIUM:</u> "I'M HEARING THAT THESE KIDS GET THIS AROUND THE AGE OF ONE, THE AGE OF ONE IS WHEN IT IS SCHEDULED. YOU KNOW HOW THEY DO A 3 MONTH, 6 MONTH, 9 MONTH...THESE KIDS ARE ONE. THE ONLY WAY THEY WOULDN'T GET IT RIGHT THEN IS IF THEY WERE SICK OR WHATEVER, AND THE DOCTOR TURNED THEM AWAY. BUT THEY ARE SCHEDULED TO GET THAT VACCINE WHEN THEY ARE AROUND ONE. IT IS OUT OF A NEEDLE, BECAUSE IT STABS THE SKIN. IT'S NOT AN ORAL THING THAT'S GIVEN. I SEE IT STAB THE SKIN. I SAW A LITTLE FAT LEG, AND THEY GOT IT LIKE THAT (DEMONSTRATES WITH HAND). SO, I SEE A SMALL CHILD, AND I FEEL LIKE THEY CRY A LITTLE, NOT A LOT, AND THEY DO RUN FEVER. YOU KNOW HOW SOME SHOTS REALLY HURT. IT HURTS, BUT NOT A WHOLE LOT. BECAUSE SOME OF THOSE SHOTS HURT MORE THAN WE THINK."

<u>Laura:</u> "Is it a live vaccine?"

<u>MEDIUM:</u> "I SEE IT MOVING WHEN YOU SAY THAT. SO IT IS LIVE, IT'S MOVING. IT'S NOT JUST AN INGREDIENT.

YEAH, IT'S CULTURED AND LIVE. IT IS LIVE, IT'S MOVING...IT LOOKS LIKE, YUCK, LITTLE LONG WORMS. EWWW."

Laura: "Because the MMR is three live viruses, and I think it's given at 18 months."

MEDIUM: "SEE I WAS PICKING A YEAR UP...ONE."
(I looked it up when I got home, and the MMR is scheduled at 12 months.[10])

Laura: "And that is the vaccine that parents notice a change. After that MMR, their child just disappears."

MEDIUM: "BUT I THINK IT IS THE RUBELLA. THE OTHER PART, MEASLES AND MUMPS, I DON'T SEE IT. DID THEY GIVE RUBELLA ALL THE TIME?"

Laura: "I don't know when it came into the schedule. They just made it a triple jab more recently, though. They used to do them individually, I think, or not at all. They used to throw measles

---

[10]http://www.cdc.gov/vaccines/recs/acip

parties, so your kids got measles, and mumps parties. They wanted children to get those childhood diseases, because it would build up their immunity. And then some genius thought, let's vaccinate them against it, and put them all in one vial. Three live viruses in one vial. And that vaccine (MMR) didn't contain thimerosal, which is part mercury, and many parents think mercury is causing autism."

<u>MEDIUM:</u> "WE HAVEN'T PICKED UP ANYTHING ABOUT MERCURY, HAVE WE?"

<u>Laura:</u> "No, and I even asked about it last time, if it was mercury from the mining in Nevada, or mercury from Thimerosal in vaccines, but they haven't said that's it."

<u>MEDIUM:</u> "YOU KNOW, THEY HAVE BEEN MINING FOR HUNDREDS OF YEARS. THEY'VE BEEN MINING SILVER; THEY'VE BEEN MINING GOLD, THEY MINE FOR DIAMONDS. THEY STIR UP THE DIRT. BUT THAT WAS BEFORE THEY PUT ALL THE STUFF IN IT. AND IT IS NOT ALL IN THE DIRT WITHIN THE STATE; IT IS WHAT'S HAPPENING IN THE DESERT."

"WE ARE FISHING AROUND ON THINGS THAT ARE BEYOND ALL OF THIS. YOU'RE LOOKING FOR ANSWERS OF WHAT IT IS THAT YOU KNOW, AND THAT'S NOT WHERE THE ANSWER LIES."

"THE RUBELLA NEEDS TO BE LOOKED INTO. BECAUSE WHAT THEY'VE DONE...THEY'VE TAKEN IT TOO LIGHTLY. THEY'VE TAKEN THE MEASLES, MUMPS, RUBELLA VACCINE TOO LIGHTLY. THEY ARE GETTING VERY SLOPPY WITH ALL OF THAT."

(I BEGIN TO ASK A QUESTION AND SHE INTERRUPTS) "OH, OH, OH...MMM-HMMM...I JUST SAW A KID GETTING, AND I'M SURE THAT THEY DON'T JUST EAT DIRT, BUT THEY JUST ATE THE DIRT, AND I'M LOOKING AT THOSE THREE LIKE THAT, AND HOW IT CAME THROUGH THAT IT WAS VERY SLOPPY, WELL I SAW A KID EATING THE DIRT, AND HE TURNS ALL SPOTTY. IT'S LIKE ALL THE GRAY SPOTS GO ALL AROUND HIM. I'M SEEING THE CHILD JUST SITTING THERE, I DON'T SEE IF IT'S GIRL, OR BOY, IT'S JUST NAKED. THIS CHILD IS LITTLE, THE CHILD LOOKS ONE,

LITTLE, A YOUNGSTER, A BABY. AND THEN I GET A HORRIBLE HEADACHE. SOMETHING HAPPENS HERE, SOMETHING HAPPENS HERE. (TOUCHES HER FOREHEAD) A LOT OF PRESSURE, IT'S LIKE I GOT HIT WITH A SLEDGEHAMMER. THEN MY THINKING GOES TO POT. AND I NEED A LOT OF LOVE; I NEED A LOT OF LOVE. I WANT SOMEONE TO HOLD ME BECAUSE I'M VERY CONFUSED AND I NEED A LOT OF LOVE. AND THEN I BECOME AN ISSUE. I BECOME AN ISSUE. I'M NOT UNDERSTANDING EVERYTHING. I WANT TO BE LIKE MY OTHER SIBBLINGS AND I CAN'T."

"THAT'S WHY THEY ALWAYS SEEK OUT HEALING, THAT'S WHY THEY WANT TO BE HELD, BUT VERY GENTLY. YOU CAN'T JUST GO AND GIVE LOVE AND THEY DON'T ACCEPT IT. IT HAS TO COME FROM A MOTHERING. BECAUSE IT'S LIKE MOTHER AND BABY, MOTHER AND CHILD. IT'S LIKE STARTING OVER, IT'S LIKE STARTING OVER LIKE YOU ARE NAKED; YOU ARE A LITTLE BABY, BUT YOU ARE ONE. IT'S LIKE YOU'RE BORN."

"AND THAT'S WHEN THEY GO INWARD, AND THAT'S WHEN THEY START SEEKING OUT THEIR PSYCHIC. AND THEN YOU'VE GOT THE 'CRYSTAL CHILDREN' IN DEVELOPMENT. SO THAT'S WHAT THEY ARE. THAT'S WHAT A CRYSTAL CHILD IS....IS SOMEONE WHO IS DEVELOPING BECAUSE THEY HAVE NO CHOICE."

"AGAIN, ALL OF THIS, THE ROOT TO THE PROBLEM IS WHAT IS GOING ON IN THE DESERT. IT'S NOT CONTAINED. THE POWDERY SUBSTANCE IS TOO THIN. YOU KNOW, IF IT WAS A WET SUBSTANCE, IF THEY DID THE RAIN, A WET SUBSTANCE, THEY COULD CONTAIN IT, BUT THEY ARE MESSING WITH DUST. YOU'RE TRYING TO CONTAIN IT, BUT IF YOU ARE GOING TO WORK WITH IT, YOU'RE GOING TO HAVE TO MOVE IT AROUND. AND IT COMES OUT. YOU KNOW, IF YOU COULD PUT IT UNDER GLASS, AND YOU WORKED WITH IT...THIS STUFF IS SO FINE, IF THEY STUCK GLOVES IN THERE, THOSE GLOVES WOULD NEED TO BE IN THERE AS WELL TO STAY. BUT THEY ARE MESSING WITH SOME THINGS THAT ARE VERY SMALL, THAT THEY CAN'T DO THAT."

"SO, THEY HAVE TO OPEN THOSE...VATS...I HEAR VATS...I HEAR THE WORD VATS. AND THE CONTAINERS THEY ARE USING...THEY ARE METAL CONTAINERS, WHEN THEY SHOULD BE, LIKE SOME TYPE OF A...YOU KNOW LIKE FLOWERS, HOW YOU PACKAGE THEM IN PAPER, AND YOU CAN BEAT ON IT, AND YOU SEE THE POWDER COMING OUT? THAT'S WHAT THEY'RE DOING. THAT'S HOW THEY'RE HANDLING THAT, INSTEAD OF PUTTING IT INTO A MORE SEALED CONTAINER. BUT SEE, THEY'RE DOING THAT THINKING THAT WHILE THE PRODUCT IS THERE...AND I DON'T SEE HOW THEY CAN CALL IT A PRODUCT, BUT THAT'S WHAT THEY'RE DOING; THEY'RE MINIMIZING THE EVIL THAT IT HAS...THE KILLING POWER THAT IT HAS."

"SEE, THE PRESIDENT (BUSH), HE DOESN'T KNOW WHAT ELSE TO DO. WHAT DO YOU DO? SEND THE AIRPLANES OVER THERE AND THEY TRY TO SHOOT YOU DOWN. YOU GO OVER THERE AND TRY TO HELP THE PEOPLE, AND THEY WON'T HELP THEMSELVES. AND WE KEEP SENDING OUR MEN OVER THERE, AND THEY KEEP KILLING THEM, ALONG WITH THEMSELVES BECAUSE THEY DON'T CARE FOR THEIR LIFE. IF THEY DON'T CARE FOR THEIR LIFE...'OKAY, THEN IT

WILL BE OVER FOR THEM' IS THE ATTITUDE... BECAUSE THERE IS NOT A SOLUTION. PEOPLE HAVE LOST THEIR OWN SOUL. PEOPLE HAVE LOST THEIR OWN SOUL TO WHOEVER THEY THINK THEY ARE PRAYING TO. THEY THINK THAT'S WHO IS TELLING THEM TO DO WHAT THEY DO. AND THE THING OF IT IS THEY ARE LOSING SIGHT OF WHO THEY ARE PRAYING TO. IT'S LIKE THE GOVERNMENT FEELS LIKE THE PRESIDENT DOESN'T HAVE ANY CHOICE, SO THEY ARE TAKING OTHER ALTERNATIVE ROUTES. THE ONLY THING IS THEY ARE HARMING US. WE ARE HARMING OURSELVES."

(George Bush was still the President of the U.S. at the time of these readings.)

"BUT YOU NOTICE WHERE TEXAS IS VERSUS WHERE NEVADA IS? I'M BEING TOLD THAT, AND I KNOW NOTHING ABOUT THE WEATHER, IF WE DO SOME RESEARCH, THE WIND BLOWS UP. SO, IT WILL GO UP INSTEAD OF DOWN, AND TEXAS IS NOT AS AFFECTED. AND THEY FEEL LIKE IF IT STARTS HERE, AND GOES UP THAT WAY...THEY ARE TRYING TO KEEP IT IN THE DESERT, BUT THAT'S NOT HAPPENING. THAT SUCKS, BECAUSE HE (BUSH) THOUGHT

ABOUT ALL OF THAT TOO. IF YOU DO A LITTLE RESEARCH, A MAJORITY OF THE TIME, THE WIND BLOWS UP AND NOT DOWN. IT GOES UP TO LIKE MICHIGAN AND GOES UP."

Laura: "The Midwest, that's where I'm from. The incidence of autism has skyrocketed there."

MEDIUM: "OVER THERE?"

Laura: "Wisconsin, where I'm from, has one of the highest autism rates in the country."

MEDIUM: "THERE YOU HAVE IT."

Laura: "Are they doing this testing in other places, or just in Nevada?"

MEDIUM: "NEVADA."

Laura: "Just here."

<u>MEDIUM:</u> "THEY ARE NOT DOING TESTING. THEY'RE DOING IT. THEY'RE MAKING IT. IT'S NOT A TEST."

"OKAY, HERE'S ANOTHER ONE...WHY DO YOU THINK THEY TRY TO SEND EVERYTHING TO YUCCA MOUNTAIN? (PROPOSED NUCLEAR WASTE DUMP IN NEVADA) WE GOT THE CRAP HERE ANYHOW."

<u>Laura:</u> "Are they doing anything at Area 51? It's restricted anyway."

<u>MEDIUM:</u> "AREA 51 IS A WHOLE OTHER STORY. IT'S A WHOLE OTHER SET OF EXPERIMENTS. IT'S ANOTHER BOOK. IT'S A WHOLE DIFFERENT STORY. AND THEY COULD CARE LESS IF THE CONTAMINATION AND ALL THAT BLOWS OVER THAT. ALL OF THAT IS MILITARY. MILITARY HAS TO DO WITH WORLD. IT HAS TO DO WITH UNIVERSE. IT HAS TO DO WITH OTHER PLANETS. THAT'S WHAT THE GOVERNMENT IS ABOUT. IT HAS TO DO WITH BIGGER THINGS."

"WE ARE ON THE OUTSKIRTS OF NEVADA. IT HAS TO HAVE SOME OUTSKIRTS, BECAUSE THEN YOU'RE GOING TO HAVE ALL THE OTHER STATES SCREAMING. IF THEY MOVED US ALL OUT OF HERE, AND DEMANDED THAT WE ALL MOVED OUT OF HERE, THEN THE BORDER STATES WOULD BE COMPLAINING. BUT SEE, SINCE THERE IS POPULATION HERE, THE BORDER STATES ARE NOT MIXING THEMSELVES UP WITH THAT LINE."

"THE ONLY THING IS THAT WIND THAT BLOWS UP, IT'S AFFECTING ALL THOSE STATES. CALIFORNIA, AND EVEN THE STATES UP THERE; WASHINGTON...I JUST HEARD, 'I DON'T WANT THAT SHIT UP THERE.' SO THEY MUST HAVE SOMEBODY RUNNING THAT STATE THAT'S FOUL-MOUTHED."

"IF THEY TRIED TO DO ANYTHING JUST FOR CONVENIENCE, THEY MIGHT HIT THE CAROLINAS. YOU KNOW, LIKE A WORKING PLACE. BUT RIGHT NOW, IT'S PRETTY MUCH IN NEVADA. AND EVERYBODY THAT'S GETTING AFFECTED IS UPSTATE, BECAUSE IT IS BLOWING

UP TOWARDS THE GREAT LAKES, AND MICHIGAN BECAUSE OF THE WAY THE WIND IS BLOWING."

"AND TEXAS IS WHERE OUR PRESIDENT (BUSH) LIVES AND THEY TOOK THAT INTO ACCOUNT WITH THE WINDS. I'M PICKING UP THAT THEY KNEW THIS AFTERWARDS, SO THEY WERE GRATEFUL THAT THEY LIVED IN TEXAS. BUT STILL, THE FACT IS, THAT'S WHERE OUR PRESIDENT LIVES, AND SO HE'S SEEING ALL THIS HAPPENING, BUT I DON'T SEE A LOT OF ACTION TAKING PLACE."

"I JUST SEE A LOT OF MOTHERS WEEPING...I SEE A LOT OF CHILDREN THAT ARE BEING HARMED. YOU KNOW THESE ARE THE CHILDREN WHO ARE SUPPOSED TO RUN OUR NATION."

"YOU NEED TO DO A STUDY OF THE WIND. YOU NEED TO DO A STUDY OF THE WIND AND THEN YOU NEED TO MAKE YOUR HYPOTHESIS OF HOW IT'S AFFECTING THE RUN OF THE WIND THAT BLOWS UP...AND THIS IS SO YOU CAN GET SOME FACTS...STARTING...WE DROVE RIGHT THROUGH IT...STARTING THERE. THEY SHOWED ME AROUND THAT

GROCERY STORE, AND ALL AROUND THERE, THAT'S WHERE YOU BEGIN YOUR WIND STUDY. AND SEE HOW ON A NORMAL BASIS HOW IT COMES INTO PLAY."

(Starting in Hawthorne, NV.)

"AND THEY NEED THE HEAT. THEY NEED THE HEAT TO MAKE IT WORK, SO YOU ARE GOING TO SEE MORE OF THIS HAPPENING IN THE SUMMERTIME THAN IN THE WINTER. AND ONE WAY TO SEE THAT IS TO CHECK OUT THAT GROCERY STORE, AND SEE HOW STOCKED UP THEY ARE IN THE WINTER VERSUS IN THE SUMMER, BECAUSE THEY NEED THE HEAT. YOU KNOW HOW IF SOMETHING IS TOO COLD IT DOESN'T...YOU HAVE TO KEEP THINGS AT A CERTAIN TEMPERATURE. THEY NEED THE WARMTH, THAT'S WHY THEY DECIDED, 'OH, WE'LL USE THE DESERT, WE'VE GOT THE RIGHT CLIMATE, WE'VE GOT THE DRY. BECAUSE THIS IS NOT LIQUID, IT'S POWDER, IT'S NOT A RAIN. THE ONLY THING IS...IF IT WAS A RAIN, A LIQUID, THEY'D BE ABLE TO CONTAIN IT BETTER THAN THEY ARE BECAUSE THIS IS DUST. DUST IS BIGGER THAN WHAT THEY ARE MAKING."

Laura: "So will these kids ever be healthy and talk? What is their prognosis? Like my son, what's going to happen to him?"

MEDIUM: "THESE KIDS ARE GOING TO HAVE TO BE UNDERSTOOD. THEY'RE GOING TO HAVE TO BE UNDERSTOOD BECAUSE THEY'RE SOULS THAT ARE TRAPPED."

"THIS IS A DISEASE THAT THEY GOT. THIS IS NOW SOMETHING THEY NEED TO FIND A CURE FOR. IT'S A DISEASE; IT'S NOT SOMETHING THAT THEY ARE BORN WITH. THEY ARE AFFECTED AND IT HAS TO BE DEALT WITH. I'M GETTING...LIKE YOUR LITTLE BOY...I PICK UP 40, IN THE AGE OF THE 40'S. I REMEMBER SOMETHING CAME THROUGH IN THE AGE OF THE 40'S."

Laura: "It was 45."

MEDIUM: "SO SOME KIND OF BREAKTHROUGH."

Laura: "That's 30 years from now."

<u>MEDIUM:</u> "WELL IT'S GOING TO END, THAT'S A GOOD THING. BUT WHAT TO DO BETWEEN NOW AND THEN? YOU HAVE TO GIVE THEM A LOT OF LOVE. YOU HAVE TO GIVE THEM A LOT OF LOVE, AND IT HAS TO COME FROM YOU. IT HAS TO COME FROM THE PARENT."

"AND I'M SEEING THAT BABY AGAIN, YOU KNOW THE NAKED BABY, BUT THE CHILD IS ALREADY A YEAR OLD. IT'S LIKE THEY ARE BEING BORN."

"SO, SOMETHING HAPPENS TO THEM, AND THEY'RE DIFFERENT BECAUSE OF SOME DISEASE THAT THEY GOT. THE'RE INNOCENT, THEY'RE INNOCENT. THEY'RE TOTALLY INNOCENT."

<u>Laura:</u> "We were in Southern California when Trevor was that age. He was three when we moved here (Nevada)."

(He had already been diagnosed with autism in CA at age three; eight months before we moved to Nevada.)

<u>MEDIUM:</u> (MEDIUM'S WORDS) "HE WAS THREE WHEN YOU MOVED HERE? AND WHEN DID THAT HAPPEN TO HIM, WHEN HE WAS IN SOUTHERN CALIFORNIA?"

<u>Laura:</u> "Before he was two. He stopped talking and stuff when he was about a year-and-a-half. It's probably just gotten worse since we've been here."

<u>MEDIUM:</u> (MEDIUM'S WORDS) "WHAT PART OF CALIFORNIA?"

<u>Laura:</u> "Thousand Oaks. That's why I'm confused...we didn't even live here then. I wonder if the wind pattern swirls around and then back up. If you've ever seen those meteorologists' maps of the wind, the wind goes down and around, then up... they swirl."

<u>MEDIUM:</u> "STUDY THE WINDS...THAT'S WHAT WE WERE TOLD. AND YOU ARE SAYING THAT A LOT OF THEM (CHILDREN WITH AUTISM) ARE UPSTATE...STUDY THE WINDS AND THEN YOU'LL SEE, BECAUSE THAT ALREADY CAME THROUGH ABOUT THE WINDS. BUT THE THING IS THAT THE NATURAL WAY FOR THAT WIND TO BLOW IS UP

THIS WAY AND UPSTATE. AND IF IT'S GOING AROUND LIKE THAT, AND THEN GOING UPSTATE, YOU ARE GOING TO FIND A LOT OF KIDS CONTAMINATED IN THAT LOWER AREA."

Laura: "Southern California and the Bay Area (San Francisco) have had huge autism increases."

MEDIUM: "CHECK THE WINDS, CHECK OUT THE WINDS."

Laura: "Oh, yeah, because it was closer to Vegas, it was down. Where we drove...it wasn't by Reno, it was down in the middle."

MEDIUM: "BUT IF YOU STUDY HOW THE WINDS BLOW FROM THAT AREA, YOU'RE GOING TO FIND THAT'S WHERE THE KIDS ARE CONTAMINATED."

"IT HAS NOTHING TO DO WITH ONE IMMUNE SYSTEM BEING STRONGER THAN THE OTHER (GENETICALLY), IT HAS TO DO WITH HOW THESE KIDS GOT OUT AND ABOUT. YOU KNOW IF THERE IS A PERSON THAT IS A HOMEBODY AND STAYS AT HOME, AND NEVER WENT ANYWHERE, AND

WAS PRETTY MUCH ON CONTROLLED AIR, THOSE PEOPLE...THEIR KIDS ARE ALRIGHT. BUT THE ONES THAT GOT OUT AND ABOUT, THOSE KIDS...AND WITH THE SHOT COMBINATION...AND THEY WERE RUNNING THE FEVER. IF THEY MADE IT TEN DAYS...I DON'T KNOW, I GOT TEN DAYS, AND THEN I GOT A MONTH."

(SHE ASKS OUT LOUD) "WELL, WHICH ONE IS IT? TELL ME."

"OKAY, IF THEY MADE IT TEN DAYS, THEN THEY WOULD BE OKAY. BUT THE PARENTS WOULDN'T SEE ANYTHING FOR PROBABLY A MONTH. SO, LETS SAY IF YOUR CHILD GOT THE SHOT, AND YOU KEPT THEM IN...AND I HEARD TEETHING, SOMETHING ABOUT TEETHING...AND THEY WERE NOT OUTSIDE...THEY DIDN'T HAVE ANYTHING HAPPEN TO THEM. BUT THE ONES THAT WERE OUT AND ABOUT, AND HAD PARTICLES FALL ON THEM, IN COMBINATION WITH JUST GETTING THE VACCINATION; THOSE WERE THE ONES THAT GOT AFFECTED."

"SO, THERE ARE SOME CHILDREN WHO DON'T GO TO DAYCARE, WHO DON'T GO HERE AND THERE, WHO ARE JUST

MORE INSIDE. THAT'S WHY IT'S CREATED CONFUSION AS TO...IT CAN'T BE, BECAUSE WHY DID THIS KID NOT GET IT AND THIS KID DID? IT'S THE DIFFERENCE OF GETTING ONE KID OUT OF THE HOUSE...ONE KID BEING IN A PLASTIC BUBBLE AND THE OTHER NOT BEING IN A PLASTIC BUBBLE."

Laura: "Can the dust particles be transferred from person to person?"

MEDIUM: "GOOD QUESTION. OKAY, WHAT I'M SEEING IS THAT IT GOES TO THE SKIN...THAT'S WHY THEY ARE MAKING IT SO FINE...IT HAS TO PENETRATE THE CLOTHES. IT HAS TO PENETRATE THE CLOTHES, AND THEN IT HAS TO PENETRATE THE SKIN. AND SO AFTER IT PENETRATES THE SKIN, IT JUST SITS THERE. OKAY, IF IT'S PENETRATING THE CLOTHES, AND THAT'S WHY IT'S SO FINE BECAUSE IT HAS TO GO THROUGH THE CLOTHES. LIKE THE ONES IN THE MILITARY, THEY ARE WEARING ALL OF THEIR THICK MILITARY CLOTHES. THEN IT LANDS ON THE SKIN, AND THEN THEY GET SICK."

(SHE ASKS OUTLOUD) "OKAY, HOW DOES THAT TIE BACK TO THE MUMMY THING? I'M PICKING UP IT'S OUTER, SOMETHING OUTER..."

"OKAY NOW I'M GETTING THE WIRY GUY. AND HE'S TALKING TOO FAST AND I DON'T EVEN UNDERSTAND WHAT HE'S SAYING. OKAY, LET ME JUST SAY WHAT I HEAR. HE'S SHOWING ME A BLACKBOARD AND ALL THIS STUFF. I DON'T KNOW WHAT ALL OF IT IS. MAYBE NEXT TIME WE WILL BRING A BLACKBOARD, OR SOMETHING TO WRITE ON, IS WHAT HE'S TELLING ME. SOMETHING BIG AND WE'LL JUST WRITE IT OUT AND MAYBE YOU CAN PHOTOGRAPH IT AND STICK IT IN YOUR BOOK. SO THAT SOMEONE THAT UNDERSTANDS IT WILL LOOK AT IT AND WILL BE LIKE, 'OH, OKAY THAT MAKES SENSE.' BECAUSE FOR YOU TO GO DO RESEARCH ON ALL THIS STUFF, THE WINDS, AND THIS, AND THAT...THIS, WHAT HE'S GOING TO GIVE US, IS SOMETHING FOR SOMEONE ELSE TO LOOK AT. I DON'T KNOW IF WE NEED TO PUT IT ON THE BACK COVER, SO IT'S RIGHT THERE FOR SOME MATHEMETICIAN TO LOOK AT, BECAUSE THIS IS NOT FOR US, IS WHAT I'M BEING TOLD."

"I SEE THE ROOT OF, AND...OKAY, I DID A LOT OF MATH, BUT NOT ALL OF THIS WHAT HE'S SHOWING ME. I HAVE NO IDEA WHAT ALL OF THIS STUFF IS. IT'S FORMULAS...AND IT'S LIKE A STORY TO HIM. TO HIM, HE'S LOOKING AT IT AND IT'S MAKING PERFECT SENSE."

"THIS WIRY GUY IS VERY WIRY, HE'S VERY SMART. WHEN HE SHOWS IT TO ME AND I PUT IT ON PAPER, IT'S GOING TO LOOK LIKE ART TO ME. BUT IT'S A STORY IN MATHEMATICS, IS WHAT HE'S SAYING. I'LL TELL YOU WHAT THIS IS FOR LATER, IS WHAT HE'S TELLING ME. AND WHAT HE'S SAYING IS THAT IT IS A SOLUTION TO A PROBLEM. I (THE MEDIUM) ASKED IF THIS IS A SOLUTION TO THE 45-YEAR-OLD PERSON BEING WELL, AND HE SAID, I WILL TELL YOU THEN WHAT ALL OF THIS IS."

"YOU HAVE ANOTHER QUESTION?"

<u>Laura</u>: "When I write the book, should I write it as fact or fiction?"

<u>MEDIUM:</u> "WE'LL TALK ABOUT THAT LATER. BECAUSE WHATEVER IT IS RIGHT NOW, IT WOULDN'T MAKE SENSE TO US...TO YOU OR ME...IS WHAT I'M BEING TOLD. SO, WAIT TO MAKE THE DECISION. THE DECISION IS ALREADY MADE. BUT IT'S NOT READY TO SHARE. AND THEN I SEE THE WORD... (SPELLS IT OUT) F-A-C-T. AND THEN I SEE THE QUOTATION MARK AND THE DOT, DOT, DOT, OF WHAT'S TO FOLLOW, OKAY."

"YOU KNOW, A LOT OF WHAT'S IN CARTOONS COMES TRUE, IS WHAT THEY SAID. A LOT OF WHAT'S IN CARTOONS COMES TRUE. IT COMES FROM PEOPLE TAPPING IN AND THEY CALL IT CREATIVITY, AND IT'S GLIMPSES OF THE FUTURE. AND THAT'S WHY SO MANY TIMES, PEOPLE LOOK AT THINGS AND THEY THINK IT'S NOT REAL, AND THEN IT TURNS OUT TO BE REAL. NOW, WE ARE NOT READY FOR THIS TO BE REAL, BUT WE WILL BE BY JANUARY. AND THAT'S SOON, AND I SEE 2008."

"AND YOU'LL BE TALKING TO PEOPLE ALSO. THERE ARE SOME PEOPLE THAT YOU ARE GOING TO BE TALKING TO THAT WILL ENLIGHTEN SOME OF THE THINGS THAT HAVE

COME THROUGH FROM SPIRIT TO MAKE YOU A BRAVER SOUL."

"THEY ARE GIVING US BIG FLAGS...AMERICAN FLAGS, AND THEY'RE FLYING. YOU KNOW, I'M BEING TOLD THAT NEVADA IS PART OF THE UNITED STATES. IT'S PART OF WHERE WE ARE SUPPOSED TO BE LIVING. AND THE FLAGS ARE FLOWN HERE."

"THE WHOLE ARGUMENT ABOUT ALL OF THIS STUFF, IS THAT IF THEY DON'T DO IT HERE, WHERE DO THEY DO IT? WHERE DO THEY DO IT, IF THEY DON'T DO IT THERE? THE WINDS ARE NOT RIGHT IN CALIFORNIA, CLOSE TO THE WATERS. IT WOULD CONTAMINATE THE WHOLE COUNTRY IF IT WAS PREPARED IN CALIFORNIA BECAUSE OF THE WINDS. ALSO, IT'S NOT HOT ENOUGH THERE. IT NEEDS WARMTH TO KEEP EVERYTHING DRY. AND IT CANNOT BE HUMID, AND THIS IS A PLACE THAT IT'S NOT HUMID. YOU LOOK AT ALL THE STATES ALL AROUND, THERE'S HUMIDITY. TEXAS IS HUMID, FLORIDA IS SUPER HUMID. CALIFONIA IS HUMID. IT HAS TO BE HERE. BUT WHAT DO

YOU DO, THROW IT IN A BUBBLE, AND THROW EVERYBODY OUT? AND THEN SCARE EVERYBODY?"

(TIMER GOES OFF. WE ALLOTTED ONE HOUR OF TIME FOR EACH SESSION)

"THE LAST WORDS I HEARD WERE… I'M TRYING TO BRING YOU UNDERSTANDING."

(CD ends)

***

Later Discoveries

The medium made me my copy of the session as we chatted again. As crazy as all of this sounded, something resonated that it was real and that this book needed to be written. Notice how the information came through. We did not ask for these particular spirits. They came to us. I was expecting one of my deceased family members to come through with information about autism for the book, not those who did. As I said earlier, draw your own conclusion. Obviously, this was a big deal in the spirit world too.

I questioned what they were saying and why they were telling it to me. Perhaps it was because I was open to it and wanted to help my beloved child. I believed that spirit communication was not only possible, but also a very valid way to get information. I had been getting readings on a regular basis for years to connect with my late husband and to get future information. If you can communicate with departed loved ones, I reasoned, why not others in spirit that you didn't know personally? The process is the same. Any other parent of a child with autism who didn't have my background would probably have laughed it off and never gone back.

It became one of my life's missions to find out what happened to my angel, my firstborn son. I vowed to not leave any stone unturned in order to pull him out of his cocoon and bring him back to me. I knew he was in there somewhere. As long as spirit was willing to give me those answers, I was willing to listen and see what came through. Desperate times call for desperate measures.

I listened to the CD again on the drive home, and immediately started to do some research on the computer when I got home. I was still a healthy skeptic and needed more proof. I tried to find some information to back up some of the messages that came through in the reading. I was still somewhat in denial that this could really be happening in this country.

The Wind Patterns

As suggested, I studied the winds. First, I looked at current animated weather from our local news stations, and from what I could tell, the winds blew to the northeast of Nevada. These winds are called "Westerlies" according to Wikipedia. Wind direction is reported by the direction from which it originates on the Earth's surface. In the Northern Hemisphere, from the equator at 0° to 30° N. latitude, the prevailing wind pattern is Northeasterly Trade winds, right to left when looking at a map. From 30° N. latitude to 60° N. latitude, the prevailing wind pattern is Westerlies, left to right when looking at a map. (Most of the U.S. is in this 30° to 60° N. latitude range, except southern Florida, part of Texas, Hawaii and Alaska.)

I wondered how the wind from the desert in Nevada could blow to Southern California, where Trevor was contaminated, if we had a predominantly Westerly wind pattern. I knew from living in Nevada that the winds through the Sierra Nevada Mountains could be wild and dangerous. I also remembered that when I lived in Southern California; we would get fierce, hurricane-force winds, called the Santa Ana winds, which actually blew east to west, toward the ocean, instead of the usual west to east winds, toward shore. These Santa Ana winds were responsible for a lot of wildfires, including many that I experienced firsthand. I wondered where these winds were coming from. Could they be coming from the deserts in Nevada?

I found a FAQ page on the UCLA Atmospheric and Oceanic Science's website, which answered the question, what are Santa Ana winds? "Santa Ana winds are dry and warm (often hot) winds in the Southern California area that blow in from the desert-which includes the Great Basin of the western United States, incorporating Nevada and part of Utah."[11] So the winds did originate in Nevada! That would explain how the "dust" traveled

---

[11]http://www.atmos.ucla.edu/fovell/ASother/mm5/SantaAna/santa_ana_faq.html

west from Nevada to Southern California, since wind typically blows from west to east.

I also found a picture titled "Dusty Skies over Southern California" taken from NASA's MISR (Multi-angle Imaging SpectroRadiometer) in space. The accompanying article said, "The strength of the winds varies greatly from place to place, and the Santa Anas can be sufficiently strong enough to pick up surface dust."[12] The picture showed dust covering the Pacific Ocean and curving upward toward the northeast.

I also found that a similar wind pattern known as "Diablo Winds" start in the Great Basin, (Nevada desert) and then blows toward San Francisco. Wikipedia defines a Diablo wind as "a relatively recent term for a hot, dry offshore wind from the northeast that typically occurs in the San Francisco Bay area of Northern California during the spring and fall. The same wind pattern also affects other parts of California's coastal ranges. The Diablo winds are created by the combination of strong high pressure at the surface over the Great Basin, strongly sinking air

---

[12] http://www.photojournal.jpl.nasa.gov/catalog/PIA03445

loft, and lower pressure off the California coast."[13] The winds can blow up to 100 mph, and blow far out over the ocean. From there, winds circulate in a huge wheel counterclockwise, and then the Westerlies blow across the United States from west to east.

Knowing that the typical wind pattern from Nevada blows to the northeast, I looked at a U.S. map. The state directly to the northeast of Nevada is Idaho, potato country. Idaho is also directly east of Oregon. So, that means if the wind pattern is reverse, in the case of Santa Ana or Diablo winds, the wind still blows west and then north over the Pacific Ocean before heading east. Idaho gets it that way too. No wonder the potatoes are so contaminated.

It was hard to find a lot of websites with wind pattern information, and then I found out why. Prior to 9/11, anyone was allowed to view an online model of air patterns in the United States. Now, thanks to Homeland Security, the National Oceanic and Atmospheric Administration maintains that information, and it is closed to the public. Researchers who study wind patterns must login with a password. Across the country, public resources

---

[13]http://www.en.wikipedia.org/wiki/Diablo_wind

like the air-pattern model are being sealed for fear they might potentially fall into terrorist hands.[14]

A lot of information can be found by studying pollution and ozone, however. I was very surprised to find that pollution and greenhouse gasses from China have been detected in the Sierra Nevada Mountains. Estimates are that a third of California's air pollution and a fifth of Oregon's come from China. Sensors in the Sierra Nevada Mountains have identified huge Chinese pollution clouds that traverse the Pacific.[15] It is more than 6,000 miles from China to CA. The point is that if pollution can travel thousands of miles traveling by wind, as proven in this study, it makes this whole theory given in the readings more probable. The "dust" could blow across the whole U.S.!

I also found that dust from the Sahara desert in Africa blows via the westward-moving Trade winds. Over 50% of the African dust that reaches the United States affects Florida. Dust events have been linked to a decline in the health of coral reefs across

[14]http://www.uaf.edu/journal/extreme/Patriot/cathy.html

[15]http://www.infinitehealthresources.com/Store/Resource/Article/85/1/1307.html

the Caribbean and Florida.[16] This could explain the increase in autism in Hawaii. The trade winds blow from the U.S. in that direction. I had questioned why Hawaii had an increase. The wind blows that direction, and as shown in the previous examples, dust from the desert and pollution can travel thousands of miles, even across oceans. I'm no meteorologist, but I could see how the scenario in the readings could really happen that way.

Autism Statistics

Next, I looked up the latest autism rates across the country. Not surprisingly, the states with the highest increases in autism were the same states that follow the path of the wind from Hawthorne, NV. The states with the highest autism rates were the more northern states, from coast to coast. In 2003, the top ten states per capita of children with autism were Oregon, Minnesota, Indiana, Massachusetts, Maine, Maryland, Michigan, California, Connecticut and Wisconsin.[17] All northern states. From the same website, I also found statistics on cumulative growth in autism cases among children aged 6 to 22 by state. The top 5 states (all in the path of the wind from NV, where it is being

[16] U.S. Geological Survey (2006). Coral Mortality and African Dust.

[17] http://www.statemaster.com

created) were Ohio, Nevada, Wisconsin, Maryland, and New Hampshire. The top state, Ohio, had a 23,291% increase!

Just before this book came out, I found more current autism prevalence statistics by state. From the Fighting Autism website, the top ten states of autism prevalence in Public Schools for eight-year-olds in 2008-2009 were: Minnesota, Oregon, Maine, Connecticut, Rhode Island, Pennsylvania, Indiana, Massachusetts, New Jersey, and Wisconsin. Nevada followed at number 11. As predicted, the least prevalent states are all southern states.[18] All states are affected, but the northern states more than the southern states. California leads with the number of autism cases in Public Schools for ages 3-22 in 2008-2009 with 53,050. That's where we lived when my son was "contaminated." I wonder how many others moved out of state?

The most current data came out shortly before this book was released. A new study published October 5, 2009 in the American Academy of Pediatrics' journal *Pediatrics* found a parent-reported Autism prevalence rate of ***one in every 91 American children,*** including ***one in 58 boys.*** The study used data

---

[18] www.figfhtingautism.org/idea/autism-state-rankings-prevalence.php

gathered as part of the 2007 National Survey of Children's Health (NSCH), a national survey directed and funded by the Health Resources and Services Administration (HRSA) and Centers for Disease Control (CDC).[19] This is one percent of all U.S. children! Another interesting thing that came from this study was that out of every 160 children whose parents reported that they had an ASD (Autism Spectrum Disorder), 60 of them (37.5%) no longer have an ASD.[20] This begs the question, how does one recover from a genetic disorder?

According to the Autism Speaks website, roughly 24,000 children a year are diagnosed with autism in our country! In an article from the Age of Autism website on December 17, 2009 titled *CDC Brings Bad Tidings: 40,000 Children Diagnosed With Autism In This Year Alone* shows just how bad the autism prevalence is getting. This rapid increase in such a short period rules out better diagnosis and genetics.[21]

---

[19]http://www.autismspeaks.org/donate/we_need_answers_.php
[20]http://www.huffingtonpost.com/david-kirby/autism-rate-now-at-one-pe_b_256141.html
[21]http://www.ageofautism.com/2009/12/-cdc-brings-bad-tidings-40000-children-diagnosed-...

Also, just before this book was released, the new Autism Statistics were released by the Centers for Disease Control. They announced on December 18, 2009 that one in 110 American Children has autism, up from one in 150. The data was extracted from screenings of health and educational records in 2006 from 8-year-olds (birth year 1998). This is the year my son Trevor was born. The CDC previously looked at autism rates of 8-year-olds in 2002 (birth year 1994). In the span of just four years, the rate of autism in the United States increased by an alarming 57 percent![22] So, somewhere between one in 110 and one in 91 is the current autism rate. What if this is the environmental factor that everyone is looking for?

The economic implications of autism should alarm us all, even if you don't have a child with autism. The lifetime cost of caring for a child with autism is $3.5 to $5 million. The annual U.S. cost is $90 billion.[23] Yes, billion! Who is going to pay for all of these children when they are adults and their parents die? Autism affects all of us! So does contaminated topsoil that we grow food in.

---

[22]Estepp, Rebecca, "New Autism Statistics- CDC: One in 110 American Children has Autism, *Morbidity and Mortality Weekly Report*, Dec. 18, 2009.
[23]http://www.usatoday.com/news/health/2008-11-03-autism_N.htm

Vaccines

I also looked up more about the vaccine schedule. In the reading, they said that the vaccine that contained the ingredient that was combining with the biological warfare was given at 12 months and that it was added to the schedule later. I discovered later that the MMR vaccine is given at 12 months, and then a second dose is given between ages 4 and 6.[24] I also found some interesting history of the vaccine schedule. According to The Children's Hospital of Philadelphia's website, it said, "In the early 1950's there were four vaccines: diphtheria, tetanus, pertussis and smallpox. Because three of these were combined into a single shot (DTP), children received five shots by the time they were 2 years old, and not more than one shot at a single visit.

By the mid-1980's, there were seven vaccines: diphtheria, tetanus, pertussis, measles, mumps, rubella and polio. Because six of these vaccines were combined into two shots (DTP and MMR), and one, the polio vaccine, was given by mouth, children still received five shots by the time they were 2 years old and not more than one shot at a single visit. Since the mid-1980's, many

[24]http://www.cdc.gov/vaccines/recs/acip

vaccines have been added to the schedule. Hib vaccine was added in the late 1980's. Again, I discovered later that the MMR was added in the 1980's.

In the 1990's, hepatitis B, and varicella vaccines were added and the polio vaccine shot (IPV) replaced the oral vaccine (OPV). In the year 2000, the pneumococcal vaccine was added and since 2004, the influenza, hepatitis A and rotavirus vaccines were added. Now children could receive as many as 24 shots ***(36 now)*** by 2 years of age and five shots in a single visit!"[25] Not only is it five shots per visits, but some of those shots are triple-jabs, making it more like 8 shots in a single visit. At the one year visit, not only do they get the MMR, they also are scheduled to get Polio, DTP, Hib, and Hepatitis B.[26] What do you think that does to a baby's immune system?

The following study came out shortly before this book was published. It is a Special Report called *Autism and Vaccines around the World* put out in April 2009 by Generation Rescue, Inc. Keep in mind that the data is from 2006; the autism rate has

---

[25] http://www.chop.edu/consumer/jsp/division/generic.jsp?id=75700

[26] http://www.cdph.ca.gov/programs/immunize/Documents/table1-2HibChanges.pdf-win

gone up since then. It concluded that The United States has the highest number of mandated vaccines for children under 5 in the world (36, double the Western world average of 18), the highest autism rate in the world (1 in 150, 10 times or more the rate of some other Western countries), but only places 34th in the world for its children under 5 mortality rate.[27] This study isn't exactly comparing apples to apples because of the years and methods of data collection in various countries, but it does show that we have the highest autism rate of any country. Their conclusion is that it gives credibility to the relationship between vaccines and autism. However, correlation doesn't mean causation. They don't know about the biological warfare.

After hearing the cause of autism in the readings, I was so grateful that I had followed my instincts and did not allow my second child, Damon, to get the MMR shot. I stopped vaccinating him altogether at 15 months. He was sick when his MMR was due at 12 months and didn't get it then, which was the same time I left the pediatrician they were seeing. By the way, your child can still attend school without being fully vaccinated. You just have to

[27]http://www.rescuepost.com/files/grautism_and_vaccines_world_special_report1.pdf

fill out a vaccine waiver with the school district. No one tells you that at the time. They just make you feel like an unfit parent if you question things. What happened to parental choice and informed refusal? The CDC even has a list on their website by state of Childcare and School Immunization Requirements Exemptions Allowed.[28] This list is also on Generation Rescue's website.[29] Some states allow medical, religious, or philosophical exemptions so your child doesn't need to be fully immunized to attend daycare or school.

I didn't have Damon vaccinated any further mainly because a lot of parents of children with autism, including me, saw their first child regress after receiving the MMR vaccine. I did not want to play Russian Roulette with his life after seeing my older son disappear. I didn't know for certain at the time if he had some "genetic predisposition," and that the MMR vaccine was possibly the "trigger" that could cause autism, as many theories I had read suggested. I just couldn't take that chance. I know my older son was not born autistic, he became that way.

---

[28] http://www.2a.cdc.gov/nip/schoolsurv/irExemptions.htm

[29] http://www.generationrescue.org/vaccine_information/vaccine-exemptions.htm

Plus, after researching more and studying homeopathy, I felt comfortable with my decision. Many of the childhood diseases that they vaccinate for are treatable with homeopathic remedies, or they are not life threatening. Vaccinating was more of a risk than not vaccinating. Remember, it isn't called a "recommended" vaccine schedule for nothing. There is a lot of money at stake.

MS and the Polio Vaccine

I found it very interesting that the President who came through, who had Polio, mentioned that Multiple Sclerosis in young women is caused from toying with the Polio vaccine. Not only has my sister been diagnosed with MS, I also know four other young women in their 20's or 30's diagnosed with MS. I did a little research, and I found a few websites that mentioned the possible link.

One website stated that "The tremendous reduction of paralysis from polio has seemed to parallel a rise in the incidence of multiple sclerosis in our culture. These epidemiological changes caused George Vithoulkas, one of the world's most well-known homeopaths, to speculate that the rise in multiple sclerosis is due to the polio vaccine."[30] Hopefully the information in this reading will end up in the right hands to lead to more research into this link and a cure for MS as well.

***

[30]http://realmedicine.ca/index.php?file=ms

CHAPTER THREE

MEDIUM: "TODAY IS DECEMBER 6, 2007, AND LAURA AND I ARE HERE TO CHANNEL THIS BOOK, AND RIGHT NOW WE ARE CALLING IT 'THE MUMMY.' WHAT WAS THE TOPIC? IT WAS ABOUT HEALING..."

Laura: "Healing...present and future."

MEDIUM: "HEALING, PRESENT AND FUTURE. AND YOU HAD ASKED ABOUT IF THE BOOK WAS FICTION OR NON-FICTION. AND THAT WAS CROSSING MY MIND A LOT SINCE THE LAST MEETING, AND I JUST PICK UP, 'IT IS TRUE. IT IS TRUE.' SO IT IS NOT SOMETHING THAT IS MADE UP. IT IS TRUE. I JUST PICK UP THAT IT IS TRUE, OVER AND OVER, OKAY."

(SHE DUMPS SOME SAGE ON THE TABLE) "I LIKE TO PUT MY HANDS IN SAGE NOW. I DON'T ALWAYS BURN IT (NATIVE

AMERICAN TRADITION CALLED SMUDGING TO CLEAR THE ENERGY) BUT I BREAK IT UP, SO IF YOU HEAR CRACKLING ON THE RECORDING, THAT'S WHAT IT IS."

"OKAY. HERE WE GO. LET'S DO THIS. WE WANT A REALLY STRONG COMMUNICATION. (SHE SAYS A PERSONAL PRAYER.) I ASK FOR THE HIGHEST AND BEST SPIRITS TO COME THROUGH NOW. OKAY, WHEN I ASKED FOR THE SPIRITS TO COME THROUGH, THE HIGHEST AND THE BEST, I FELT THIS ENERGY COME AROUND ME LIKE THAT, AND THEN THIS TALL BEING STANDS BEHIND ME. I FEEL LIKE HIS ARMS ARE RIGHT HERE, CROUCHED OVER ME, LIKE HE'S LOOKING AT WHAT I'M DOING WITH MY HANDS. HE PUTS HIS HEAD IN MY HEAD TO TAKE A LOOK. CUZ HE WAS TRYING TO USE MY EYEBALLS, MY PHYSICAL EYEBALLS. THAT'S WHAT THEY HAVE TO DO IN ORDER FOR THEM TO BE ABLE TO USE THE PHYSICAL SENSES, AND SEEING IS PART OF A PHYSICAL REALITY. FEELING, EATING, THE HUNGER AND ALL THOSE THINGS HAVE TO DO WITH THE BODY. AND I KNOW IT'S A MALE, AND I KNOW THAT'S WHAT HE WAS DOING. I HEAR A VERY LOW VOICE."

"AND I FEEL THAT HE'S A FRIEND OF THE WIRY ONE. SO, THEY KNOW EACH OTHER. AND, IN PUBLIC, THEY JUST SHAKE HANDS, BEHIND CLOSED DOORS; THEY ARE MORE AFFECTIONATE BECAUSE THEY ARE MORE OF A FRIEND THAN TO THE WORLD THEY LEAD ON. BECAUSE THEY HAD TO DO WITH A LOT OF THINGS THAT HAD TO DO WITH SCIENTIFIC THINGS. THEY DIDN'T WANT THE WORLD TO THINK THAT THEIR MIND WAS CLOUDED BECAUSE OF FRIENDSHIP. SO, THEY KEPT IT BUSINESS, BUT BEHIND CLOSED DOORS THEY WERE REALLY, TRULY GREAT FRIENDS IN A BEAUTIFUL WAY. I FEEL LIKE HE CARED, AS IN TAKE CARE OF...THIS PERSON WOULD TAKE CARE OF THE WIRY ONE. SO, HE KNOWS A LOT THAT WENT ON...."

"AND NOW I'M PICKING UP THE WIRY ONE. I THINK THAT HE WAS BRINGING HIM THROUGH, AND ACKNOWLEDGING THAT THIS IS A GREAT FRIEND. WITHOUT THIS PERSON, HE DOESN'T FEEL THAT HE WOULD HAVE ACCOMPLISHED THE THINGS THAT HE DID BECAUSE OTHER PEOPLE DIDN'T HAVE FORESIGHT OF WHAT HE COULD DO. AND THAT'S A LOT OF THE SAME THING THAT WE HAVE GOING ON HERE.

BUT WE ARE DOING IT ON A DIFFERENT MEASURE IS WHAT HE'S SAYING."

"THEY'RE TELLING ME THAT YOU (LAURA) ARE GOING TO HAVE TO...THERE ARE SOME THINGS THAT YOU ARE GOING TO HAVE TO SHUT DOWN IN ORDER TO GET YOUR FOCUS AND COMPLETE THIS PROJECT. AND IT'S JUST ONE OF YOUR EARS. IT'S LIKE THE HEARING STOPPED, LIKE YOU'RE IN YOUR HEAD INSTEAD OF LISTENING. BUT THE OTHER EAR WAS OKAY. SO, IT'S JUST ONE OF THE EARS. SO, DON'T THINK ANYTHING IS WRONG WITH YOU, IF THIS IS A REALITY EXACTLY LIKE THEY ARE SAYING. IT IS JUST A WAY TO GET YOU FOCUSSED ON WHAT YOU'RE DOING. JUST GO WITH THE FLOW, AND THEN AFTERWARDS, YOU'LL SEE YOUR CONNECTION WITH ALL THE MATERIAL. BUT AS YOU'RE GOING ALONG, JUST DO IT. DON'T QUESTION IT UNTIL THE COMPLETION, AND THEN WHEN YOU HAVE THE FULL EXPERIENCE ON PAPER, FOR THE WORLD TO GREET, THEN YOU'VE DONE THE RIGHT THING."

"CUZ IT'S AFFECTING THE BOTH OF YOU...IT'S AFFECTING THE BOTH OF YOU. SO, STEP BACK AND LOOK AT IT AS A

BUBBLE. AND YOU ARE ON THE OUTSIDE OF THAT BUBBLE. CUZ YOU'RE AFRAID OF SOMETHING THAT HASN'T HAPPENED YET. AND YOU'RE COMING INTO KNOWLEDGE THAT YOU CAN PREVENT MANY THINGS IN YOUR OWN PERSONAL LIVES; BUT DON'T RUN AWAY FROM IT. INSTEAD, APPLY THE SPONGE, AND CLEAN IT UP. YOU KNOW, JUST CUZ THE DISHES ARE DIRTY, DOESN'T MEAN YOU THROW THEM AWAY. YOU CLEAN THEM UP AND USE THEM AGAIN. THAT'S WHAT YOU'RE SUPPOSED TO BE DOING...THE BOTH OF YOU. SO, FEAR NOT."

<u>Laura</u>: "Okay."

<u>MEDIUM</u>: (THE WIRY ONE SPEAKING) "I LIKE TO BE CALLED 'THE WIRY ONE.' THAT'S THE NAME I GAVE YOU FOR ME IN THE BEGINNING. I JUST SEE A LOT OF SCRIBBLING. YOU DON'T HAVE THAT CHALKBOARD YET."

(MEDIUM'S WORDS) "WE'LL BRING ONE, WE'LL BRING ONE. OKAY. OH, MY WRIST WAS JUST LIKE...HE WAS JUST JOLTING IT."

Laura: "It looked like he was making you write in the air."

MEDIUM: "I DON'T THINK HE PAID ATTENTION. OKAY, NOW THIS IS ME (THE MEDIUM) TALKING. I DON'T THINK HE PAID ATTENTION, HE KIND OF SNAPPED ME OUT OF IT BECAUSE...MY WRIST...IT WAS LIKE HE JOLTED IT, AND I DON'T THINK HE PAID ATTENTION WHEN HE WAS DOING THIS, HE WOULD JUST GO INTO A FRENZY AND START WRITING ALL THIS STUFF DOWN. AND THAT'S WHAT HE WAS DOING TO ME. LIKE ALL OF A SUDDEN, IT WAS LIKE HE WAS WRITING ON THIS CHALKBOARD. SO, WE NEED TO GET THAT. WE NEED TO PUT IT ON OUR LIST. I'LL PICK ONE UP, OR YOU CAN PICK ONE UP, BUT WE NEED SOME CHALK TOO."

Laura: "I can pick one up on my way home."

MEDIUM: "HE REALLY DID A JOB TO MY WRIST! OKAY, HERE WE GO. I ASK FOR THE HIGHEST AND BEST TO COME THROUGH NOW. I'M HERE...I'M HERE, IS WHAT I HEAR HIM SAYING. HE SAYS, 'WHY DON'T YOU LAY DOWN?' AND I'M

LIKE...NO; I'M NOT GOING TO LIE DOWN. (LAUGHS) THAT WAS WEIRD."

(Perhaps a joke referring to the medium that was mentioned in Chapter One, known as The Sleeping Prophet because he laid down as he channeled.)

"THIS IS COMING FROM HIM WITH A LOT OF LOVE. THIS IS A WAY THAT HE FEELS LIKE HE CAN HELP THE WORLD ONCE AGAIN. I WAS INCLUDED IN A LOT OF THINGS THAT HAPPENED THAT MY INFORMATION WAS USED AND I DIDN'T EVEN KNOW IT, IN A LOT OF AREAS. THERE WAS LOTS OF MONEY MADE FROM THE THINGS THAT I CAME UP WITH, BUT MY WHOLE THING WAS THE VISIONS THAT I NEEDED TO PUT OUT THERE."

(MEDIUM'S WORDS) "OKAY, TELL US ABOUT THE BOOK. TELL US WHAT WE ARE SUPPOSED TO BE DOING ABOUT THE BOOK."

"WE ARE BEING TOLD ALL OF THIS INFORMATION BECAUSE IF WE START QUESTIONING THE FACT THAT WE ARE HAVING THE MEETINGS, AND THE BOOK, AND WHERE IS

THIS GOING, AND WHAT DO WE DO WITH IT AND ALL THAT...WE ARE DOING WHAT WE ARE SUPPOSED TO BE DOING."

(THE WIRY ONE) "LET'S GET TO WORK, LET'S GET TO WORK. YOU BRING THE BLACKBOARD NEXT TIME. WE NEED TO KEEP IT IN ORDER. SO THE INFORMATION THAT WE GET TODAY, WE ARE GOING TO SKIP WHAT'S SUPPOSED TO BE FOR THE NEXT PART, AND WE ARE GOING TO JUMP ON TO THE NEXT PART. SO, YOU ARE GOING TO HAVE TO FLIP-FLOP AROUND. THIS ONE (#3) IS GOING TO BE THE FOLLOWING ONE (#4), AND THE FOLLOWING ONE (#4) IS GOING TO BE THIS ONE (#3)."

***

CHAPTER THREE- PART TWO

(Note to reader: Because of the instructions to have the rest of this reading be Chapter 4, the remainder of Chapter 3 is actually the reading from our next session, which was four days later.)

MEDIUM: "OKAY, WHAT'S TODAY?"

Laura: "December 11th."

MEDIUM: "TODAY IS DECEMBER 11, 2007, AND THIS IS OUR FOURTH SESSION FOR THE BOOK, BUT THIS IS SUPPOSED TO BE THE THIRD CHAPTER. LET'S SAY A PRAYER, LAURA, AND THEN WE'LL GET STARTED. (SHE SAYS A PERSONAL PRAYER). IT FEELS SCARY, I DON'T KNOW WHY. LET ME SET

THE TIMER. IT FEELS SCARY, WHY LAURA? DID YOU FEEL IT? DID YOU FEEL THAT? I FEEL VERY SHAKY."

Laura: "I've felt queasy all day."

MEDIUM: "I ASK FOR A WHITE LIGHT OF PROTECTION AGAINST FEAR. I ASK FOR THE HIGHEST AND BEST SPIRITS TO COME THROUGH NOW. OKAY, WHEN I ASKED FOR A WHITE LIGHT OF PROTECTION AGAINST FEAR, THEN I FELT BETTER AND WHEN I ASKED FOR THE HIGHEST AND BEST, I SAW THE WIRY ONE RIGHT AWAY, AND SOME OTHER PEOPLE WITH HIM. I FEEL LIKE IT'S THE SAME THREE, LIKE THAT PRESIDENT, AND SOMEBODY ELSE, BUT THERE'S THREE. THERE'S GOING TO BE SOMEBODY ELSE THAT'S GOING TO COME THROUGH FOR SOME OF THE OTHER CHAPTERS AS WE GO ALONG, BUT THESE ARE THE THREE THAT WE ARE SUPPOSED TO BE DEALING WITH RIGHT NOW."

"AAH, THE CHALKBOARD, IS WHAT I HEAR. AND YOU KNOW THAT COMES FROM THE WIRY ONE. HIS NAME IS REALLY (SAYS A DIFFERENT PRONOUNCIATION) IT'S NOT LIKE WE

PRONOUNCE IT. SO WE ARE SAYING IT WRONG, IS WHAT HE'S TELLING ME. SO, THE ACCENT IS OFF IS WHAT HE'S TELLING ME. THAT'S WHY HE PREFERS, YOU KNOW HOW HE SAYS 'THE WIRY ONE'...BECAUSE WE'RE MISPRONOUNCING HIS NAME. THAT WASN'T WHAT HE WAS CALLED."

"I BECAME BIG IN LIFE AFTER I CROSSED OVER. AFTER I CAME TO SPIRIT, I BECAME BIG. BECAUSE WHEN I WAS HERE ON THE PHYSICAL PLANE, I WASN'T KNOWN AS MUCH AS I'M KNOWN NOW BECAUSE THEY HAD TO EXPLORE MY NOTES AND CALCULATIONS AND THEN THAT'S WHEN PEOPLE STARTED UNDERSTANDING THAT I WASN'T JUST PULLING MY HAIR OUT FOR NOTHING."

"BUT I HAD FRIENDS IN HIGH PLACES BECAUSE WHAT I KNEW MADE SENSE TO THEM. SO THEY KEPT ME CLOSE AND DEAR. HE'S TALKING ABOUT (HIS FRIEND). WASN'T HE TELLING US ABOUT THAT BEFORE?"

<u>Laura</u>: "He said (the name) last time."

<u>MEDIUM:</u> "OKAY, WELL HE'S TALKING ABOUT HIS FRIENDS. BECAUSE HE'S GOING OVER HIS FRIENDS, AND THE PEOPLE AROUND HIM. NOW (THE FRIEND HE MENTIONED), THAT ONE WAS HIS PERSON BEGINNING TO PUT HIM OUT THERE AND SAY 'LOOK AT THIS GUY. LOOK WHAT HE DOES. HE KNOWS THIS AND THAT. THIS PERSON INTRODUCED THE WIRY ONE TO THE WORLD ON A LEVEL OF WHAT HE COULD DO ON A HIGHER MENTAL PLANE. BECAUSE BY LOOKING AT HIM, YOU WOULD THINK, 'MAN, THIS GUY'S A JOKER.' I WAS ASKING HIM WHY HE WAS SAYING A JOKER, AND HE SAYS BECAUSE IT WOULD BE LAUGHED OFF...UNEXPLAINED STUFF WOULD JUST BE LAUGHED OFF. HENCE, THE JOKER."

(MEDIUM'S WORDS) "LET'S TALK ABOUT THE BOOK. WHAT ARE WE SUPPOSED TO PUT IN THE BOOK?"

"ALL OF THAT, (WHAT HE TOLD US ABOUT HIMSELF) IS BECAUSE YOU NEED DESCRIPTION OF HIM IN A CHANNELED MANNER TO PEG HIM LIKE HE REALLY IS...AS HE SAW HIMSELF, INSTEAD OF HOW OTHERS SAW HIM. BECAUSE WHY NOT BETTER THAN THE PERSON HIMSELF, IS WHAT HE'S SAYING, OKAY."

"I AM HEARING 'VESSELS'...SOMETHING ABOUT VESSELS, LIKE SHIPS, BUT VESSELS. VESSELS WOULD BE HUGE. MORE CRAP IS COMING AND IT'S IN VESSELS. SO, SOMEHOW, I DON'T KNOW IF WE HAVE SOME POLLUTANTS OR SOMETHING IN OTHER PARTS OF THE UNITED STATES AND WE ARE GOING TO BRING THEM AROUND, AND THEY ARE GOING TO BE IN VESSELS. THAT WAY THEY HAVE A SHORTER LAND TRAVEL. BUT THEY'RE COMING IS WHAT HE'S SAYING."

"OUR PRESIDENT (GEORGE BUSH) IS GOING TO MAKE A LOUD EXIT. THE PRESIDENT WE HAVE NOW IS GOING TO MAKE A VERY LOUD EXIT. HE'S NOT JUST GOING TO TAKE HIS GOODBYE AND GO. HE WANTS A LOUD EXIT. YOU KNOW EVERY PRESIDENT, HIS HISTORY GOES INTO BOOKS, AND HE WANTS MORE. SO, HE'S GOING TO HAVE A VERY LOUD EXIT. THERE'S GOING TO BE MORE THINGS THAT HE'S GOING TO DO TO ROCK THE WORLD."

"HE ALSO WILL TALK A LOT ABOUT HIS FATHER. BECAUSE HE CREDITS A LOT OF HIS BELIEFS AND THE BASE OF THE

WHOLE STRUCTURE...HAS TO DO WITH THE FAMILY'S TRAIN OF THOUGHT. WHICH IS MEDIOCRE, IS WHAT THE WIRY ONE SAYS. HE'S NOT A POWERFUL MIND. HE'S NOT A MIND THAT'S LED COMPLETELY BY THE HOUSE. HE'S MEDIOCRE...SO HE'S NO GENIUS, AND HE'S NOT STUPID EITHER. HE TRIES TO OVERCOME STUPIDITY. BECAUSE NOT KNOWING IS NOT AN EXCUSE."

"HE (BUSH) IS FOR EDUCATION...BUT HE DOES LIKE THE POWER, AND THE MONEY, OF COURSE. BUT THEY'RE OKAY...THAT FAMILY IS OKAY. HE COULD HAVE MORE OR NOT HAVE MORE, AND HE'S OKAY. BUT RIGHT NOW, HE WANTS TO GO OUT WITH A BIG BANG BECAUSE HE'S HISTORY...HE'S HISTORY, HE'S IN THE BOOKS. AND HE WANTS MORE. HE WANTS GOOD LIGHT SHED UPON HIM, SO THIS WOULD TELL ME THAT HE WOULD HAVE A CREATION OF SOMETHING WHERE HE GETS GOOD LIGHT, SO IT SHOULD BE POSITIVE INSTEAD OF NEGATIVE. IF IT'S JUST GOING OUT WITH A BANG, AND IT DIDN'T MATTER HOW, THEN WE SHOULD WORRY. BUT WHAT I'M SEEING IS THAT HE WANTS TO GO OUT IN GOOD LIGHT."

"I'M GETTING AGAIN ABOUT THE POTATOES. DON'T EAT THE POTATOES. ALSO, WITH THE POTATOES, LIKE THE SAYING, 'YOU ARE WHAT YOU EAT,' THE POTATO IS WHAT IT EATS. BUT THE CARROTS, THEY HAVE SOMETHING ELSE IN THE CHEMISTRY OF THE CARROT; IT'S NOT AS CONTAMINATED AS THE POTATO. YOU WILL TASTE THAT A CARROT DOES NOT TASTE LIKE A CARROT IF IT IS TO NOT BE EATEN. BUT IF IT TASTES LIKE A CARROT, THEN THAT'S OKAY. BUT THE CHANGEOVER NEEDS TO BE MADE ON HOW NUTRITION IS CONSUMED IN THE BODY, BUT THE POTATO IS A BIG, AND I SEE, NO. A BIG NO."

Laura: "I just ate some yesterday."

MEDIUM: (MEDIUM'S WORDS) "THE FIRST FEW DAYS I STAYED AWAY FROM IT BUT THEN AFTERWARDS, I ATE THE POTATO."

Laura: "Me too. Any potatoes, from anywhere?"

MEDIUM: "THE POTATOES FROM THE SOUTH, YOU WOULDN'T ESPECIALLY GO BUY THEM BECAUSE THEY DON'T

LOOK GOOD. YOU KNOW THEY'VE GOT THE HOLES. THEY ARE THE ONES THAT AREN'T GROWING PRETTY BECAUSE THAT AREA IS NOT A POTATO LAND. BUT WHERE THE POTATOES DO GROW, IT'S TOO CLOSE TO THE CONTAMINATION."

(Idaho is directly northeast of Nevada.)

"AND IT'S IN THE GROUND, SO THE GROUND IS A ROOT, AND THE ROOT IS THE DIRT, AND THE DIRT IS THE ROOT, AND THAT'S WHY YOU DON'T WANT TO EAT IT. AND THE POTATO CHIP, THE POTATO AU GRATIN, THE POTATOES IN THE BOX, THE POTATO THAT YOU EVEN ADD WATER TO AND ALL THAT...THEY'RE BUYING THEM FROM THE SOURCE OF WHERE THEY'RE GENERATING ALL THE POTAOES, WHICH IS A PROBLEM. BECAUSE THE POTATOES ARE EATEN, AND ALL THAT STUFF (THE CONTAMINATION) WE CONSUME. IT'S ALMOST TO US LIKE CANNIBALISM. YOU KNOW WHAT HAPPENS TO YOUR BODY WHEN YOU ARE A CANNIBAL?"

Laura: "When you eat other humans?"

<u>MEDIUM</u>: "WHAT HAPPENS IS THE BODY DESTROYS ITSELF BECAUSE IN TRYING TO DIGEST SELF, IT THEN DETERIORATES THE REST OF THE BODY BECAUSE IT STARTS CONSUMING OTHER...AND THEN THE PERSON BECOMES SICKLY, AND IT EATS UP THEIR JOINTS, AND THEN THEIR BONES AND THEN THEIR TEETH. BUT FIRST YOU'LL SEE IT IN THE TEETH AND HAIR. SO PEOPLE, WHO HAVE EATEN, WILL SEE THINNING OF THE HAIR. SO YOU SHOULDN'T EAT...DON'T EAT SELF. BUT IT STARTS EATING ITSELF, AND IT STARTS WITH THE BONES. AND THIS HAS TO DO WITH ANY ANIMAL. THAT'S WHY YOU HAVE THE DOGS AND ANIMALS THAT DON'T LIVE SO LONG BECAUSE IT'S SELF (OTHER ANIMALS) IN THE FOODS THAT THEY EAT. BECAUSE ALL OF THAT IS IN THERE. UNLESS YOU GO TO THE EXTREMES OF FINDING THEM PURE FOOD INSTEAD OF FOOD THAT HAS OTHER ANIMAL, OF SELF, OF DOG EATING DOG."

<u>Laura</u>: "Nice."

<u>MEDIUM</u>: "I SEE ONE OF YOUR SONS AND I SEE A LOT OF LITTLE STARS AROUND HIM. I JUST SAW A VISION OF

HIM SITTING THERE, AND I SAW JUST TINY, LITTLE BITTY, TINY, TINY SPARKLES OF STARS AROUND HIM, AND I SAW HIM IN THE DARKNESS AND I JUST SAW THE LIGHT FROM THE STARS. HE'S A SUBJECT...HE'S A SUBJECT, AS IN THE SUBJECT OF STUDY. YOU KNOW WHAT? HE IS. CUZ THAT'S KIND OF WHAT WE'RE WRITING A BOOK ABOUT."

Laura: "Are they watching him? Are they studying him?"

MEDIUM: "HE'S A SUBJECT OF THE BOOK."

Laura: "Oh, I got it. He's the subject of the book."

MEDIUM: (PICKS UP THE CHALK AND DRAWS ON THE BLACKBOARD BEHIND HER) "I JUST GOT A LITTLE LIKE THAT (DRAWS A SHAPE ON THE BOARD) OR LIKE THAT (DRAWS ANOTHER ONE) I DON'T KNOW. AND I GET THE FIVE, AND I GET SOME KIND OF LINE THERE. AND I SEE SMILES...I SEE A SMILE WITH HIM."

"YOU WANT TO ASK SOME QUESTIONS? DO YOU HAVE ANY QUESTIONS?"

<u>Laura:</u> "Yeah, I have a bunch of questions."

<u>MEDIUM:</u> "I'M BEING TOLD THAT YOU'LL COVER THREE. BECAUSE I'M BEING TOLD THAT YOU'VE BEEN GUIDED WITH YOUR QUESTIONS, WHAT IS SUPPOSED TO BE ASKED TODAY. SO, YOU'LL COVER THREE. SO, WHATEVER IT IS THAT YOU'RE ASKING, IS GOING TO BE ENOUGH INFORMATION TO COVER THAT WE'RE NOT GOING TO HAVE TIME TO DO EXTRA STUFF IS WHAT HE'S SAYING. AND HE'S (THE WIRY ONE) THE ONE WHO MAINLY IS CONCENTRATED HERE. IT'S NOT SO MUCH ABOUT THE PRESIDENT AND ALL THAT, IT'S MORE ABOUT HIS KNOWLEDGE, AND UTILIZING IT."

<u>Laura:</u> "Okay. How long have they been producing this biological warfare in Nevada?"

<u>MEDIUM:</u> "11." (ALSO DRAWS THE NUMBER 11 ON THE BLACKBOARD.)

<u>Laura:</u> "11 years. (Since 1996.) And why has autism increased in every state and other countries as well if it is only being carried by the wind?"

<u>MEDIUM:</u> "THE OTHER COUNTRIES ALREADY HAVE BAD...THEY CONTAMINATE THEMSELVES BECAUSE THEY DON'T HAVE THE GOOD HYGEINE. AND SO IT'S CONTAMINATION. OTHER COUNTRIES THAT YOU GO TO, THE BAD HYGEINE IS ALREADY THERE. WHAT'S GOING ON HERE IS MULTIPLIED OF THE THINGS THAT THEY GET THERE. OVER THERE, THEY GET IT DURING A WHOLE LIFETIME. SO, THESE PEOPLE, OVER THERE, THEY'RE NOT GETTING THIS KIND OF THING AT A CERTAIN AGE. IT HAPPENS THROUGH THE YEARS."

"THIS, (AUTISM) WHAT'S HAPPENING HERE, IS LIKE, BING, BING. (DRAWS TWO LINES ON BLACKBOARD). BUT OVER THERE, IN OTHER COUNTRIES, IF YOU MAKE YOUR STUDIES, IT'S LIKE THE PEOPLE GET WORSE AND WORSE AND WORSE. IT'S NOT HEREDITARY, SO IT'S NOT BEING PASSED FROM ONE TO THE OTHER. IN OTHER COUNTRIES, IT HAPPENS GRADUALLY."

"AND IT'S MORE THE INLAND PEOPLE, BECAUSE THE ONES THAT LIVE BY THE WATER, POOR/RICH, WHATEVER THEY MAY BE, EAT MORE OUT OF THE WATER. IF THERE ARE DEAD ANIMALS, THEY JUST LEAVE THEM THERE, AND THEN THE BIRDS EAT THEM, AND SPREAD THEIR GERMS, AND DEAD COWS AND ALL OF THAT. AND THEY JUST ATTRIBUTE THE DEATH BECAUSE THERE'S NO FOOD. THE POISONS AND ALL OF THAT, THEY'RE CREATING THEM IN THEIR OWN PLACE."

"THAT SHOULD NOT BE HAPPENING IN AMERICA. A LONG TIME AGO, WE LEARNED THAT CLEANLINESS DOES MAKE US LIVE LONGER. GO BACK IN TIME, AND MOST OF THE PEOPLE, OUR FOREFATHERS, LIVED AND DIED AT VERY YOUNG AGES, AND A LOT OF IT HAD TO DO WITH CONTAMINATION. IT HAD TO DO WITH THAT THINGS WERE NOT SANITARY. THE ONLY THING IS WE HAVE SO MUCH INVESTED IN THE MEDICAL FIELD THAT WE SAVE THESE PEOPLE, AND THEN THEY END UP LIVING IN AN ODD POSITION."

(Life expectancy rose dramatically in the United States over the past century. Final data for 2003, the most recent available, show that life expectancy at birth for the total population has reached an all-time American high level, 77.5 years, up from 49.2 years at the turn of the 20th century.[31])

"YOUR NEXT QUESTION?"

Laura: "So what about in our country...ADD (Attention Deficit Disorder) and ADHD (Attention Deficit Hyperactivity Disorder), and all of these other neurological disorders...what's causing that? Other types of contamination that don't include the biological warfare?"

MEDIUM: "ADD (WRITES IT ON THE BLACKBOARD). YOU KNOW, THAT'S JUST A BRAIN. THAT DOESN'T HAVE TO DO WITH THIS (CONTAMINATION). THIS, ADD, DOESN'T HAVE TO DO WITH WHAT YOUR SON HAS..."

Laura: "Autism."

---

[31]http://www.aging.senate.gov/crs/aging1.pdf

<u>MEDIUM:</u> "IS LIKE HERE TO HERE (POINTS BACK TO THE TWO MARKS SHE DREW ON THE BOARD EARLIER, SIGNIFYING TWO AGES). HE'S GOOD... (POINTS TO FIRST MARK) THEN HE'S NOT (POINTS TO SECOND MARK). THIS IS ALWAYS THERE (POINTS TO ADD), THAT CAME IN. THIS WASN'T THERE (POINTS TO AUTISM FIRST AGE MARKER) THIS IS THERE NOW (POINTS TO AUTISM SECOND AGE MARKER) THIS IS THERE (ADD). TWO DIFFERENT ANIMALS. TWO DIFFERENT SUBJECTS, TWO DIFFERENT TOPICS. NOT THE SAME THING."

<u>Laura:</u> "So it's not caused by contamination."

<u>MEDIUM:</u> "NOT THIS. NOT ADD, NOT ANXIETY. IT'S JUST PROBLEMS. IT'S JUST A DIFFERENT WAY OF LEARNING. SOME PEOPLE SHAKE FAST, SOME PEOPLE SHAKE SLOW. IT'S JUST A VIBRATION THAT THEY ARE IN. BUT THESE PEOPLE ARE NEEDED (POINTS TO ADD), THESE PEOPLE ARE NEEDED BECAUSE THEY MAKE THINGS HAPPEN. THEY'RE IN A HURRY. THAT WAY, THE ONES THAT REST GET SOMEBODY TO TELL THEM TO HURRY UP. IT'S DIFFERENT."

<u>Laura:</u> "The reason I ask, is that they are trying to lump them all into the same 'spectrum' and call them 'Autism Spectrum Disorders,' lumping ADD, ADHD, and what my son has (autism) as the same thing to a different degree. And I don't agree with it."

<u>MEDIUM:</u> "WHAT A GREAT IDEA TO COP EVERYTHING OUT. NO, IT'S DIFFERENT. THIS (ADD) IS NOT THE SAME AS THAT (POINTS TO AUTISM AGE MARKERS). THIS SUBJECT CAME IN AS IT WAS (ADD). THIS SUBJECT (AUTISM) TURNED INTO THAT. NOT THE SAME."

<u>Laura:</u> "Good explanation, thank you. Was that my third question?"

<u>MEDIUM:</u> "HE SAYS, 'THIRD CHAPTER.' DO YOU HAVE ANOTHER QUESTION THAT HAS TO DO WITH THE BOOK?"

<u>Laura:</u> "The only other question I have is just about the whole believability factor...How do I present this to people without being laughed at? How do I prove it?"

<u>MEDIUM:</u> "OKAY, START WITH THE CITY. (DRAWS A SYMBOL FOR IT ON THE BLACKBOARD) START WITH THE

CITY. AND YOU GOT PROOF OF THAT. PUT IN THE MEDITATION (DRAWS A SYMBOL FOR THAT) AND THEN THE CITY. AND THIS IS YOUR HOOK TO GET THE READER TO READ. BECAUSE YOU HAVE TO HAVE A HOOK. IF YOU DON'T HAVE THIS, YOU HAVE NO BOOK. SO, START WITH THE CITY, AND THEN DO THIS (POINTS TO MEDITATION SYMBOL). SOME OF THIS, YOU'RE GOING TO DO BACKWARDS. LIKE IN A MOVIE, YOU TELL THE END, AND THEN YOU PRESENT THE BEGINNING. SO, IT WILL BRING SOME SENSE, AND BRING IT TOGETHER. SO, SOME OF IT YOU'RE GOING TO HAVE TO TURN IT AROUND, AND IT'S BECAUSE IT PREPARES THE MIND OF THE READER."

<u>Laura:</u> "I don't really follow...the city and the meditation part?"

<u>MEDIUM:</u> "OKAY. IN NEVADA, WE FOUND THAT THERE WAS A CITY."

<u>Laura:</u> "Hawthorne."

<u>MEDIUM:</u> "THERE WAS A CITY UNDERGROUND, AND THEN TELL ABOUT IT."

Laura: "Okay."

MEDIUM: "AND THEN TELL ABOUT THE MEDITATION, AND THEN DO YOUR RESEARCH."

Laura: "Oh, by meditation, you mean the reading."

MEDIUM: "THE READING...WHAT WE PICKED UP, THROUGH SPIRIT, ABOUT THE CITY. AND THAT LED YOU TO DISCOVER IT IN THE PHYSICAL. SO IT LED TO DISCOVERY. AND THEN, SOME OF THE OTHER THINGS, YOU'RE GOING TO HAVE TO TELL THE END, AND THEN TELL THE BEGINNING. HAVE YOU EVER SEEN A MOVIE THAT THEY SHOW IN REVERSE, AND THEN IT STARTS MAKING SENSE? BUT YOU NEED THE END FIRST, AND THAT'S WHAT'S GOING TO HAPPEN. SO, PART OF THIS IS COMING LIKE IT'S SUPPOSED TO, BUT THE BEGINNING ISN'T. BUT THIS IS CHAPTER THREE...WHAT WE ARE DOING NOW. BUT THE OTHER ONES ARE GOING TO BE FLIP-FLOPPED AROUND."

"YOU KNOW, BACK IN THE DAY, THERE WAS A LOT OF MISCOMMUNICATION. BACK IN THE DAY WHEN I WAS BRINGING THE INFORMATION THROUGH TO DIFFERENT PEOPLE, AND THEY WERE USING ME IN WARFARE. THERE WAS A LOT OF MISCOMMUNICATION. SO THEY TOOK MY MATERIAL TO OTHERS, AND THEN THEY DREW FROM THAT. AND THEN THEY CAME UP WITH THE DIFFERENT THINGS THAT THEY DID. THIS IS NOT GOING TO HAPPEN."

"THIS IS NOT GOING TO HAPPEN THIS TIME SO I'M BEING VERY CAREFUL HOW I GIVE YOU THE INFORMATION BECAUSE IT'S NOT TO BE MANIPULATED TO HURT THE WORLD. IT'S SUPPOSED TO HELP. IT'S SUPPOSED TO HELP THE CHILDREN. CUZ THERE IS A TURN AROUND. THERE IS A TURN AROUND TO THE SITUATION. THEY ARE NOT CALLING FOR IT RIGHT NOW."

"AND THIS BOOK WILL BE OLD. THIS BOOK WILL BE OLD, AND IT WILL STILL BE THERE. AND IT WILL BE GONE BACK TO FOR REFERENCE. AND THEY ARE GIVING ME A 50-YEAR PLUS BACK, AND THE BOOK WILL BE IN EXISTENCE. SO, IT

WILL CONTINUE TO BE PICKED UP AS PUBLISHED. BUT IT HAS TO DO WITH THE WIRY ONE, IS WHY."

Laura: "I have a question. Okay, so you talk about kids being cured of autism when they are in their forties, but then..."

MEDIUM: "***YOUR*** KID, NOT KIDS."

Laura: "Okay. But then, you talk about going into the future. If we can go into the future, why can't we grab that remedy, and bring it in now?"

MEDIUM: (STARTS DRAWING LINES ON THE BLACKBOARD AS SHE TALKS) "IT WOULD BE LIKE US HAVING A WHOLE MEDICAL UNIT, AND ONE PERSON DISCOVERS ONE THING, ONE PERSON DISCOVERS ANOTHER THING, ONE PERSON DISCOVERS ANOTHER THING, AND THEN THEY TIE THEM BACK. AND THAT DOESN'T WORK, AND THIS DOESN'T WORK, AND THEN THEY TIE SOMETHING ELSE BACK. IT'S GOING TO TAKE A LOT OF EXPERIMENTS. THIS IS NOT SOMETHING THAT JUST CAN BE...AND I FEEL GRIEF, I FEEL GRIEF."

"IF WE WROTE IT DOWN IN THIS BOOK, AND WE PUT IT TOGETHER...WHICH IT WILL; THAT IS GOING TO BE WHAT'S GOING TO HAPPEN. BUT THEY WON'T HAVE THIS REMEDY UNTIL ALL THIS HAPPENS." (POINTS TO THE LINES SHE JUST DREW.)

"BECAUSE THERE IS A LOT OF CONTROL. JUST LIKE WHEN I WAS HERE, AND MY WORK DIDN'T...I WAS MORE KNOWN AFTER I WAS GONE, AND OTHERS TOOK MY WORK AND TOOK IT A STEP FURTHER AND MORE STEPS FURTHER, AND FURTHER AND FURTHER. THEN, THEY DID WHAT THEY WERE SUPPOSED TO DO WITH IT. SAME THING WITH WHAT WE ARE DOING HERE. SO, IT'S NOT LIKE WE CAN SAY 'WELL, THIS IS WHAT WORKS, AND WE CAN TAKE IT SOMEWHERE AND THEY WILL PUT IT TOGETHER AND SAY GIVE THEM THE SHOT OR GIVE THEM THE TABLET."

"BECAUSE THERE WILL BE TWO FORMS. THERE WILL BE A TABLET AND A SHOT. AND THIS IS QUICK (THE SHOT), AND THIS IS MORE SUBTLE (THE TABLET). AND THIS IS

WHY THERE ARE TWO. THIS IS QUICK, AND THIS IS MORE SUBTLE."

Laura: "Is it homeopathic?"

MEDIUM: "IT'S LIKE A SHOT...TO SAY IT'S HOMEOPATHIC OR NOT...IT'S INGREDIENTS, AND THEY'RE IN THERE. NO...NO. IT'S LIKE A FIRE WITH A FIRE (HOMEOPATHY IS BASED ON LIKE CURES LIKE), AND WE ARE NOT TALKING ABOUT HOMEOPATHIC PROBLEMS, WE ARE TALKING ABOUT PROBLEMS THAT WERE DEVELOPED BY CHEMISTS. BECAUSE THE PROBLEM IS THAT THEY TOOK SOMETHING NATURAL THAT BIODEGRADED AND THEN THEY ADDED OTHER THINGS TO IT TO MAKE IT A KILLER. AND THAT'S WHAT WE ARE DEALING WITH. THE ONLY THING IS, THESE PEOPLE ARE SHUT DOWN. THESE PEOPLE ARE SHUT DOWN...MUMMIFIED."

"I HEAR '06. I HEAR '06...IT SKYROCKETED. PEOPLE ARE TAKING PRECAUTIONS. SO, THINGS ARE CHANGING. THE BIG RISE WAS IN 2006, BUT PEOPLE ARE TAKING MORE PRECAUTIONS, SO THE CHILDREN OF 2007 WILL BE THE

PROOF OF THE GRAVY. WHEN THEY SEE THAT THERE IS A DECLINE, THEN THEY'LL KNOW THAT THESE PEOPLE ARE DOING SOMETHING TO PREVENT THE PROBLEM."

(There was a 57% increase in autism of children born in 1996 than children born in 1994 according to the CDC.)

Laura: "They're not vaccinating."

MEDIUM: "YOU NEED TO REMEMBER, IT'S PART OF THE SOLUTION. IT'S NOT A COMPLETE SOLUTION. THAT'S WHY THERE ARE STILL NUMBERS. IF IT WAS SOLUTION, THERE WOULD NOT BE NUMBERS. SO IT'S PART OF THE SOLUTION, OKAY."

"YOU GET A SHOT OF A VIRUS TO PREVENT A VIRUS. OR YOU DO NOT GET A SHOT FOR A VIRUS, AND THEN YOU GET THE VIRUS. THEN YOU GET THE CONTAMINATION. BUT THE THING IS, THE VIRUS MAY COME LATER, (WHEN THEY'RE OLDER) WHERE THE BODY IS MORE IMMUNE, AND WHEN THAT (THE CONTAMINATION) HITS, IT'S NOT GOING TO ATTACK AS BAD."

"IT'S LIKE A CHILD GETTING A COLD, AND THEIR LUNGS FILL UP, AND IF THEY ARE SIX MONTHS, OR ONE MONTH OR A YEAR...IT'S ONLY A FEW MONTHS IN BETWEEN, BUT IT MAKES A HUGE...NO, HE SAID A ***GRAVE*** DIFFERENCE BECAUSE OF THE SIZE OF THE LUNG. SO, WHEN THEY ARE BEING VACCINATED AND THEY'RE SO YOUNG, THEY DON'T HAVE A CHANCE."

"SO, THE KIDS THAT GET VACCINATED, AND THEY KEEP GETTING FEVERS AND ALL KINDS OF STUFF AND DON'T GET VACCINATED UNTIL LATER...THEY'RE THE ONES THAT YOU'RE SEEING THAT MADE IT THROUGH THE VACCINATIONS. THESE KIDS ARE TOO YOUNG, AND THEY CAN'T EVEN FIGHT IT OFF. BUT, THEY STILL HAVE A NEURAL PROBLEM, BUT IT'S NOT AS EASILY DETECTED IN YOUR KIDS THAT YOU'RE CALLING 'THE CRYSTAL CHILDREN.'"

<u>Laura:</u> "So, there's a degree of severity with the biological warfare?"

<u>MEDIUM:</u> "IT HAPPENS ALL IN ONE DUMP. IT'S LIKE...WHEN IT HAPPENS...IT'S LIKE ALL IN ONE DUMP. LIKE YOUR SON, IF THIS WAS GOING TO HAPPEN TO HIM IT'S NOT LIKE IT WOULD BE A LITTLE MORE, LITTLE MORE, LITTLE MORE. IT'S LIKE ***BAM!*** AND IT'S DONE. SO, WHAT HAPPENS TO EACH ONE, IT'S A DUMP. LET'S SAY THE CHILD HAS A FEVER, AND HE DOESN'T GET HIS VACCINATIONS, AND HE WAS OLDER, AND IT WAS A DUMP, AND THAT'S WHAT HE GOT. THEN, THIS CHILD IS YOUNGER, AND HE GETS A BIG DUMP. BECAUSE IT'S LIKE THE COLD, AND THE SIZE OF THE LUNG. BUT WE'RE TALKING ABOUT IMMUNE SYSTEM. AND THIS IS TALKING IN ABC'S. THIS IS VERY ELEMENTARY."

(MEDUM'S WORDS) "CAN I HAVE THE ERASER? (THE BLACKBOARD WAS ALL SCRIBBLED UPON). YOU KNOW, I REALLY FEEL LIKE THE BLACKBOARD WAS A PRACTICE FOR TODAY. SO THAT'S OKAY."

"A LOT OF THE HOLDBACK FOR US IS MONEY, BECAUSE THERE ARE SO MANY LAWS, RULES AND REGULATIONS. SO, A LOT OF IT IS MONEY, BUT THE THING OF IT IS...ALL OF

THIS IS GOING TO HELP SOMEONE SPEED UP THE PROCESS OF GETTING A CURE."

"SO, YOUR ANSWER IS...THERE IS A CURE OUT THERE. THERE WILL BE A CURE. AND THAT'S WHY WE'RE SUPPOSED TO LOOK INTO THE FUTURE. SOME PEOPLE THINK, OH, YOU SHOULDN'T BE LOOKING INTO THE FUTURE, BUT I (THE WIRY ONE) DID IT BACK THEN. THAT'S HOW I WAS ABLE TO BRING EVOLUTION TO THE WORLD, BECAUSE WE WERE WAY BEHIND."

"YOU CAN SEE THESE CHILDREN'S SOULS BY LOOKING INTO THEIR EYES. YOU CAN SEE THAT THEY ARE IN THERE INSIDE OF THE SHELL THAT THEY ARE IN. AND THAT'S WHAT MAKES PEOPLE WORK EVEN HARDER, BUT THESE CHILDREN WILL BE BORN TO THE ONES THAT IT MAKES THE DIFFERENCE ON THE INVESTMENTS, AND THAT'S COMING."

"A LOT OF PEOPLE ARE IN DENIAL, BUT THEY CAN'T GIVE UP ALL OF THEIR KIDS. BECAUSE THEY ARE COMING IN GREATER AND GREATER NUMBERS."

"NOT VACCINATING THEM IS GOING TO BE A PARTIAL SOLUTION, BUT IT IS NOT THE SOLUTION. THIS IS GOING TO CONTINUE BECAUSE THE VIRUS COMES, WHETHER IT'S GIVEN TO THEM, OR NOT."

"BECAUSE AT A CERTAIN AGE, THEY GET...IT IS THE MEASLES, MUMPS AND RUBELLA. I WAS GETTING THAT, AND THEN..."

Laura: "Which one specifically is it? I've been trying to figure it out and a lot of the symptoms are the same." Is it Rubella?

MEDIUM: "RUBELLA IS THE HARSHEST. MEASLES ALSO ATTACKS THE SYSTEM, AND IT EXPLODES OUT WITH THE MEASLES, WHAT WE SEE."

Laura: "Because Rubella is German Measles."

MEDIUM: "BUT THE RUBELLA IS THE WORST, THE MEASLES IS SECOND, AND MUMPS IS THE LOWEST. BECAUSE THE MUMPS IS ATTACKING ONE AREA. YOU KNOW THAT'S

ATTACKING THE BIRTH SYSTEM? AND I ASKED WHAT DOES THE FAT FACE HAVE TO DO WITH THE GENITAL ORGANS AND ALL OF THAT?"

<u>Laura:</u> "Well, mumps can affect the glands of the testicles. In boys, they can swell up."

<u>MEDIUM:</u> "OKAY, MUMPS IS CONCENTRATED, AND THE MEASLES IS ALL OVER. RUBELLA IS THE WORST. (SHE HAD WRITTEN MMR ON THE BLACKBOARD) THIS, (POINTS TO MUMPS) HITS THE BODY, BUT IT'S HITTING A CERTAIN AREA. THIS, (POINTS TO MEASLES) HITS THE WHOLE IMMUNE SYSTEM."

<u>Laura:</u> "So, can the biological warfare combine with the virus from any of those childhood diseases and cause autism?"

<u>MEDIUM:</u> "IT HAS TO DO WITH THE RUBELLA. THAT'S THE ONE THAT IS HEIGHTENED. BUT THEN THEY ARE THROWING ALL OF THAT TOGETHER (CIRCLES MMR ON BLACKBOARD) AND SLOPPING IT. NOT GOOD, NOT GOOD."

"IT'S NOT THE MUMPS. BECAUSE I HEARD, IF YOU TOOK THIS (MUMPS) OUT, YOU HAVE NO CONSEQUENCE. YOU PUT THESE (MEASLES AND RUBELLA) SEPARATE, OR TOGETHER, THERE'S CONSEQUENCE. BUT THE RUBELLA, THAT'S THE TOUGH ONE. BECAUSE IF YOU WERE TO GET THE MEASLES YOU WOULD BE REALLY DOWN, BUT IF YOU GET THIS ONE (RUBELLA), YOU'RE ON YOUR ASS. YOU'RE DOWN, YOU ARE DOWN. SO, YOUR IMMUNE SYSTEM IS HIT HARD. THIS (MEASLES) HITS YOU, BUT NOT LIKE THAT (RUBELLA)."

"THE VIRUSES ARE DIFFERENT, SO THEY THROW THEM TOGETHER, AND THROW A LITTLE SPRINKE IN IT, AND YOU'VE GOT PROBLEMS. AND THE SPRINKLE COMES FROM CONTAMINATED SOIL, DUST, FLYING THROUGH THE AIR, THAT'S BEING CREATED FOR WARFARE."

"BUSH KNOWS. BUSH KNOWS."

<u>Laura:</u> "Then why isn't he doing anything about it?"

<u>MEDIUM:</u> "HE DOESN'T KNOW ABOUT THIS (POINTS TO DRAWING ON BLACKBOARD ABOUT VACCINES). HE KNOWS ABOUT THE CONTAMINATION."

"HE DOESN'T CARE ABOUT INDIANS."

<u>Laura:</u> "Native American Indians?"

<u>MEDIUM:</u> (SHAKES HEAD YES) "HE IS VERY MUCH INTO SEPARATING BLACKS AND INDIANS, EVEN THOUGH HE DOESN'T SAY IT."

<u>Laura:</u> "Segregation?"

<u>MEDIUM:</u> "HE'S ONE PRESIDENT THAT LET IT GO BACK. I DON'T KNOW HOW THAT IS...BUT I'M HEARING HE'S LETTING IT GO BACK. IT'S SLIDING. SO, IF YOU CHECK THE NUMBERS IN SOLDIERS, A LOT OF BLACK. HE SENDS THEM. THERE ARE A LOT OF PROMISES, AND HE'S TAKING THEM AND HE PUTS THEM IN THE WORST PLACES. A LOT OF WOMEN IN NEVADA, IN THE UNDERGROUND CITY. A LOT OF BLACKS TO GET KILLED. A LOT OF NEVADANS TO GET

KILLED...BECAUSE WE ARE COMPLAINING. AND THEN WE'VE GOT WHERE IT'S ACCESSIBLE. IT'S RIGHT THERE. TRAINING, AND IT'S RIGHT THERE. (POINTS TO DRAWING ON BLACKBOARD SHE DREW OF UNDERGROUND CITY) IF YOU'RE SOMEWHERE ELSE, IT'S A LONG WAY TO COME FOR TRAINING (DRAWS LONG LINE TO UNDERGROUND CITY) AND THEN BACK THERE. SO IT'S CONVENIENCE."

(MEDIUM'S WORDS) "ALSO, OH, WHAT A JERK. YOU KNOW I NEVER THOUGHT THAT ABOUT BUSH. I DON'T THINK YOU SHOULD PUT THIS IN THE BOOK...OR YOU MAY, I DON'T KNOW. BUT I'M PICKING THIS UP, AND WE'RE SUPPOSED TO BE PICKING UP INFORMATION FOR THE BOOK. BUT THIS I WOULD HESITATE TO PUT IN THE BOOK."

"NEVADA IS COMPLAINING, BECAUSE WE DON'T WANT SHIT HERE. (VARIOUS FORMS OF CONTAMINATION). AND NEVADA IS TRASH. (WRITES ON BLACKBOARD) NEVADA GAMBLES! PROSTITUTES! BAD! HE'S CHRISTIAN (BUSH). BAD! YUCK! NEVADA SUCKS! THAT'S WHAT HE THINKS. BUT HE DOESN'T REMEMBER...FAMILIES. SEE, THEY SAY THE DESERT, AND THERE'S NOBODY THERE... BUT THEY'RE NOT

PAYING ATTENTION TO WHAT THEY'RE DOING. BUT AS FAR AS BUSH GOES, NEVADA IS THE STATE OF LEAST IMPORTANCE, ALONG WITH THEIR PEOPLE BECAUSE THAT'S WHAT HE THINKS OF IT. IT IS GAMING, IT IS PROSTITUTION. IT IS ALL OF THOSE THINGS THAT CHRISTIANITY IS AGAINST."

Laura: "Nice."

MEDIUM: "THE PROBLEM BEING HERE, (NEVADA) AND ALL OF THIS RIGHT HERE, SO SMALL, AND IT'S SPREADING EVERYWHERE; THAT'S WHAT'S GOING TO BRING HELP. BUT IT'S TOO BIG TO FIGHT. IT'S TOO BIG TO FIGHT IN A DAY. IT'S TOO BIG TO FIGHT IN TEN YEARS."

Laura: "How do we fight? Now that we know?"

MEDIUM: "HE'S OUT OF THERE (BUSH)... WITH A BIG BANG, BECAUSE HE WANTS TO BE WELL HISTORIED."

"OH, AND WE ARE GOING TO HAVE THE NEXT PRESIDENT BE A LOT OF YADDA, YADDA, YADDA; EMPTY WORDS. A LOT

OF PROMISES AND EMPTY WORDS IS GOING TO BE OUR NEXT PRESIDENT."

(This was recorded before the 2008 Presidential election, in which Barack Obama was elected.)

Laura: "Who is it?"

MEDIUM: "I DON'T KNOW, I SEE A NOSE. SO WHOEVER IT IS DOESN'T HAVE THE BEST OF NOSES. OKAY, LET'S NOT DO THE NEXT PRESIDENT. BECAUSE THE NEXT PRESIDENT WILL COME, AND THEN WE PUBLISH THE BOOK, AND THEY ARE LIKE, OH, THAT PRESIDENT WAS ALREADY HERE, SO THAT DOES US NO GOOD."

"NOW BUSH GOING OUT WITH A BANG, THIS HAS TO DO WITH WHAT WE ARE TALKING ABOUT. I'M NOT BEING TOLD WHAT, BUT IT HAS TO DO WITH WHAT WE ARE TALKING ABOUT, OKAY. MY GOD, DOES HE NOT SEE THE PEOPLE? YOU'RE A GOOD PERSON. YOU'RE NOT A BAD PERSON JUST BECAUSE YOU'RE HERE WITH THE GAMING AND THE PROSTITUTION."

"OKAY, YOU HAVE ANOTHER QUESTION?"

Laura: "What do you want to tell the world? How can we use your ideas to help?"

MEDIUM: "OKAY, RIGHT NOW, IT DOESN'T SEEM LIKE YOU'VE GOT AN ARRAY OF INFORMATION, BUT YOU DO HAVE AN ARRAY OF INFORMATION THAT IS GOING TO TIE BACK TO WHAT YOU'RE GOING TO LOOK UP. SOME OF IT IS GOING TO MAKE SENSE, AND SOME OF IT IS NOT SUPPOSED TO MAKE SENSE. YOU CAN'T INCORPORATE THE FUTURE BECAUSE THE FUTURE IS NOT HERE YET. SO, YOU CAN ONLY INCORPORATE THE PAST, AND THE REASON THAT I'M GIVING YOU THINGS THAT TIE BACK TO THE PAST AND TIE BACK TO THE CURRENT, IS BECAUSE IT'S GOT TO MAKE SENSE TO THE READER."

"THE REASON THAT THIS INFORMATION IS LIKE IT IS...IS THAT YOU'VE GOT TO HAVE THE PROBLEM AND THE SOLUTION, AND YOU'VE JUST GOT TO WORK YOUR WAY THROUGH THE MIDDLE. IT'S LIKE HAVING THE VISION OF AN END, AND BY READING THE BOOK YOU CAN HAVE THAT.

THE ONLY THING IS THAT THE END RESULT WILL BE IN THE BEGINNING, BUT THE SOLUTION...IT WILL BE TURNED OVER. AND THAT'S JUST FOR THE UNDERSTANDING OF THE MIND, BECAUSE THE FUTURE AND CURRENT BEING MIXED UP AS IT'S COMING THROUGH."

"THAT PART IS FOR YOU, LAURA, SO THAT YOU'RE ABLE TO PUT THIS INTO SOME ORDER AND COMPOSITION, OKAY. YOU NEED TO GET YOUR FINGERS GOING. THEY'RE TELLING ME YOU HAVEN'T TYPED ANY OF THIS."

Laura: "No."

MEDIUM: "THEY'RE SAYING THAT YOU NEED TO GET YOUR FINGERS GOING. BECAUSE ONCE YOU START...YOUR BEGINNING SHOULD BE JUST TRANSCRIBING EXACTLY WHAT'S COME THROUGH. INCLUDING WHAT I'M SAYING RIGHT NOW, THE BEGINNING IS TRANSCRIBING THESE VERY WORDS. YOU'RE SUPPOSED TO BE DOING THAT, BECAUSE AS YOU'RE DOING YOUR RESEARCH, YOU'RE JUST GOING TO BE THROWING PIECES HERE AND THERE, AND IT WILL BE REMINDERS AS YOU'RE GOING THROUGH AND

READING IT. IT SEEMS LIKE A LOT OF MATERIAL, BUT IT'S NOT. NOT SO MUCH THAT YOU CAN'T HANDLE, BUT IT'S ENOUGH TO GET YOU THROUGH FROM ONE STAGE TO THE OTHER. SO, EVEN THOUGH YOU CAN'T DO YOUR PART RIGHT NOW...JUST DO SOME OF THE TYPING."

Laura: "I was going to start doing that this weekend."

MEDIUM: "BECAUSE TRANSCRIBING IT, AS YOU'RE LISTENING TO IT, YOU'LL HAVE ALL THESE THINGS COME THROUGH. AND YOU MIGHT DO SMALL AND CAP., SMALL AND CAP., TO SEE WHAT'S COMING FROM YOU AND WHAT'S COMING FROM ME, OR THE OTHER PRESIDENTS OR THE OTHER SPIRITS WHO ARE GOING TO BE INVOLVED IN ALL OF THIS. AND THEN YOU CAN TURN AROUND AND YOU CAN PUT IT IN GOOD FORM. BUT JUST FOR THE SAKE OF SEPARATION, AND WHEN YOU DO YOUR INSERTS, YOU'VE GOT TO HAVE A WAY TO DIFFERENTIATE FROM ONE TO THE OTHER."

"THERE'S A LOT I'M SEEING ON THE BOOK THAT HAS TO DO WITH COPYRIGHT AND ALL OF THAT. BECAUSE THERE'S

GOING TO BE PEOPLE TRYING TO TEAR OUT INFORMATION OUT OF THERE, AND STEM OFF OF WHAT THIS IS. AND HE SAYS, 'NO CHANGE! NO CHANGE!' IT'S LIKE PUTTING A LOT OF IDEAS OUT THERE AND PEOPLE TRYING TO RUN WITH THEM. AND HE'S SAYING, 'NO CHANGE!' SO THE COPYRIGHTS ARE VERY, VERY IMPORTANT SO THAT NO ONE CAN TAKE ANYTHING OUT OF THERE AND TRY TO CHANGE IT, BECAUSE THEN WHEN THEY DO THAT, IT'S GOING TO MAKE A MESS OUT OF IT."

"THIS HAS TO BE THE BASE. IT IS THE BASE. THE FOUNDATION. A FOUNDATION OF DISCOVERY. OKAY, SO FOUNDATION OF DISCOVERY IS WHAT THIS BOOK IS...IT'S THE BASE. THE BASE. I DON'T KNOW...I'M SEEING THAT, *FOUNDATION OF DISCOVERY, CHANNELED."*

Laura: "Is that the title of the book?"

MEDIUM: "AND IT'S LIKE I SAW IT LIKE THIS (DRAWS ON THE BLACKBOARD). AND I WAS TELLING HIM, 'WELL YOU TOLD ME YOU WEREN'T GOING TO BE HERE FOR THE OTHER

CHAPTERS.' AND HE SAYS, 'YEAH, BUT I TOLD YOU, YOU WERE GOING TO MIX THEM UP.'

<u>Laura:</u> "So is that the title then?"

<u>MEDIUM:</u> "I THINK SO."

<u>Laura:</u> "Ask him again."

<u>MEDIUM:</u> "BUT I SAW IT LIKE THIS, (DRAWS ON THE BLACKBOARD) BECAUSE IT'S THIS, (DRAWS AN ARCH ON THE BLACKBOARD) AND THEN YOU HAVE FOUNDATION."

<u>Laura:</u> "Channeled." (TIMER GOES OFF)

<u>MEDIUM:</u> "WHOA!"

<u>Laura:</u> "Did he answer you?"

<u>MEDIUM:</u> "THAT'S IT. THE REASON I SAID, 'WHOA' WAS BECAUSE THEY KNOW WHEN THE TIME IS UP."

(CD ENDS)

***

Later Discoveries

The wiry one mentioned in both parts of this reading that there was a friend in spirit with him that was a great friend while they were here on earth. They shook hands in public, but behind closed doors they were close friends. His first name was given in the reading, but I took it out. I figured out who this friend is, but again, I can't say because it would expose the identity of the one I can't mention for legal reasons. Just know that I discovered lots of connections between the two friends and colleagues. The important thing to know is that the information given in the readings led to me discovering it in the physical. I didn't even know who this person was, but after reading about him, I was honored to have him helping out in this situation as well.

More on the Autism Statistics

This is where it gets interesting. In this reading, it says that they started making the biological warfare in Hawthorne, NV in 1996, which is during the time frame when autism increased 57% in the United States. If you recall, the data from the CDC study showed that autism increased 57% in four years, between the years of 1994 and 1998. The study was for children born in 1998, the year my son with autism was born, and included both health and educational records, so it is more precise than just counting the children receiving services through IDEA (Individuals with Disabilities Education Act). Coincidence?

Autism in Other Countries

I looked up the autism statistics in other countries for comparison to the United States. There is not a lot of current data available globally. But the readings were correct that it is not happening all over the world. We have the highest rate of any country. Interestingly, Canada has a high autism rate. They are the country directly north of the United States, and in the path of the way the wind typically blows from Hawthorne, NV. I'm sure the "dust" doesn't stop at the border. According to the

Autism Society of Canada's website, the current prevalence of autism in Canada is one in 165.[32]

Other countries with high autism rates include the United Kingdom and India. According to the National Autism Society in the UK, their autism rate is one in 100. Higher according to other sources. India's autism rate is one in 250, according to Action for Autism India. An estimated two million people in India have autism. And yes, they give the MMR vaccine in all of these countries. Over 90 countries currently use the MMR vaccine.

Just a thought: the United States is at war in the Middle East. We are creating biological warfare to use on our enemies, which is inadvertently causing autism here in our country according to the readings. India is in the Middle East. India has two million people with autism. Hmmm.

***

[32]Fombonne, E., et al. "Pervasive Developmental Disorders in Montreal, Quebec, Canada: Prevalence and Links With Immunizations." *Pediatrics*, 2006 Jul;118(1):e139-50.

CHAPTER FOUR

***(Note to reader:** This chapter is the remainder of the reading from Chapter Three, channeled on December 6, 2007, which I was instructed to make into Chapter Four.)*

MEDIUM: (TO THE WIRY ONE) "WHAT DO YOU HAVE ON THE AGENDA? HE'S SHOWING ME A LOT OF PEOPLE PROTESTING. A LOT OF PEOPLE NOT AGREEING WITH WHAT'S GOING ON. A LOT OF PEOPLE PROTESTING, A LOT OF PEOPLE SAYING THINGS ARE NOT RIGHT AND CONNECTING THE DOTS, AND BRINGING ANGER WITHIN THEMSELVES. AND WITH THOSE AROUND THEM, FEELING LIKE THEY SHOULD HAVE BEEN TOLD. ALTHOUGH WITHIN SOME MONTHS, THEY ARE GOING TO COOL THEIR HEELS BECAUSE THEY ARE GOING TO HAVE TO WAIT FOR THINGS

TO START HAPPENING BEFORE THEY CAN REALLY BE UPSET ABOUT IT."

"SO THERE WILL BE A PERSON THAT WILL COME THAT'S GOING TO TRY TO CORRECT EVERYTHING THAT'S GONE WRONG, BUT IT'S REALLY HARD FOR ONE PERSON TO DO IT. AS I TOLD YOU BEFORE, THE PRESIDENT CAN'T EVEN WORK BY HIMSELF, MUCH LESS ONE PERSON TRYING TO CHANGE THE WORLD. IT'S JUST NOT GOING TO HAPPEN. AND EVERYBODY GETS SCARED BECAUSE THEY THINK, 'OH, MY GOSH, IS THIS THE BAD GUY COMING INTO TOWN THAT'S SHOWING HIMSELF AS GOOD.'"

"AND IT'S JUST A LOT OF CONFUSION IN HUMANITY AS FAR AS THE SPIRITUAL REALMS GO, AND THEM ENTERING HERE INTO YOUR LEVEL BECAUSE IT'S HAPPENING. IT'S HAPPENING IN A STRONG WAY."

"THERE ARE OTHER BEINGS FROM OTHER AREAS THAT ARE ALSO COMING BECAUSE THEY DON'T WANT THE FUTURE TO BE WHAT IT'S LOOKING LIKE. IT'S LIKE THEY ARE SEEING A BABY ABOUT TO KNOCK OVER THEIR TOMMY-TIPEE CUP,

AND THEY ARE JUST GOING TO TRY TO CATCH IT. TO THEM IT'S NOT AS SEVERE AS IT IS THAT WE'RE LOOKING AT IT...AS YOU LOOK AT IT. IT CAN BE CONTROLLED AND CHANGED. BUT THE EARTH WILL DO A LOT OF IT ON ITS OWN."

"YOU'LL SEE A LOT OF PURPLE SKIES, A LOT OF PURPLE SKIES. A LOT OF PEOPLE ARE ATTRACTED TO THE COLOR PURPLE. THEY THINK IT'S A HIGH LEVEL COLOR, AND IT IS, BUT IT IS BECAUSE OF THE COLORS PEOPLE WILL BE SEEING. THE SKIES WILL BE VERY PURPLE WITH STREAKS OF THE LIGHTER, WHICH ALMOST LOOK PINK, BUT THEY ARE SHADES OF PURPLE, DIFFERENT SHADES OF PURPLE."

"I'M SEEING A LOT OF...IT LOOKS LIKE VOLCANIC STUFF....LIKE ERUPTIONS AND STUFF COMING OUT OF THE EARTH. AND THAT'S GOING TO ELIMINATE A LOT OF PEOPLE IN THE PROCESS, AND THEN YOUR GOVERNMENT IS GOING TO FIGURE OUT...HEY, YOU DIDN'T NEED TO MAKE ALL OF THIS STUFF THAT'S HARMING YOUR VERY OWN PEOPLE."

"AMERICANS HAVE BEEN PRETTY GODLY IN COMPARISSON TO WHAT OTHERS ARE DOING. NOT THAT IT IS A PERFECT AREA OF THE WORLD, BUT IT IS BETTER THAN..."

"WE HAVE AN AREA OF MILLIONS AND MILLIONS AND MILLIONS OF PEOPLE THAT WILL BE MIXED UP IN THE SOIL. IT'S JUST LIKE GETTING FLOUR, AND MIXING UP OTHER INGEDIENTS, AND THAT'S WHAT IS GOING TO HAPPEN TO MILLIONS OF PEOPLE. I GET INDIA, I GET PAKISTAN, I GET ALL ACROSS THAT AREA. THE WORSHIPPING HAS TO CHANGE. IT'S SOMETHING THAT HAS TO DO WITH THE GODS THAT THEY THINK ARE. THERE MUST BE A LOT OF IDOLS THAT THEY ARE WORSHIPPING...FIGURES, INSTEAD OF A HIGHER, REAL GOD. FIRST THING'S FIRST. IT'S JUST A WAY TO CORRECT WHAT'S GOING ON."

"YOU HAVE A QUESTION?"

Laura: "I've been looking at all of these biological warfare agents, and I'm still curious as to what it is that they are making down there. Is it anthrax?"

<u>MEDIUM</u>: "IT'S A FORM OF THAT, BUT THAT'S PRIMITIVE (ANTHRAX)."

<u>Laura:</u> "Because I've had Trevor tested for toxins energetically, and he has biological warfare in his body. One of them was anthrax; one of them was the mad cow bacteria (prions). I asked, 'Where the hell is this coming from?' Now I know."

<u>MEDIUM:</u> "IT'S THE AIR...WE'VE ALREADY TALKED ABOUT THAT. IT'S ABOUT THE AIR."

"IT'S COMING IN DUST FORM, THEY CAN'T CONTAIN IT. YOU KNOW, THINGS ARE DONE SLOPPY. JUST BECAUSE THEY ARE IN THEIR BEEHIVE UNIFORM, IT DOESN'T MEAN THAT THEY...AND ALSO, THEY THINK THAT THEY ARE OUT THERE IN THE MIDDLE OF NOWHERE, THEY HAVE NO IDEA THE MONSTER THAT THEY ARE CREATING. THEY ARE BRINGING HARM TO EVERYBODY AROUND THEM, BECAUSE THEY CAN'T CONTROL THE WINDS."

"AND THIS STUFF IS SUCH A LIGHT POWDER, THAT IT'S THINNER THAN DUST. AND IT IS OF A GRAY COLOR, SO YOU'RE GONNA SEE IT, YOU'RE GONNA RECOGNIZE THAT IT'S NOT DUST THAT YOU NORMALLY HAVE. BUT WHEN IT SETTLES, IT WILL SETTLE IN A LAYER. AND IT SETTLES ALL OVER YOUR BODY, AND IT WILL PENETRATE YOUR CLOTHING. THE NORMAL TYPE OF CLOTHING. PLASTIC...IT DOESN'T GO THROUGH THAT, AND THAT'S MAINLY WHAT THESE UNIFORMS ARE MADE OF. BUT THERE WILL BE HARM, EVEN TO THE ONES THAT ARE WORKING THERE BECAUSE THEY TAKE IT FOR GRANTED. THEY ARE SLOPPY."

"AND THEY ARE NOT PUTTING THE THINGS IN THE CONTAINERS LIKE THEY'RE SUPPOSED TO. THEY'RE SUPPOSED TO BE SQUARE, METAL CONTAINERS WITH LINERS, AND A LOT OF THEM...THEY'VE USED THE SQUARE CONTAINERS AND THEY DIDN'T PUT THE LINERS IN THEM, SO THE ONES THAT DON'T HAVE LINERS IN THEM...IT'S LIKE YOU MOVE THEM AROUND, AND EVEN WHEN YOU SET THEM FROM ONE PLACE TO THE OTHER, THAT STUFF IS SEEPING OUT. AND SOME OF THESE PEOPLE ARE HANDLING IT WITH BARE HANDS."

"THEY ARE GOING TO RETURN HOME AND THEY ARE GOING TO HAVE ALL KINDS OF PROBLEMS. BUT THEN, THEY'LL SAY, I WAS HERE AND I WAS THERE, AND THEY AREN'T GOING TO BE ABLE TO PINPOINT IT. IT'S LIKE THEY'RE ALL OVER THE PLACE, AND THE LITTLE, MINUTE WORK THAT THEY DID WITH IT IN THE DESERT, IT JUST DOESN'T SEEM LIKE IT WAS THAT IMPORTANT, OR WHAT IT IS THAT THEY ARE HANDLING. BECAUSE HALF THE TIME, THEY DON'T EVEN KNOW WHAT THEY ARE DOING. THEY ARE JUST FOLLOWING ORDERS. AND THAT'S ALL THEY ARE SUPPOSED TO DO. THEY HAVE A LOT OF FEMALES THERE. THERE'S A LOT OF FEMALES THERE, AND THEY HAVE VERY STRONG MINDS."

"FROM OCTOBER THROUGH THE WINTER, IF YOU EXPLORE THE AREA, YOU'LL SEE THAT IT KIND OF CLEARS OUT BECAUSE THE WEATHER IS NOT THE TYPE OF WEATHER THAT THEY NEED. THEY NEED DRY, THEY NEED HEAT. SO AS FAR AS YOU HAVING FEAR THAT ALL OF THIS IS GOING ON RIGHT NOW...THE BEST TIME OF THE YEAR IS WHEN THIS PLACE IS COVERED IN SNOW, OR COVERED IN WATER

BECAUSE EVERYTHING IS SETTLED AND NOT MOVING ANYMORE. SO, WE DON'T HAVE TO FEAR. YOU SHOULDN'T HAVE FEAR RIGHT NOW BECAUSE THEY ARE CLEARING OUT OF THERE."

"DON'T LET YOUR CHILD PLAY IN THE DIRT."

"AND AREA 51 IS REAL...THERE ARE BODIES THERE FROM OTHER PLACES. BUT THEY'RE THE SAME AS US. THEY'RE MADE DIFFERENT, BUT THEY'RE ALL ABOUT SURVIVAL. THEY WEREN'T GOING TO DO ANY HARM. IT WAS JUST A CRASH...AND THEN A SCARE...AND THEN IT HAPPENED AGAIN...AND AGAIN...AND THEN THEY STOPPED COMING. AND NOW, THEY'RE MORE PROGRESSED, AND THEY DO VISIT US, BUT THEY'RE WORKING WITH US ON ANOTHER LEVEL BECAUSE THEY'VE TAKEN A DIFFERENT APPROACH. BUT THEY'RE JUST TRYING TO SAVE A PLACE THAT THEY ENJOY COMING TO."

<u>Laura:</u> "That's another book. Okay, so the kids that get autism...they get the vaccine, which is a live virus, and then they are exposed to the biological warfare, that puts them in this

mummified state. You said, 'Don't let your kids play in the dirt.' What happens if they do? What's happening to the kids that didn't just get vaccinated that are exposed to it?"

<u>MEDIUM:</u> "OKAY, THE ONLY WAY THOSE KIDS WOULD GET IT (AUTISM) IS IF THEY WERE GETTING THE PROBLEM (NATURALLY) THAT THE VACCINATION WAS FOR. BECAUSE THEN THEY GOT THE LIVE VIRUS IN ANOTHER FORM. SO, IF THEY GOT THE VIRUS THE NATURAL WAY OR THEY GOT THE VIRUS FROM THE VACCINATION, AND THEN THAT IN COMBINATION (WITH THE CONTAMINATION) WILL TRIGGER IT. SO, IN ESSENCE IT IS A DISEASE COMBINED WITH WHAT THEY ARE DOING. BECAUSE THEY ARE INJECTING A LIVE VIRUS AND THE VIRUS IS EITHER GROWING OR NOT GROWING, BUT...."

<u>Laura:</u> "You can get it naturally, or by the vaccine, then it's combining with the..."

<u>MEDIUM:</u> "THE CHILDREN THAT AREN'T GETTING VACCINATED AND THEY ARE AROUND SOMEONE THAT IS

CARRYING THE VIRUS, AND THEN THE OTHER ONE GETS SICK, THE WHOLE PROCESS HAPPENS IN THE SAME WAY."

"BUT YOU NEED TO KNOW THAT IT'S NOT THE THINGS THAT THEY PUT IN THERE TO MAKE IT LAST. IT IS NOT..."

Laura: "The preservative?" (THIMEROSAL)

MEDIUM: "IT'S NOT THE PRESERVATIVE."

Laura: "It's the virus? Is it the Rubella virus?

MEDIUM: "OKAY, THIS VIRUS CAUSES A PERSON TO GET VERY FEVERISH, AND THEY ARE ACTUALLY TIRED, AND I FEEL FEVERISH. DRY MOUTH, VERY DRY MOUTH, AND THE CHILD GETS VERY WHINY. SO IT HAPPENS IN CHILDREN. IT AFFECTS THE BODY, BUT THE MIND IS GOING 100 MILES AN HOUR. SO, IT'S NOT A VIRUS THAT MAKES YOU TIRED AND SLEEPY TO THE POINT TO WHERE YOU'RE NOT THINKING. YOU KNOW WHEN YOU HAVE A COLD, YOU'RE TIRED, YOUR BODY HURTS, AND YOU JUST LIE DOWN AND GO TO SLEEP, AND YOU'RE WAITING TO GET OVER IT. THIS

IS LIKE YOU'RE A MUMMY, ALMOST LIKE A MUMMY. YOU'RE LIKE TRAPPED INTO THIS, IN YOUR BODY. AND THIS IS A DISEASE THAT WE DO GET A VACCINATION FOR, AND YOU'RE TRAPPED IN YOUR BODY, AND IT'S SICK."

"WHAT IS HAPPENING TO THESE CHILDREN…WHEN YOU HAVE THIS DISEASE, YOUR MIND IS GOING 100 MILES AN HOUR, YOU HAVE THE FEVER, YOU WANT ATTENTION, YOU DON'T FEEL GOOD, BUT YOUR MIND IS VERY ALERT. WHAT'S IN THERE IS JUST VERY ALERT. AND THAT'S ALMOST IN A MUMMY STATE. THOSE ARE THE SYMPTOMS."

"THESE KIDS ARE… WE DESCRIBED THEM AS MUMMIES, BECAUSE THEY GET TRAPPED IN THERE, AND THEIR MINDS ARE STILL GOING, BUT THEN THEY HAVE TO LEARN IN A DIFFERENT WAY BECAUSE THEY'RE NOT USING ALL OF THEIR SKILLS THAT THEY ARE SUPPOSED TO HAVE. THEY LOSE THOSE SKILLS, AND IT HAS TO DO WITH NEURO…WHEN THIS DISEASE IS COMING ON THAT YOU CAN GET THE SHOT FOR, IT'S NOT AT THAT LEVEL. SO, IT'S MAGNIFIED."

"OKAY, THIS IS ME (THE MEDIUM); I DON'T KNOW THE SYMPTOMS OF RUBELLA..."

Laura: "Me neither."

MEDIUM: "SO YOU NEED TO CHECK IT OUT."

Laura: "You could have just said yes or no."

MEDIUM: "THEY ARE NOT GIVING ME A NAME AS TO WHAT THAT IS. THE REASON THAT THEY ARE NOT GIVING YOU A YES OR NO IS BECAUSE YOU'VE GOT TO GO LOOK IT UP BECAUSE YOU'VE GOT TO SEE IN YOUR OWN MIND THAT THOSE ARE THE SYMPTOMS, AND YOU CAN SAY, 'WHOA, OKAY, NOW I CAN KEEP ON, BECAUSE I'M GETTING VALIDATION OUT OF SOME BOOK. AND IF I SAY YES OR NO, YOU'RE NOT GOING TO GO LOOK IT UP, YOU'RE JUST GOING TO SAY, OKAY, IT IS THIS, AND YOU'RE NEVER GOING TO KNOW THE SYMPTOMS OF WHAT THAT IS."

"OKAY. SO, WHAT'S HAPPENING IS, IT IS THE VERY DISEASE YOUR CHILD HAS NOW, BUT ON A VERY, VERY LOW

SCALE THAT'S ESCALATED TO SOMETHING ELSE TO WHERE THEY ARE STILL TRAPPED IN THE BODY AND THEN THEY ARE LEARNING IN DIFFERENT WAYS. DURING THE TIME WHERE IT IS A LOW DOSE, THEY JUST WANT ATTENTION, THEY ARE RUNNING FEVER, THEIR MIND IS VERY ALERT, THEY WILL NOT STAY DOWN. THEY WILL NOT REST. THEY WANT TO KEEP GOING. THEY FIGHT IT, AND FIGHT IT, AND FIGHT IT. AND SO IT BECOMES VERY CHALLENGING FOR THE PARENT. AND THIS IS A DISEASE THAT'S IN CHILDREN."

Laura: "Measles?" (Giggles)

MEDIUM: "AND I DON'T KNOW…YOU MIGHT CHECK OUT MUMPS. CUZ THEY ARE SHOWING ME THE FAT CHEEKS AND THE HEATING PADS AND ALL OF THAT."

Laura: "That vaccine…Measles, Mumps, Rubella…is all in one shot. Three live viruses.

They are all in the same vaccine, and that's usually when the parents see the child disappear, after that vaccine. And that's when they are getting it. I'll look up all three of them and see.

That's what happened to my son. After the MMR shot, he changed."

<u>MEDIUM:</u> "WELL, I SAW THE PHYSICAL SYMPTOMS OF MUMPS, THE FAT CHEEKS AND HEATING PADS TO TRY TO ALLEVIATE THE PAIN."

<u>Laura:</u> "Last time, I thought it came through that it was the Rubella...same vaccine."

<u>MEDIUM:</u> "AGAIN, MY EAR IS SHUTTING DOWN. THIS ONE IS SHUTTING DOWN. SO THERE ARE A LOT OF THINGS YOU'RE GOING TO HAVE TO BE DOING THAT HAS TO DO WITH...AND THEY ARE SHUTTING THAT EAR DOWN, SO HALF OF YOU IS...I DON'T KNOW WHAT'S GOING ON EXACTLY, BUT YOU NEED TO KNOW THAT THAT'S WHAT THEY'RE TELLING ME."

"THERE WILL BE CHANGES MADE IN THE WATERS..."

"YOU HAVE ANOTHER QUESTION?"

<u>Laura:</u> "Let's see what else they have to say."

<u>MEDIUM:</u> "OKAY, THIS IS THE WIRY ONE… I'M TRYING TO PUT IT INTO WORDS THAT YOU'LL UNDERSTAND BECAUSE I'M PRETTY MUCH OF A FREAK, AND I TALK ALL OVER THE PLACE, SO I NEED TO REALLY THINK ABOUT COHERENTLY WHAT IT IS THAT YOU NEED TO HEAR, SO YOU'LL GET IT EXACT."

"THE THINGS THAT YOU ARE WRITING ABOUT IN THIS BOOK ARE GOING TO TRIGGER A LOT OF OTHER THINGS, A LOT OF OTHER PEOPLE THAT ARE OF THE LEVEL THAT I AM, TO BE USING ALL RESOURCES. BECAUSE THE DAYS OF KEEPING ALL OF THIS SEPARATED IS GONE. WE NEED TO BRING THE MINDS, THE BODIES, AND THE SPIRITS ALL TOGETHER BECAUSE THERE IS A HIGHER LEVEL OF GENIUS, AND IT'S GOING TO HAVE TO BE INCORPORATED."

"SO, YOU MUST PUT ON THE FRONT OF THE BOOK THAT IT IS CHANNELED BECAUSE THIS KIND OF INFORMATION IS GOING TO BE SOUGHT OUT."

"AND THERE'S ONE MAN WITH MANY PEOPLE WHO ARE BEHIND HIM WHO WILL SEEK THIS OUT. SO, HE HAS SOME SORT OF A CREW. PEOPLE WHO WORK FOR HIM, BUT HE'S SHOWING ME SOME SORT OF ENERGETIC LEADER THAT IS TRYING TO SAVE THINGS. AND IT ALL STARTS WITH THE PLANTS. HE'S IN THE WASHINGTON AREA, OR THAT CORNER UP THERE...OREGON, WASHINGTON...UP THERE. THE VEGETATION AND THAT...SOMETHING GOES WRONG UP THERE. EYEBROWS ARE REALLY GOING TO BE GOING UP. AND THEY START REALLY LOOKING AT THINGS IN A BIGGER WAY THAN IT DOES IN THE OTHER PARTS OF THE NATION. AND YES, SOME OF THE POWDER IS GOING TO GO THAT WAY AS WELL. AND THAT'S WHEN ALL THE EYEBROW RAISING AND THE HEAD SCRAMBLING, AND EVERYTHING STARTS HAPPENING OVER THERE."

"THERE ARE A LOT OF SCIENTIST-TYPE MINDS IN THAT AREA. THEY KEEP A LOW PROFILE, BUT THAT'S WHERE THEY LIVE. IT HAS TO DO WITH PEOPLE THAT STUDY BIOLOGY, THAT STUDY THE PLANTS, THAT STUDY EARTH CHANGES, THE EARTHQUAKES...MEASURING THINGS. AND EQUIPMENT THAT THEY HAVE OUT TO SEA, EQUIPMENT

THAT THEY HAVE ON THE LAND. THEY'RE WATCHING THE GREENERY, THEY'RE WATCHING THE WATERS, THEY'RE WATCHING THE EARTH. AND A LOT THEY DO FROM THOSE TWO STATES. AND PEOPLE FEEL LIKE THIS IS A GOOD PLACE TO START, BECAUSE IT'S VERY GREEN. IT FEELS GOOD, IT'S TREASURED. SO WHEN THERE'S A MODALITY OF WRONGNESS, THEY FEEL IT VERY QUICKLY AND THEY SEE THE DIFFERENCE. IN OTHER AREAS, THEY JUSTIFY IT TO SOMETHING...BECAUSE OF THIS, OR BECAUSE OF THAT. THEY DON'T REALLY SEE IT. AND IN THAT AREA, THERE'S MORE TREES THAN PEOPLE."

(The closest organization I could find that fit the description is the Pacific Northwest National Laboratory. They study the environment, and one of their scientific missions is to "Prevent and Counter Terrorism and the Proliferation of Weapons of Mass Destruction."[33] They have state of the art biological warfare detection equipment.)

"DO YOU HAVE ANOTHER QUESTION?"

---

[33]http://www.pnl.gov/missions/prevent.asp

<u>Laura:</u> "I wanted to ask The Wiry One, some people in the autism community say that he was autistic...how would he explain that?"

<u>MEDIUM:</u> "I JUST HAD MORE IN MY HEAD. I HAD THOUGHTS ON TOP OF THOUGHTS, AND I GENERATED THEM AS QUICKLY AS I COULD. PUT OUT AS MANY AS I COULD. AT FIRST IT WAS VERY CONFUSING TO ME BECAUSE THERE WERE JUST SO MANY OF THEM. WHAT THE AVERAGE PERSON HAS, I'M 15 UP PER NANOSECOND. SO IN THE BEGINNING IT WAS VERY CONFUSING. AND THEN I FOUND OUT THAT I WAS JUST SUPPOSED TO PUT THEM OUT THERE BECAUSE PEOPLE WERE DOING THINGS WITH THEM THAT I DIDN'T KNOW HOW EVERYTHING WAS SUPPOSED TO BE APPLIED. I EVEN SEE IT TODAY; WITH MY THEORIES AND THINGS THAT I DEVELOPED THAT I JUST LAYED DOWN THE FOUNDATION. IT'S LIKE SAYING SOMETHING IS ROUND, AND THEN YOU MAKE A WHEEL OUT OF IT, AND THEN YOU MAKE A TIRE, AND THEN YOU MAKE ALL THESE THINGS THAT ARE TOOLS AND YOU CAN USE THEM IN MANY DIFFERENT WAYS. AND THAT'S WHAT HAPPENED WITH MY INFORMATION."

"NO...AUTISM, NO, THAT'S NOT WHAT I HAD. I WAS NOT TRAPPED IN MY OWN BODY. I WAS TOTALLY THE OPPOSITE. I WAS SCATTERED ALL OVER THE PLACE. AND I HAD SO MANY THOUGHTS GOING IN SO MANY DIFFERENT DIRECTIONS, THAT IT WAS HARD TO PUT ON MY PANTS. AND I WOULD LOOK AT MYSELF, BUT I DIDN'T LOOK LIKE TO ME WHAT I LOOKED LIKE. BECAUSE I WAS ALWAYS STEPS AHEAD OF MYSELF, IF THAT MAKES ANY SENSE TO YOU. IT WAS LIKE I WAS DOING ONE THING, BUT I WAS ALREADY DOING ANOTHER, BECAUSE I WOULD GO INTO THE FUTURE."

"AND THE FUTURE IS VERY REAL, AND THEN I WOULD COME BACK, BUT IT'S ALL IN THE MIND. IT'S NOT LIKE I HAD TO THROW MY BODY, AND MAKE IT MATERIALIZE SOMEWHERE ELSE, IT WAS JUST MY MIND GOING FORWARD. AND PEOPLE TALK ABOUT GOING INTO THE FUTURE, AND IT CAN BE DONE. BUT IT'S ALL MIND, AND THEN YOU BRING BACK THE INFORMATION."

"AND THIS IS OKAY TO DO, BECAUSE YOU'VE GOT TO HAVE A BETTER WORLD. FUTURE IS GOOD TO KNOW OR YOU

WOULDN'T BE ABLE TO APPLY THE THINGS. YOU WOULD NOT EVOLVE. IF YOU COULD NOT GO INTO THE FUTURE, YOU COULD NOT EVOLVE. YOU HAVE TO GO INTO THE FUTURE. AND WHEN YOU SEE THE FUTURE, YOU START EVOLVING BECAUSE YOU TAKE EVERYTHING AND YOU PUT IT INTO PLAY. YOU USE IT AS TOOLS."

"SO, ALL OF THESE PEOPLE WHO ARE SCREAMING ABOUT PROFITS...THEY ARE SO WRONG! WHAT IS WRONG WITH THEM? AND HE GOES, 'AAAGH!'"

"AND I'M OKAY, AND NO, I DID NOT HAVE WHAT YOUR CHILD HAS. THIS IS DIFFERENT. THIS IS FROM WARFARE. THIS IS FROM GOVERNMENTAL CONTROL. WHAT I HAD IS WHAT GOD GAVE ME; AND THERE IS A GOD, LET ME TELL YOU. IT WAS A GIFT IN ITSELF."

"ALTHOUGH LET ME TELL YOU, THE THING I DIDN'T LIKE...I DIDN'T CARE IF I COULDN'T COMB MY HAIR OR PUT MY SHIRT ON...IT'S MY PANTS THAT BOTHERED ME! CAN YOU IMAGINE GETTING HELP PUTTING YOUR PANTS ON? THAT'S WHAT BOTHERED ME THE MOST."

"YOU COULD SEE IT IN MY EYES. THAT'S ALL THAT I WANTED TO DO."

"EVERYTHING WORKS LIKE A WHEEL, AND IT TURNS, AND YOU'VE GOT THE NEXT WHEEL THAT CATCHES, AND THE NEXT WHEEL THAT CATCHES. AND THEN EVERYBODY THROWS FAULT EVERYWHERE ELSE."

"I HATE WHAT IS HAPPENING TO THE CHILDREN. IT'S NOT A NORMAL THING. IT'S NOT A GOD-GIVEN THING. IT'S NOT FAIR TO THEM; THEY ARE VICTIMS. THE PARENTS HAVE IT HEAVY ON THEIR HEART. SOME OF THEM LOSE A LOT OF LOVE. IT'S JUST A LOT OF MISUNDERSTANDING."

"THERE'S GOT TO BE CHANGES...AND I'M COMING BACK TO MAKE THOSE. NO YOU DON'T NEED SOMEBODY ELSE; YOU JUST NEED ME RIGHT NOW. I'LL BE AROUND FOR THE FIRST FIVE CHAPTERS, AND THEN THERE WILL BE ANOTHER GENTLEMAN WHO WILL COME AND STEP IN. CUZ THIS BOOK IS ALREADY PLANNED. IT'S ALREADY MADE. IT'S JUST GOING TO HAVE TO MANIFEST. AND IT TAKES

PEOPLE TO DO IT. DON'T TAKE ANY OF THE THINGS THAT COME THROUGH PERSONALLY. YOU NEED TO FIND THE REMEDY, AND PUT IT THERE."

"FORGET ABOUT EVERYBODY THAT GETS PUT INTO THE EARTH. WHAT ARE YOU GOING TO DO TO STOP IT? BUT YOU WRITE IT DOWN, AND IT HAPPENS. AND THEN WHAT? IT WILL MAKE THEM LISTEN. CUZ THEY ARE NOT LISTENING. THEY TALK ABOUT IT, AND IT GOES IN AND OUT OF THEIR MIND JUST AS FAST AS SIPPING ON A CUP OF COFFEE."

"SO MANY LITTLE BOYS....AND GIRLS...BUT NOT AS MANY."

Laura: "Why? Why are there more boys than girls?"

MEDIUM: "THERE'S SO MANY BOYS, GIRLS TOO, BUT NOT AS MANY."

Laura: "Why does it affect boys four times as much as girls."

<u>MEDIUM:</u> "CUZ THEY ARE THE ONES OUTSIDE PLAYING IN THE DIRT...THE LITTLE GIRLS ARE IN THEIR DRESSES. THEY'RE THE ONES OUTSIDE, BEING WHO THEY ARE. THEY'RE THE LITTLE BOYS. STRONG MINDS...EVEN THE STRONG-MINDED...THEY WIND UP THE SAME."

"IT'S A SHUT-DOWN; IT'S A SHUT-DOWN OF THEIR WAY TO SPEAK. A WAY FOR THEIR WRIST TO CORRECTLY WORK. YOU SEE IT ON THE OUTSIDE, AND IT LOOKS LIKE AN ANXIETY. BUT IT'S ***NOT!*** IT'S A BODY BEING THROWN AROUND BECAUSE WHAT'S INSIDE DOESN'T KNOW HOW TO COMMUNICATE WITH THE OUTSIDE BECAUSE IT'S TRAPPED."

"BUT THERE ARE WAYS TO COMMUNICATE WITH THEM. BECAUSE THEY HAVE RESOURCED TO THEIR PSYCHIC SO THAT THEY CAN EXPRESS THEMSELVES. SO LISTEN!"

<u>Laura:</u> (Fighting tears) "Telepathy?"

<u>MEDIUM:</u> "AND AUTOMATIC WRITING, TELEPATHY, ALL OF THOSE WAYS. READ ABOUT EVERYTHING THAT HAS TO DO

WITH ESP. THEY'LL USE EVERYTHING THAT'S CALLED PHENOMENA, BECAUSE THEY ARE USING THEIR PSYCHIC. ALL OF THAT FALLS INTO THE CATEGORIES OF…THE DIFFERENT THINGS THAT YOU DEVELOP IN SPIRITUALISM. WHETHER YOU CALL IT SPIRITUALIST, OR SPIRITUALISM, OR SPIRITIST…DEPENDS ON WHAT PART OF THE WORLD YOU'RE FROM."

"YOU KNOW I HAD A LOT MORE TO DEAL WITH WHEN I WAS IN MY CENTURY. SO THERE'S NOT AS MUCH AS I PUT OUT THERE AS I WOULD HAVE LIKED. THERE ARE SOME OF MY THINGS THAT GOT WATER PUT ON THEM, AND THEY WERE DESTROYED. SO NOT ALL OF MY WRITINGS AND EVERYTHING THAT I NEEDED TO GET OUT TO THE WORLD IS THERE. AND THIS IS MY OPPORTUNITY TO DO IT NOW."

Laura: "Like what?"

MEDIUM: "LIKE HELPING THE PLANET STAY TOGETHER. HELPING HUMANITY EXIST AND INTERMINGLE WITH THE ONES THAT ARE COMING, AND NOT BE FEARFUL. BECAUSE YOU WILL NOT BE CONTROLLED, IF THAT'S WHAT YOU'RE

THINKING...IT IS NOT SO. YOU WILL NOT BE OVERPOWERED. LOOK AT YOU...LOOK AT YOU WHEN YOU GET A DOG. WHAT DO YOU DO FOR THAT DOG? THINK ABOUT IT...DO YOU THINK THESE PEOPLE WANT TO HARM YOU? THEY'RE JUST DIFFERENT ENTITIES. THEY WILL TAKE CARE OF YOU. YOU JUST HAVE TO MAKE THIS BALL YOU LIVE ON STAY TOGETHER."

"BUT MANY ARE GOING TO BE GOING DOWN. THEY WILL BE MESHED INTO THE EARTH, AND MIXED UP. AND THEY WILL NOT BE BURIED IN TOMBS, OR THEIR OWN GRAVES. AND AGAIN, THEY'RE GIVING ME PAKISTAN, INDIA, AND THAT SURROUNDING AREA. SO THERE MUST BE..."

Laura: "From what? A volcano or warfare?"

MEDIUM: "I REALLY FEEL EARTHQUAKE...CUZ IT'S GOING TO EAT THEM UP. THEY ARE GOING TO BE IN THE LAND, AND I JUST SEE THEM LIKE JUST MIXED UP. THE VOLCANOS AND ALL THAT I SAW SOMEWHERE ELSE. THEY SHOWED ME THE VOLCANOS...REMEMBER THE SKIES WERE PURPLES AND PINKS, BUT THAT'S FROM THE ERUPTIONS. BUT THIS

RIGHT HERE, I DON'T SEE THAT SORT OF THING, I SEE THE PEOPLE...IT'S LIKE FLOUR, IT LOOKS LIKE FLOUR AND YOU'RE MIXING UP, AND THE PEOPLE ARE JUST GOING IN THERE."

"AND SOMEONE UP THERE IS PUTTING THEIR FOOT DOWN. THIS WORLD IS JUST TRYING TO REPAIR ITSELF. BUT YOU KNOW WHAT, IT DOESN'T HAPPEN BY ITSELF. THERE'S A HAND UP THERE IN MOTION. BUT, IT HAPPENS FROM THE SPHERES ABOVE. IT'S NOT LIKE THE HAND COMES AND SHAKES THE EARTH, IT'S LIKE IT MANIPULATES WHAT'S AROUND THE EARTH. AND THEN IT HAPPENS TO THE EARTH."

"SO, HE GOES (LICKS POINTER FINGER, AND MOTIONS LIKE IT IS TOUCHING SOMETHING HOT) 'PPPSSSTTT.' THAT'S HOW IT'S SCIENTIFICALLY PROVEN AND PEOPLE GET CONFUSED THAT THERE'S A HIGHER POWER. BECAUSE OF THE STRATEGIES. CUZ YOU'RE NOT GOING TO SEE A BIG OLD HAND SLAP THE SIDE OF THE EARTH AND SHAKE IT UP AND SQUEEZE IT. IT MANIPULATES WHAT'S AROUND IT."

Laura: "Natural disasters?"

MEDIUM: "THAT'S WHAT THEY CALL IT...BUT, SORRY! IT'S NOT NATURAL (IN A SING-SONG FAST-PACED VOICE). THAT'S HOW HE SAID IT (LAUGHING). THAT'S HOW I HEARD IT."

"HE LIKES US. THE WIRY ONE LIKES US."

Laura: "We're cool."

MEDIUM: "HE'S LAUGHING. HE LAUGHS. HE'S A MAN OF LAUGHTER. HE'S JUST CRACKING HIMSELF UP. OKAY, WELL PUT (HE SAYS) A MAN WHO CRACKS HIMSELF UP. SO HE THINKS THAT HE'S FUNNY. YEAH, BUT IT'S BECAUSE HE'S OF HIGHER INTELLEGENCE. SEE, HE CAN LOOK BACK. HE CAN DO AND LOOK AT HIMSELF AT THE SAME TIME. AND THAT TAKES TALENT. THAT TAKES TALENT FOR YOU TO BE ABLE TO SEE YOURSELF AT THE SAME TIME AS YOU CRITIQUE YOURSELF, AND YOU KEEP RIGHT ON GOING. (WHISPERING) 'I DID THAT.' I DID THAT ON A REGULAR BASIS. BUT THANK GOODNESS I WASN'T THE ONE OF

FASHION...BUT I COULD TELL YOU ALL ABOUT IT. BUT FOR ME TO STRUT IT? NO WAY."

"YOUR BOY (LAURA'S SON) WILL COME AROUND IN HIS 40'S. THIS IS A DISEASE, AND THERE WILL BE A CURE. THIS IS NOT SOMETHING THAT HAS KILLED A CHILD. IT'S SOMETHING THAT HAS CRIPPLED IT. SO THESE CHILDREN WILL SNAP OUT. THERE ARE TOO MANY. TOO MANY ON THE AGENDA TO NOT DO RESEARCH AND TRY TO FIGURE IT OUT. THESE KIDS THEMSELVES WILL HELP FIND THE REMEDY IF YOU WILL JUST LISTEN TO THEM THROUGH THEIR WAY OF COMMUNICATING. BECAUSE THEY'RE TRAPPED INSIDE...THEY ARE MUMMIES."

"YOU'VE NOT LOST YOUR CHILD...YOU'VE NOT LOST YOUR CHILD, YOU NEED TO UNDERSTAND THAT. YOUR CHILD IS THERE. YOU NEED TO CONTINUE TO SEND ALL THE LOVE AND SUPPORT. AND HE HAS A VERY UNDERSTANDING BROTHER."

Laura: (Choked up) "Yeah."

<u>MEDIUM:</u> "A VERY SUPPORTIVE BROTHER. AND THAT WILL GO ON AND ON AND ON THROUGHOUT THEIR LIFETIMES. THERE WILL BE A LOT OF INTRODUCTIONS THAT THE BROTHER WILL MAKE TO THE OTHER TO GIVE HIM SOME THRILLS. SO THOSE ARE TIMES YOU WON'T WANT TO BE AROUND."

<u>Laura:</u> (Laughing) "Great. How does he explain the people who say that they've 'recovered' their autistic child? Did they even have the same thing that we're talking about?"

<u>MEDIUM:</u> "THESE WERE MOSTLY GIRLS. AND IT'S BECAUSE THEY WEREN'T AFFECTED AS MUCH BECAUSE THEY DIDN'T GET THE DOSAGE (OF THE DUST) THAT THE OTHERS DID. SO THESE ARE MOSTLY GIRLS...THE ONES THAT ARE RECOVERING, THOSE ARE THE GIRLS. BECAUSE IT WAS JUST A LITTLE BIT, NOT LIKE YOUR SON, AND THE MANY BOYS THAT ARE VERY, VERY TRAPPED WITHIN THEMSELVES. SO IF YOU DO A STUDY, YOU'LL SEE THAT IT'S MOSTLY GIRLS THAT ARE COMING AROUND."

(The percentage of girls who apparently lost their original label is 44.5%, compared to 34.6% of boys who lost their original ASD label.[34])

<u>Laura:</u> "So are they continuing to be poisoned every time they're in the dirt? Is it making it worse?"

<u>MEDIUM:</u> "IT DOESN'T HELP. IT DOESN'T HELP, BUT WHEN THE CRASH COMES, IT IS WHEN YOU'RE DOWN. IT'S LIKE GETTING KICKED WHEN YOU'RE ALREADY DOWN...AND SOMEONE TRIES TO KILL YOU. THAT'S WHAT HAPPENING. IT TAKES OVER DURING A WEAK PERIOD. AND WHEN THAT INJECTION...WHEN THEY'RE PUT INTO THAT WEAK STATE, AND THEN THEY'RE ATTACKED...BEING IN THE WRONG PLACE AT THE WRONG TIME...THAT'S ALL IT IS. IT'S NOT SOMETHING THAT'S FROM BIRTH. IT'S NOT SOMETHING IN THE GENES. IT'S JUST BEING AT THE WRONG PLACE AT THE WRONG TIME."

---

[34] http://www.huffingtonpost.com/david-kirby/autism-rate-now-at-one-pe_b_256141.html

<u>Laura:</u> "How do you explain all these boys...for instance Jenny McCarthy just wrote a book about how she recovered her son from autism with biomedical intervention, speech therapy, and diet?"

<u>MEDIUM:</u> "SO DID SHE GET IN HIS HEAD SOMEHOW? FROM COMMUNICATING WITH HIM. THAT'S WHAT THEY ARE TELLING YOU TO DO. YOU NEED TO COMMUNICATE WITH HIM. YOU NEED TO LISTEN TO THE LAST FEW MINUTES OF WHAT ALREADY CAME THROUGH, AND THAT ANSWERS YOUR QUESTION. I'VE ALREADY TOLD YOU. BECAUSE IT WILL BE ABOUT YOU WORKING TOGETHER. LISTEN TO THE LAST FEW MINUTES AND YOUR ANSWER IS THERE. CUZ I ALREADY TALKED ABOUT THAT."

<u>Laura:</u> "The ESP and automatic writing and telepathy?"

<u>MEDIUM:</u> "AND THAT COMMUNICATION WITH EACH OTHER...YOU'LL HAVE BREAKTHROUGHS. THE MIND IS THERE...DO YOU NOT UNDERSTAND WHAT A MUMMY IS?" (TIMER SOUNDS OFF)

"OKAY…BYE, BYE…IS WHAT HE SAYS. (LAUGHING) HE WAS SAYING SOMETHING IN A REALLY STRONG WAY, AND THEN IT TURNED AND HE WAS LIKE A KID SAYING, OKAY…BYE, BYE."

(CD ends)

***

Later Discoveries

Don't skip this section. What you are about to read may seem boring or pointless, but it will help you connect the dots. Since this reading stated that the form of biological warfare they were creating in the underground facility in Hawthorne, NV was a form of anthrax, I started to study anthrax and the history of biological warfare. BINGO!

History of Biological Warfare

I found another very interesting connection with this material and the President who came through in the readings. I was looking for information about the history of biological warfare and found that American biological weapons development began in 1942. The President from the readings placed George W. Merck (former president of the pharmaceutical giant Merck & Co.) in charge of the effort to create a biological weapons development program. This was another A-ha! moment for me. Another reason this President was coming through to help us out was that he was involved with our country's biological weapons program.

In response to Japan's full-scale germ-warfare program, the U.S. began research on biological weapons. The main military facility that was used at this time to develop BW was Fort Detrick, MD. On their own website, it says "From the moment of its birth in the highest levels of government, the fledgling biological warfare effort was kept to an inner circle of knowledgeable persons. George W. Merck was a key member of the panel advising The President and was charged with putting such an effort together. Merck owned the pharmaceutical firm that still bears his name."[35]

1972 Biological and Toxin Weapons Convention

I discovered that under President Nixon, the U.S. initiated and signed the Biological and Toxin Weapons Convention (BWC). The BWC prohibits the development, production, stockpiling, and acquisition of these weapons. The BWC thus supplements the prohibition on use of biological weapons contained in the 1925 Geneva Protocol. Opened for signature on April 10, 1972 and entering into force on March 26, 1975, The BWC is commonly portrayed as the first international treaty to ban an entire class of weapons. As of June 2000, it had 144 states parties, including the five permanent members of the United Nations Security Council, plus a further 18 signatory states. The United Kingdom, the United States and the Russian Federation are the depositaries of the Convention.

In the preamble to the BWC Convention it states, "Determined, for the sake of all mankind, to exclude completely the possibility of bacteriological (biological) agents and toxins

[35]http://www.detrick.army.mil/cutting_edge/chapter04.cfm

being used as weapons, convinced that such use would be repugnant to the conscience of mankind and that no effort should be spared to minimize this risk." Article I states, "Each State Party to this Convention undertakes never in any circumstances to develop, produce, stockpile or otherwise acquire or retain: (1) Microbial or other biological agents, or toxins whatever their origin or method of production, of types and in quantities that have no justification for prophylactic, protective or other peaceful purposes; (2) Weapons, equipment or means of delivery designed to use such agents or toxins for hostile purposes or in armed conflict."[36]

Did the United States stop its offensive biological weapons program after signing the BWC? I did more research about the history of biological warfare, and what I discovered was pretty appalling. One article I found was from the Houston Chronicle, titled. *"Secret Germ Warfare Tests Produced Chilling Results."*[37] This was just after the anthrax mail scare post 9/11, on Nov. 9, 2001. It said that "The Army kept the biological-warfare tests secret until word of them was leaked to the press in the 1970's.

---

[36]http://www.fas.harvard.edu/~hsp/1972.html

[37]Carlton, Jim, "Secret germ warfare tests produced chilling results" *Wall Street Journal*. (Nov. 9, 2001).

Between 1949 and 1969, when President Nixon ordered the Pentagon's biological weapons destroyed, open-air tests of biological agents were conducted 239 times, (in the U.S.) according to the Army's testimony in 1977 before the Senate's subcommittee on health. In 80 of those experiments, the Army said it used live bacteria that its researchers at the time thought were harmless, such as the Serratia that was showered on San Francisco. In others, it used inert chemicals to simulate bacteria." Then it went on to say, "The possibility cannot be ruled out that peculiarities in wind conditions or ventilation systems in buildings might concentrate organisms, exposing people to high doses of bacteria." Imagine how many tests they've done on an unsuspecting public since then! They mentioned in the readings that starting with Watergate was when diseases were put into the people.

Further validation that the U.S. did not stop producing biological warfare was in a movie by Dr. Leonard Horowitz called *The CIA, Hollywood, and Bioterrorism.* It was about the history of bioterrorism with lots of information. One article highlighted was from the prestigious scientific magazine *Nature* and said "In 1969, the use of biological warfare was renounced as a political ploy. By 1970, a year after Nixon ratified the Geneva Protocol; nothing had changed except the public's perception of chemical biological warfare risk. Rather than receive the promised annual cut in biological warfare research funding, the DOD's BW budget increased from $21.9 to $23.2 million. The stockpiled bioweapons Nixon pledged would be rapidly destroyed remained intact in Pine Bluff, Arkansas, and the announced transition of Fort Detrick from a BW testing facility to a solely defensive NIH run health research lab had not occurred."[38]

Even now, this offensive work continues. I found a damaging article titled "U.S. Corporations Aren't Disclosing Biological Warfare Research Work" from *Political Affairs* magazine from 6-22-07 states "A number of pharmaceutical corporations and biotech firms are concealing the nature of the biological warfare research work they are doing for the U.S. government. Since their funding comes from the National Institutes of Health, the recipients are obligated under NIH guidelines to make their activities public. Not disclosing their ops raises the suspicion that they may be engaged in forbidden kinds of germ warfare research. According to the Sunshine Project, a nonprofit arms

[38] www.liveleak.com/view?i=377_1195303011

control watchdog operating out of Austin, Texas, among the corporations holding back information about their activities are: Abbott Laboratories, BASF Plant Science, Bristol-Meyers Squibb, DuPont Central Research and Development, Eli Lilly Corp., Embrex, GlaxoSmithKline, Hoffman-LaRoche, **Merck & Co.**, Monsanto, Pfizer Inc., Schering-Plough Research Institute, and Syngenta Corp of Switzerland. In case you didn't know it, the White House since 9/11 has called for spending $44 billion on biological warfare research, a sum unprecedented in world history, and an obligating Congress has authorized it. Thus, some of the deadliest pathogens known to humankind are being rekindled in hundreds of labs in pharmaceutical houses, university biology departments, and military bases." It went on to say that "In 2006, the NIH got $1.76 billion for biodefense, much of it spent to research anthrax."

I couldn't believe it! Now, I am not saying that this is proof, but I wondered after reading all of this if Merck is the pharmaceutical company that was mentioned in the first reading that said that U.S. Presidents automatically get stock in? It started with the Nixon Administration. The President of Merck, the world's largest vaccine manufacturer, was America's biological weapons director during World War II. Talk about a conflict of interest. Did I mention that Merck also manufactures the MMR vaccine? Maybe someone with inside knowledge can validate more on this one.

U.S. Military and Biological Warfare

I found a frightening article sourced from the Wall Street Journal titled, "*Biological Warfare: Incredible, Deadly Viruses are Manufactured with Little Difficulty.*" It quoted a passage from the book, *"AIDS: The End of Civilization,"* by Dr. William Campbell Douglass which says, "With the advent of genetic manipulation (i.e., recombinant engineering), some most incredible and deadly viruses can now be manufactured with little difficulty. One devastating possibility would be to combine the highly-contagious influenza virus with the genes of either the anthrax toxin, the botulism toxin, or the toxin from plague. If this type of designer virus were unleashed upon a population, infection of almost all of the populace would be certain, especially in the cities, and death would very quickly follow. There would be no treatment and diagnosis would be difficult. This is not science fiction. This is today's reality."

The article went on to say, "The reports of chemical and biological warfare experiments that have allegedly been carried out against innocent American civilians by the scientists working in the defense industry and our own military are numerous and staggering in their implication. More and more of these stories are surfacing through declassified documents, leaks, and testimonials of some of the victims involved." [39]

I found another interesting article about cleanup at Fort Detrick from CBS News from May 28, 2003. The article is titled *"Buried WMDs Found...In Maryland: Cleanup at Ft. Detrick Has Unearthed Secrets of U.S. Biowar Work."* The article states "U.S. weapons experts are struggling to deal with the remnants of a decades-old biological weapons program. They are trying to find potentially dangerous materials—once shrouded in secrecy—with only poorly kept records and fading memories to go on. Thousands of tons of hazardous substances like anthrax are at stake. Only the hunt is not in Iraq. It's in Maryland.

According to the Washington Post, the U.S. Army has spent two years and $25 million cleaning up an area of central

---

[39] http://www.geocites.com/area51/Shadowlands/6583/project085.html?200719.

Maryland's Fort Detrick that was used as a target range and waste dump. In what has become the Army's biggest remediation project ever, the cleanup of Area B has unearthed vials of live bacteria and nonvirulent anthrax. Some 2,000 tons have been scooped out of the ground to date." It went on to say, The site is so toxic that cleanup crews wear respirators and the materials sometimes burst into flames as they are dug up. At one point, digging released a gas that sent workers to the hospital. The very small amount of anthrax that was found in vaccine form could not have spread the disease. But cleanup crews have also unearthed old lab rats, syringes and drums and canisters with unidentified contents. The documentation for where this came from does not exist."

This was validating to me because it shows history that our military has been involved in creating biological warfare, specifically anthrax that polluted the soil, which had to be dug up and removed. This was one of the messages from our readings of what is happening now to our topsoil, only on a much grander scale.

The United States has a rich history of getting the world's top biological warfare specialists (war criminals) to come to our country and work for us. There is plenty of literature out there on Project Paperclip, including the book *Lab 257: The Disturbing Story of the Government's Secret Plum Island Germ Laboratory* by Michael Carroll. In the book, it says, "Nearing the end of World War II, the United States and the Soviet Union raced to recruit German scientists for postwar purposes. Under a top-secret program code-named Project Paperclip, the U.S. military pursued Nazi scientific talent like forbidden fruit, bringing them to America under employment contracts and offering them full U.S. citizenship. The recruits were supposed to be nominal participants in Nazi activities. But the zealous military recruited more than two thousand scientists, many of whom had dark Nazi party pasts." This was in 1945. Many of the Nazi scientists went to work at Ft. Detrick. They were given immunity from prosecution for war crimes and secret identities in exchange for work on top secret U.S. government projects, including biological warfare experiments.

One of these Nazi scientists was Dr. Erich Traub. In the book, *The Nazi Hydra in America: Suppressed History of a Century* by Glen Yeadon and John Hawkins, it claims that "In 1949, Nazi scientist Erich Traub applied to work under the Project Paperclip program. Within months, Traub was invited for a talk with Germ Warriors from Fort Detrick, the Army's biological warfare headquarters in Frederick, MD. A former declassified summary confirmed the meeting occurred, but the CIA denies the summary exists and claims that if it did, it would withhold it for reasons of national security. Almost all documents concerning Traub and the Army's biowarfare at Plum Island have been destroyed or remain deeply buried in the government's secret vaults. The few documents that remain show that Traub worked with more than 40 lethal viruses on large test animals. He was at Plum Island from 1949-53. Reports of a Nazi scientist releasing infected ticks come from a former employee of Plum Island. Plum Island is two miles offshore from Old Lyme, Connecticut, home of Lab 257, where secret biological experiments were conducted with the most deadly strains of bacteria and viruses. Both Lyme disease and West Nile virus first appeared in the general area."

The U.S. government also offered Japanese war criminals and scientists who performed human medical experiments salaries and immunity from prosecution in exchange for data on biological warfare research. The following disturbing information comes from an article by journalist Christopher Reed titled *The United*

States and the Japanese Mengele: Payoffs and Amnesty for Unit 731 Scientists. "The Japanese Imperial Army group called Unit 731 was led by Army General Dr. Ishii Shiro. He was the chief of Japan's well financed scientifically coordinated and government approved biological warfare program from 1932-45. Ishii rose to general and supervised deliberate infection of thousands of captives with deadly diseases. He also conducted grotesque surgeries, but the unique medical specialty of Ishii and his surgical team were dissections, without anesthetic, on an estimated 3,000 live, conscious humans."

The article also stated that the Japanese performed "open-air germ tests on captured Chinese and Russian men, women and children. Some were bound to stakes in a large field and bombarded with anthrax. Others were subjected to germs of bubonic plague, cholera, smallpox, typhus and typhoid, and women to syphilis. Its biological warfare (BW) was also illegal, since all such experiments were banned by the 1925 Geneva Convention, which Japan signed but did not ratify."

The article continues to say "At Fort Detrick, Maryland, the main U.S. installation for BW, records remain on file of the thousands of tissue slides, preserved organs (some labeled 'American') removed from living bodies with medical schedules and reports on perverse surgical procedures on screaming and writhing human specimens."

The most concerning thing in the article was "The disclosure of two documents previously marked Top Secret and dated July 1947. They show not only full U.S. participation in allowing the Japanese medical torturers who escaped to Tokyo to go free in exchange for information, but that the Pentagon actually paid them. As General Charles Willoughby, chief of U.S. Military Intelligence gleefully noted to his headquarters, these pay-offs were 'a mere pittance...netting the U.S. the fruit of over 20 years' laboratory tests and research' in this 'critically serious form of warfare.'"

There is a lot more disturbing and incriminating information in this article and others regarding this topic. The point is that after World War II, the U.S. paid and protected biological warfare experts from both Germany and Japan in exchange for information. But wait, it gets even worse.

Anthrax and the Soviet Union

Since it was mentioned in the readings that what they are creating in the underground military facility in Hawthorne is a form of anthrax, I did some more research specifically about anthrax. This led me to an article from the Canadian website CBC News Online from Feb. 18, 2004 titled *Red Lies: Biological Warfare and the Soviet Union.* The article said that during the Cold War, "While the world worried about the nuclear threat, the Soviet Union was secretly amassing the largest biological weapons program in global history. It involved thousands of scientists, who spent two decades turning deadly diseases like anthrax and smallpox into weapons of mass destruction. It mentioned that the largest documented outbreak of human inhalation anthrax happened in Sverdlovsk, at a secretive military base called "Compound 19" in the Union of Soviet Socialist Republics in 1979. 68 people died. It was concluded that the escape of an aerosol of anthrax pathogen at the military facility caused the outbreak.[40]

The Soviet government claimed the deaths were caused by intestinal anthrax from tainted meat for thirteen years, until 1992, when President Boris Yeltsin admitted, without going into

[40]*Science* 1994, Volume 266, Pages 1202-1208

details, that the anthrax outbreak was the result of military activity. All of the victims were clustered in a straight line downwind from the military facility. Livestock in the same area also died of anthrax.

Former first deputy chief for Biopreparat (the civilian part of the Soviet Biological weapons program), Dr. Ken Alibek, who defected to the U.S., says that the anthrax airborne leak had been caused by workers at the military facility who forgot to replace a filter in an exhaust system. He also says that if the wind had been in the opposite direction that day, toward the city of Sverdlovsk, that the death rate could have been in the hundreds of thousands.[41]

Another fascinating piece of information I found regarded the aforementioned Soviet defector Ken Alibek. In the *Red Lies* article it stated that after the 1979 incident "During a scientific exchange visit to the United States, Alibek came to the unsettling conclusion that the U.S. was not engaging in similar biological weapons research. With the CIA's assistance, Alibek defected to the West, bringing with him firsthand scientific

[41]http://www.pbs.org/wgbh/pages/frontline/shows/plague/sverdlovsk/

knowledge of the Soviet's secret program. Alibek says, 'They were shocked; shocked because you know they couldn't imagine that the Soviet Union had such an enormous, very powerful and sophisticated offensive program.' In the years since the Sverdlovsk accident, Alibek and a research team had taken the Soviet military's anthrax and made it even more deadly. He developed a process to take ground up anthrax spores and coat each particle in plastic and resin. It kept the anthrax aloft four times longer, increasing its ability to infect people."[42]

It gets worse. The article continued to say that "While scientists here (U.S.) were researching improvements to Russia's anthrax vaccine, they created a deadly invention. In the December 1997 issue of the medical journal *Vaccine,* the Obolensk (a Russian lab) scientists claim to have 'inadvertently' developed a new genetically altered strain of anthrax. Its most frightening attribute, this new strain overpowers Russia's anthrax vaccine, rendering it completely useless. America's vaccine is different. But if this new anthrax defeats one vaccine, there's a fear it could defeat the other. At Fort Detrick, the study set off alarm bells."

---

[42] http://www.cbc.ca/news/background/bioweapons/redlies.html

Then the clincher: "After scientists at Biopreparat created their new 'super anthrax' the U.S. government asked for a sample to test it against the North American vaccine. The Russians turned the request down flat. By 2001, the U.S. had still not received a sample. But on September 4, 2001 *The New York Times* ran an article titled "U.S. Germ Warfare Research Pushes Treaty Limits." It reported that the U.S. government was launching its own program to create genetically modified anthrax, at a laboratory of the Battelle Memorial Institute in West Jefferson, Ohio. In the article it says that "The 1972 biological weapons treaty forbids nations from developing or acquiring weapons that spread disease, but it allows work on vaccines and other protective measures. Over the past several years, the United States has embarked on a program of secret research on biological weapons that, some officials say, tests the limits of the global treaty banning such weapons."

It went on to say that "Earlier this year, administration officials said, the Pentagon drew up plans to engineer genetically a potentially more potent variant of the bacterium that causes anthrax, a deadly disease ideal for germ warfare." Then the part that really caught my eye, "At about the same time, Pentagon experts assembled a germ factory **in the Nevada Desert** from commercially available materials. Pentagon officials said the project demonstrated the ease with which a terrorist or rogue nation could build a plant that could produce pounds of the deadly germs."

Interesting that they choose Nevada to produce secret biological warfare, isn't it? Makes you wonder what they are **not** admitting to. So, the U.S. recruited biological warfare specialists from Germany and Japan after World War II, and Soviet biological warfare specialists after the breakup of the Soviet Union. Do you still think the information given in the readings is impossible? Read on...

I found some information on the NTI (Nuclear Threat Initiative) website about a biological facility that the Soviet Union used for open-air testing of BW agents called Vozrozhdeniye Island in the Aral Sea. It said that "From 1936 to 1992, Vozrozhdeniye Island was the major proving ground in the Soviet Union for the open-air testing of BW agents developed at different Soviet BW facilities. A variety of BW agents were tested on the island, including the microbial pathogens that cause plague, anthrax, Q-fever, smallpox, tularemia, and Venezuelan equine encephalitis, as will as botulinum toxin. Some of the pathogens tested in aerosol form were genetically modified strains that produce atypical disease processes and are resistant to existing medications, potentially complicating diagnosis and treatment. In addition to common pathogenic strains, special strains developed for military purposes were tested on the island."

This last description of what the Soviets were testing on the island seems more along those lines: aerosol form, genetically modified strains that produce atypical disease processes, complicating diagnosis and special strains for military purposes. Since then, I am sure that our advances in biotechnology have created an even more horrifying version than we can even imagine. Is it even detectable by today's biosensing equipment? They said in the readings that it was new technology and we didn't have recognition of it.

The following part of the article also got my attention because of the information given in the readings about why they are doing the BW work in the Nevada desert at a secret underground military base. The article said, "Vozrozhdeniye Island was apparently chosen for open-air testing of biological weapons because of its geographic location and climate conditions. The shores of the Aral Sea are predominantly large, sparsely populated deserts and semi-deserts, which hindered unauthorized access to the secret site. The island's sparse vegetation, hot, dry climate, and sandy soil- all reduced the possibility that the pathogenic microorganisms would survive and spread."

There was more. "In 1998, information was revealed regarding viable anthrax spores on the Vozrozhdeniye Island, which caused a new wave of concern regarding the environmental condition of the island. It's also notable that during the late 1980's, large quantities of anthrax spores that had been mass-produced and stockpiled in Russia were transported to the island for decontamination and burial. In the aftermath of the September 11 attacks, the U.S. government recognized the urgency of decontaminating the anthrax burial sites to eliminate the threat of terrorist access. Moreover, because oil companies are interested in drilling on the island for petroleum and natural gas, these activities could stir up contaminated dust that could blow across to the mainland."[43] Contaminated dust, blowing...Sound familiar?

In Ken Alibek's autobiographical book, *Biohazard: The Chilling True Story of the Largest Covert Biological Weapons Program in the World- Told from Inside by the Man Who Ran It,* he acknowledges the activities on Vozrozhdeniye Island, which they called Rebirth Island. He says that "Our teams would spend four or five months there, living in Army barracks and testing that year's supply of biological weapons." He describes how they would spray aerosol bioweapons on monkeys tethered to posts and how men in biological protective suits would retrieve them and examine them to see if they died of anthrax, Q fever, brucellosis, glanders, or plague.

Genetic engineering of biological weapons has been going on for a long time. According to Ken Alibek's book, as early as 1970 in the Soviet Union, "Scientists had been studying peptides, strings of amino acids which perform various functions in our bodies, from regulating hormones and facilitating digestion to

---

[43]http://www.nti.org/e_research/profiles/Kazakhstan/Biological/facilities_vozrozhdenie.html

directing our immune system. One important group of peptides, called regulatory peptides, is activated during times of stress or heightened emotion- anger, love, fear- or to fight disease. Some regulatory peptides affect the central nervous system. When present in large quantities, they can alter mood and trigger psychological changes. Some can contribute to more serious adverse reactions such as heart attacks, strokes, or paralysis when overproduced. In a series of trailblazing experiments, the scientists found a way to duplicate in the lab the genes for a handful of regulatory peptides with known toxic properties. One of these was found capable, when present in large quantities, of damaging the myelin sheaths protecting the thousands of nerve fibers that transmit electric signals from the brain and spinal cord to the rest of the body. Unknown in the West, we called it myelin toxin."

He continued, "As with all peptides, it was hard to obtain enough for useful experimentation. Genetic engineering solved this problem: scientists could synthesize the genes that code for the production of myelin toxin, reproduce them artificially in the lab, and insert them into bacterial cells. If a bacteria strain compatible with myelin toxin could be found, the transplanted genes would multiply along with the bacteria." They found a suitable bacterial host for myelin toxin in the bacteria *Yersinia pseudotuberculosis,* closely related to *Yersinia pestis,* the bacteria that causes plague.

They did successful tests on animals and found that a single genetically engineered agent had produced symptoms of two different diseases, one of which could not be traced. He says, "A new class of weapons had been found. For the first time we would be capable of producing weapons based on the chemical substances produced naturally by the human body. They could damage the nervous system, alter moods, trigger psychological changes, and even kill. The mood-altering possibilities of regulatory peptides were of particular interest to the KGB- this and the fact that they could not be traced by pathologists. Victims would appear to have died of natural causes."

A few months later, they successfully transferred the gene for myelin toxin to *Yersinia pestis.* A toxin-plague weapon was never produced before the Soviet Union collapsed, but the success of this experiment set the stage for further research on bacteria-toxin combinations. Did you get all of that? For decades, they have had the capability of combining genetically modified human toxins and bacteria that are untraceable. Imagine the possibilities today. They said in the readings that the biological weapon they are creating in the underground base in Hawthorne is a modified form of anthrax that is to be delivered in an aerosol form and that it will look like the victims died of natural causes. As you can see, this is possible!

Just a thought here, if people died immediately after exposure to this BW, as they did in the Sverdlovsk anthrax leak, it wouldn't look like natural causes, would it? It isn't supposed to be immediately lethal. Maybe that's why our children aren't dying from exposure to what they are making now, but are being crippled by it, causing autism.

Also in Ken Alibek's book *Biohazard,* according to his own biography it says "Since he defected to the United States in 1992, he has briefed the U.S. military intelligence and he is now working in biodefense." Are you following the time line? The man who weaponized and genetically modified anthrax for the Soviet Union defected to the U.S. with our government's assistance in 1992, and briefed our military intelligence. Then, according to the readings, the U.S. started creating a modified version of anthrax in a dust form in an underground facility in Hawthorne, NV in 1996. That is when the autism epidemic exploded in the United States. Still think it's a coincidence?

In Ken Alibek's book he explains "The most effective way of contaminating humans is through the air we breathe, but this has always been difficult to achieve. Soviet scientists combined the knowledge gained from postwar biochemistry and genetic research with modern industrial techniques to develop what are called "aerosol" weapons- particles suspended in a mist, like the spray of an insecticide, or a fine dust, like talcum powder." He goes on to say, "Primitive aerosols lose their virulence and dissipate quickly. In our labs, we experimented with special additives to keep our agents from decaying when transported over long distances and to keep them alive in adverse weather conditions. These manipulated agents, more stable and more lethal, were our biological weapons."[44] The scenario described in the readings doesn't sound so crazy now, does it? It doesn't take

---

[44]Alibek, Ken with Handelman, Stephen *Biohazard: The Chilling True Story of the Largest Covert Biological Weapons Program in the World- Told From Inside by the Man Who Ran It* (1999, Delta) pp. 20-21.

a genius to figure out the obvious implications of what is going on today.

Britain and Biological Warfare

Just when I thought it couldn't get any worse, it did. I came across another historical incident involving anthrax testing and soil contamination that happened on Gruinard Island, a small Scottish Island, now referred to as "Anthrax Island." In 1942, during World War II, Gruinard Island was the site of a biological warfare test by British military scientists from Porton Down. The British government bought the island to test anthrax bombs on 80 sheep to see if the sheep would survive the anthrax bombs and to test the long-lasting contamination of anthrax spores in the soil. The sheep became infected with anthrax and died within days of exposure.

After the tests were completed, British scientists concluded that a large-scale release of anthrax spores would thoroughly pollute German cities if used during the war, rendering them uninhabitable for decades afterward. The anthrax spores used on Gruinard Island remained viable in the soil for decades, 48 years to be precise. Decontamination attempts on the island following the biological warfare testing were unsuccessful due to the durability of the anthrax spores. As a result the island was quarantined for many years afterwards. Visits to the island were strictly prohibited, except by Porton Down personnel checking the level of contamination.

Starting in 1986, a determined effort was made to decontaminate the island, with 280 tons of formaldehyde solution diluted in seawater being sprayed over all 196 hectares of the island, and the worst-contaminated topsoil around the dispersal site being removed.[45] Some of these experiments were recorded on 16mm color movie film, which was declassified in 1997. You can watch it yourself on You Tube and other websites. The men are wearing full-body Biohazard suits with masks, you see the bombs explode, a cloud emerge, and the sheep dying. It is very disturbing.

For me, this information validated the fact that anthrax remains viable in the soil for decades and that they used ***seawater*** to decontaminate it. The readings told us that saltwater would be used to decontaminate the soil in our country

---

[45]http://en.wikipedia.org/wiki/Gruinard_Island

in order to grow food. It was told to us in the readings that the topsoil is very contaminated, and that potatoes and other root vegetables were contaminated. This made more sense now, knowing that anthrax remains viable in the soil for decades!

From the previously mentioned article *Red Lies*, it says that in 1989, the late Vladimir Pasechnik, the Administrative head of Biopreparat in the Soviet Union, and their number one bioweaponeer, was whisked out of Moscow by British agents and defected to Britain. Pasechnik said "I came to the conclusion that one possible way to stop the program will be to bring the news about it to the Western side." Dr. Christopher Davis was a biological weapons expert with British intelligence who said, "He (Pasechnik) confirmed how much of a cover-up we'd been subject to. You've got a very strong impression of a deliberate planned program. We're talking 25 to 30,000 people working on the program, maybe more in different capacities over a large number of years. It is sometimes difficult to convey the sheer magnitude of it. It wasn't just big, it was massive." After defecting, Pasechnik worked at Porton Down, Britain's chemical and biological warfare defense establishment until he died under mysterious circumstances. Yes, the same Porton Down that did the Gruinard Island anthrax test during WWII.

The reason I am bringing up Britain is because the UK, which includes Britain, has a very high autism rate, has a similar vaccination program to the U.S., and is our ally. So, if the two top Soviet bioweapons specialists who admittedly created genetically modified anthrax in their country, then defected, one to the U.S. and one to Britain, and shared their secrets...you do the math.

In the book *Biohazard*, regarding where the biological weapons specialists went after the Soviet Union broke up, Ken Alibek says, "At least twenty-five former specialists in the Soviet Union's biological warfare program are now in the United States. Many more have gone to Europe and Asia. I've heard that several went to Iraq and North Korea. A former colleague, now the director of a Biopreparat institute, told me that five of our scientists are in Iran. The disastrous economic conditions in Russia have driven many of our brightest scientists and technicians to seek work wherever they can get it."

I understand that our country is involved in this work in the name of National Security, but at what cost? Protecting our people is one thing, harming our own children in the process is quite another. Fears of a biological attack by a hostile neighbor or terrorist group have given us the excuse to continue this work and try to one-up our enemies. All of this is a flagrant violation of the 1972 Biological and Toxic Weapons Convention. Are there consequences to this, or do we just look the other way? It truly is "repugnant to the conscience of mankind" as the BWC stated.

Is this alarming anyone? It should. There are also some serious Human Rights violations going on here! It saddens me to say this, but our country has become so passive and desensitized, that nothing seems to register anymore. I am hoping that this material will put a fire under some people, particularly the parents and loved ones affected by autism. This is not just about our children; it is about our country's future. This is not going to stop until we do something about it. It is only going to get worse. Or we can keep doing what we've always done, and get the same results. Nothing to see here, move along!

More Clues

I was never that interested in aliens or UFO's before these readings, but since they came up in the readings, the subject got my attention. Shortly before this book was published, I noticed an interesting episode of UFO Hunters was airing on the History Channel called "Area 52." I taped it and watched it later. In the episode, they were trying to show that Dugway Proving Ground, a military base in Utah, was taking over as the new Area 51, so they referred to it as Area 52. They suggested that UFO activity including reverse engineering was taking place at this high security facility.

What got my attention was a local reporter interviewed on the show named Lee Davidson, who said that "During the Cold War Era, there was chemical, germ and radiological weapons testing done at Dugway Proving Ground. The Army denied that anything dangerous was happening. In the last 20 years, they were able to use the Freedom of Information Act to dig up what actually did happen. In World War II, they used human guinea pigs to test germ warfare on volunteers from the Seventh Day Adventist Church. They lined them up along the side of the road along with Rhesus monkeys and real guinea pigs and spread germs over them such as Q-Fever and Parrot fever to see if they would be infected. They were infected, but didn't die. They were told it was defensive work only. They found that they were doing offensive work as well." Now they use private contractors to do a lot of the work there because the Freedom of Information Act does not apply to private contractors. The point is that the Army denied anything was going on, but then it took interested people 20 years to prove otherwise. This shows a pattern of deceit by the military. This is what I expect once this information comes out, denial.

Another pair of interesting guests on this program was two friends who were interested in UFOs. They went out on the perimeter of Dugway to investigate activity. They had pictures that they had taken of over 80 vehicles, including Hummers, driving in a convoy that disappeared ***underground***. One of the hosts said that in the 1990's, satellite imagery of military bases and access to it became very sophisticated, so it makes sense that they moved their operations underground into subterranean test facilities. To me, this showed that it is probable that secret military operations are done underground. If underground activity is happening at Dugway, why not at other facilities such as

Hawthorne? They don't want anyone to see what is going on. If you go to Google Earth, satellite images allow you to see places very clearly from any angle. You wouldn't be able to see it if it was underground, right?

Psychic Spying

If you think it is a long shot to believe that the information in this book could have come through a psychic or medium, read on. I found that both the U.S. government and the Soviet Union have been using psychic spies for years. One very interesting book called *Remote Viewing: What It Is, Who Uses It, and How To Do It* by Tim Rifat states that even as far back as 1972, "To perfect their psychic spying, the Soviets developed practical, reliable forms of ESP, clairvoyance and telepathy for espionage, surveillance and industrial spying. Results were outstanding, a spy's Holy Grail, by means of which secret U.S. underground bases such as Dulce, Area 51, and Pine Gap could be mapped and documents within U.S. top secret files and computer systems read."[46] Notice the reference to secret underground bases? I did.

There is plenty of information out there about former U.S. Government Remote Viewers as well. Joe McMoneagle is the most interesting Government remote viewer I have come across. He worked for the Star Gate project, and wrote many books about it if you're interested in this topic. This information is a lot to take in. There is a huge learning curve here for those who don't understand psychic phenomena, so I am trying to explain parts of it along the way. It was pretty astonishing to see that even our government used psychics and remote viewing to gain an edge, and I'm sure they still do.

Interestingly, even in Ken Alibek's book *Biohazard,* there is a reference to the KGB using psychics. When Soviet bioweaponeer Pasechnik defected to England, they used a psychic to locate his whereabouts. The psychic was correct when he described him as being on a big island, very close to the sea; as well as other

---

[46]Rifat, Tim *Remote Viewing: What It Is, Who Uses It, and How To Do It.* (Vision Paperbacks, 2001) p. 10

detailed information.[47] This is another validation that even the military sees the value in this type of work and has been using it to their advantage for years.

Alternative Communication

It was mentioned in this reading that there are ways to communicate with children with autism, including telepathy, automatic writing, and other types of phenomena. I can validate this myself because seven months after this reading I met an amazing woman who is a psychic medium who does alternative communication in which she can communicate with people who can't speak. This includes people with autism, Alzheimer's, people in comas, and animals. She started as an animal communicator and had horses that she took to a school for special needs children. When she had a child with autism put on her horse's back, the horse told her that the child understood what the horse was thinking. The child couldn't speak, but could telepathically communicate with the horse. This is how she learned to speak with children with autism telepathically.

---

[47] Alibek, Ken with Handelman, Stephen *Biohazard: The Chilling True Story of the Largest Covert Biological Weapons Program in the World- Told From Inside by the Man Who Ran It* (1999, Delta) p. 143

I had her do a phone reading for me about Trevor, and I was totally blown away by the accuracy. She mentioned things that she could not have possibly known. For example, she mentioned that he had a brown fuzzy bear that he slept on like a pillow, that his favorite food was spaghetti, and that there was a noise in his room bothering him (the vent). All of these things were true, and much more.

I was so impressed that three months later, I attended a class where she taught people how to do what she does. It was very informative, and I learned a lot. I can see this work being done to teach parents and caregivers of children with autism how to communicate with them telepathically. It works and it can be learned.

Other Validations

I tried to find out which one of the viruses in the MMR vaccine gave the symptoms described in the reading. The closest description I could find was for the Rubella virus, except for the description of the active mind. The symptoms of Rubella included mild rash, fever, swollen lymph glands, and joint pain, especially in the small joints of the hands. Many children with autism have issues with small motor skills like writing, and tend to "stim" with their hands and fingers. They mentioned in the reading that what happens to the children causes them to not be able to use their wrist correctly.

I also read that autism is sometimes caused when the mother gets German measles (Rubella) during pregnancy. I found that to be interesting. I have always believed that traditional autism is a different kind of "autism" than what we are dealing with. It is not even the same at all. My son wasn't born this way, something happened "to" him. Basically, if a person has problems with communication, socialization, and has sensory issues, they're on the "Autistic Spectrum." No one looks for other causes of the symptoms. They just slap a label on them, and get them on the waiting list for services. So incredibly sad.

I was glad that I asked the question, "Why do boys have autism four times more than girls?" That was always the one thing that prevented me from fully believing the autism/mercury connection. It didn't support the statistics. I had even heard theories that testosterone attracts mercury and estrogen repels it, but I still wasn't convinced. Also, even after I detoxed mercury homeopathically from my son, his symptoms didn't magically disappear. In addition, when they took mercury (thimerosal) out of vaccines, the autism rates didn't drop, they went up. The theory from the readings somehow made sense "Boys are the ones playing in the dirt, and the little girls are in their dresses." Living in sunny Southern California at the time, my son was outside all the time, playing in the sandbox, at the park, the beach, you name it. If the topsoil that they're playing in is contaminated, or if the particles are actively falling on them, they're done. My son was probably outside playing right after his MMR vaccine, exposing him to both ingredients. Wrong place at the wrong time.

It was also validated in this reading that the biological warfare that was detected in my son's body was coming from the air. I dug up the notes from Trevor's previous QXCI sessions. The QXCI is a bioresonance device that records the body's reactivity to over 90,000 frequencies in less than 4 minutes. It is a diagnostic as well as a healing tool. It electronically measures the biological energies of the body and gives an assessment of the stressors on the system. I decided to try it out because it can be done at a distance, the patient doesn't need to be present, which was great for Trevor. I knew how it worked theoretically because of my experience in energy healing; I had done plenty of distance healings that worked.

Some of the more frightening items that came up on Trevor's first assessment were: *Bacillus anthracis* (anthrax), *Dengue fever virus, Borrelia burgdorferi* (Lyme disease), *West Nile virus, Lassa fever virus, Coxsackie virus, Mycoplasma, Rickettsia, Prion bacteria* (Mad Cow), *Monkeypox virus.* You get the picture. This was frightening to me because these things shouldn't be detected in a child's body. But what if they were clues as to what happened to him? The practitioner said that my son had the most things in him that she had ever seen in one person. Also, in a later session, the computer posted on the screen, "Your patient is poisoned!" The program is a type of artificial intelligence. Now, at the time, I wasn't sure how much of this was accurate, but I began looking into some of it. A good friend of mine also took her son with regressive autism to do the QXCI during the same time period we did, and his results also said that he had anthrax and biological warfare in his body. When we compared notes, we couldn't figure out why they had this in their bodies and questioned the accuracy of it.

There is a list of "Pathogens with Biological Weapons Potential" on a website I found.[48] Interestingly, all of these pathogens that Trevor has in his body are on the list. The practitioner said that it didn't mean that he "had" all of these diseases, but he had been exposed to them. So, maybe this previous experience to all of this made me a little more open to believing what was coming through in the readings than most other people would have. Most people would have laughed it off and called her a "quack."

***

48 http://www.cbwinfo.com/Biological/BWList.html

CHAPTER FIVE

MEDIUM: "OKAY, TODAY IS DECEMBER 13, 2007 AND TODAY WE ARE GOING TO CHANNEL ANOTHER CHAPTER OF THE BOOK. RIGHT NOW WE ARE JUST REFERRING TO IT AS 'THE MUMMY.' LAURA IS HERE, AND SHE'S GOING TO TRIGGER THE QUESTIONS SO THAT WHEN I MAKE THE CONNECTION I CAN GET THE ANSWERS. SO FAR, WE'VE BEEN CHANNELING IN PEOPLE WHO ARE VERY INTERSTED IN THE WORK WE'RE DOING. AND WHAT WE'RE ASKING FOR IS THAT THE BEST OF THE BEST COME THROUGH TO HELP IN THIS SITUATION SO THAT WE CAN HELP HUMANITY, AND HELP THESE KIDS, THE PARENTS, AND EVERYBODY THAT'S INVOLVED WITH THE INFORMATION THAT YOU'VE DECIDED TO GIVE US. OKAY, HERE WE GO LAURA. (SHE SAYS A PERSONAL PRAYER.) I ASK FOR THE HIGEST AND BEST SPIRITS TO COME THROUGH NOW."

"OKAY, WE HAVE MY SPIRIT CONTROL HERE, THE WIRY ONE IS HERE, HE HAS SOME FRIENDS. HE TELLS ME HE'S GOING TO BE INTRODUCING THEM AS WE GO ALONG. AND I SAID TO HIM, 'OH, SO YOU'RE THE ONE THAT'S KIND OF LEADING THIS WHOLE GROUP OF SPIRITS.' SO, HE'S GOING TO BE INTRODUCING THE NEXT ONES THAT ARE COMING THROUGH, AS THEIR TURN COMES ALONG."

"HE'S SAYING THIS IS ***HIS*** BOOK. SO, SOMETHING HAS TO BE ON THERE THAT HAS TO DO WITH HIM. EITHER A PHOTOGRAPH, OR HIS NAME MENTIONED OVER AND OVER, HE SAID THIS, HE SAID THAT. SO HE WANTS TO TAKE HIS CREDIT FOR WHAT HE'S DOING. 'HEY, IF I PLANTED THE SEED, AND I GREW THE TREE, I SHOULD,' IS WHAT HE SAYS. HE SAYS THIS TREE THAT HE'S PLANTED IS GOING TO GROW A LOT OF FRUIT, AND SO MUCH FRUIT IS GOING TO BE ON THIS TREE, THAT IT IS GOING TO BE FALLING TO THE GROUND. SO, THERE WILL BE MORE THAN ENOUGH."

"AS YOU GO ALONG, YOU'RE GOING TO SEE. THERE'S GOING TO BE DIFFERENT PEOPLE STEPPING IN TO HELP WITH THE DISTRIBUTION AND PUBLICITY. YOU HAVE A LOT OF IDEAS

LAURA, IS WHAT HE'S SAYING AS FAR AS THE DISTRIBUTION, AND PLACES TO GO TO TAKE IT TO. AND SOME TYPE OF LEVEL OF TESTING. MORE INVOLVEMENT IN THAT AREA, IN THAT VEIN. THAT'S STEMMING TOO. HE'S SHOWING ME A VEIN, LIKE A LEAF, YOU KNOW HAS VEINS LIKE THAT."

(TO LAURA) "SO, YOUR STORY IS GOING TO BE THAT THE SUBJECT MATTER DREW YOU TO IT BECAUSE OF YOUR CHILD, AND THEN FINDING OUT THE THOUSANDS AND THOUSANDS OF OTHER CHILDREN AND PARENTS THAT ALL CAN UNDERSTAND, AND NEED UNDERSTANDING. SO THIS BOOK IS GOING TO GO IN TWO DIFFERENT DIRECTIONS. TWO VERY, VERY DIFFERENT DIRECTIONS. ONE HAS TO DO WITH THE CHANNELING, AND THE INTEREST WITH ALL OF THAT, AND THE OTHER HAS TO DO WITH THE HEALING, AND THE WIRY ONE."

(THE WIRY ONE TALKING) "A LOT OF TIMES WHEN I START GETTING INFORMATION FOR MY PROJECTS, I GET LOST. I FEEL VERY LOST. I FEEL LIKE I DON'T KNOW WHAT IS

WRONG WITH ME. I JUST FEEL LIKE GOING TO SLEEP, AND THEN WAKING UP AGAIN, AND GOING TO SLEEP."

"AND I COMB MY HAIR, BUT I THINK I PUT MY HANDS IN IT A LOT, AND THAT'S WHY IT LOOKS ALL WIRY TO YOU."

"AND I LIKE MY PICTURE MADE BY THIS ONE FELLOW. HE DID CALM ME DOWN. HE MADE ME FEEL GOOD. BUT I DIDN'T LIKE OTHER PEOPLE TO MESS WITH ME AND TAKE PICTURES OF ME."

"AND IT'S A THRILL BEING HERE. NOT ONLY IS IT A THRILL BECAUSE WE'RE FETCHING SOME INFORMATION THAT WILL HELP YOU PEOPLE THERE NOW, BUT IT ALSO IS AWARENESS THAT I AM ALIVE. THAT I'M NOT JUST NONEXISTENT. IT PROVES MY THEORIES THAT I TRIED TO GET ACROSS IN MY EQUATIONS AND IN MY WORDS, AND MY WORK. SO I AM HERE TO PROVE ALL OF THAT."

"THERE WILL BE SOME PEOPLE THAT WILL BE VALIDATING THAT I AM THE ONE THAT'S TALKING THROUGH YOU BECAUSE I DO STILL HAVE FAMILY IN GENERATIONS

FORWARD. AND THEY'LL HAVE DOCUMENTATION OF SOME OF THE THINGS, OF THE PERSONALITY THAT I HAVE, THAT YOU ARE CAPTURING WITHIN THE PAGES. WRITE THAT DOWN, OKAY."

"YOU HAVE SOME QUESTIONS, LAURA?"

Laura: "I still want to know what the solution is."

MEDIUM: "YOU WANT THE END OF THE BOOK. THAT'S NOT GOING TO HAPPEN. YOU'RE ON THE WRONG CHAPTER. LET'S BACK UP A LITTLE BIT. OKAY, LET ME GET YOU STARTED IN THE RIGHT DIRECTION. I'M SEEING YOU AS YOU ARE TYPING SOME OF THIS STUFF, YOU'RE GOING TO BE TYPING OTHER THINGS IN THERE, SO REMEMBER...LOWER CASE, UPPER CASE, SO THAT YOU CAN PULL THEM OUT BECAUSE AS YOU'RE TYPING IT'S GOING TO CAUSE YOU TO THINK. SO, GO AHEAD AND BE MAKING YOUR INSERTS."

"THIS BOOK IS ALREADY WRITTEN. THE HAND OF WHAT'S PUTTING IT TOGETHER IS ALREADY AT WORK."

Laura: "Is he going to be helping me when I'm putting it together?"

MEDIUM: "I'M HELPING THE WHOLE WAY THROUGH. YOU'RE NOT DOING IT BY YOURSELF. IT'S ALREADY WRITTEN, IT'S JUST GOT TO BE CONJURED INTO THE EXISTENCE OF THE PHYSICAL REALM."

"SOME OF THE THINGS THAT WE'VE BEEN TALKING ABOUT THAT YOU'RE LEARNING...OF HOW TO HELP YOUR CHILD...SOME OF THESE THINGS YOU'RE GOING TO BE INCORPORATING, AND THEY ARE GOING TO BE MAKING HIM BETTER. SO, YES, THERE WILL BE SOME CHANGE IN YOUR SON AS WE GO ALONG BY YOU INCORPORATING THE THINGS THAT I'M REVEALING TO YOU."

"SO NO, YOU'RE NOT GOING TO WAIT UNTIL HE'S 40 YEARS OLD, AND NEITHER ARE ANY OF THE OTHER PEOPLE THAT INCORPORATE THE SUBJECT MATTER INTO THEIR LIVES. BUT AS THEY DO, IT WILL HELP THEIR CHILD, BUT NOT UNTIL LATER WILL THEY HAVE A FULL, FULL RECOVERY. BUT THAT DOESN'T MEAN THAT THEY WON'T BE ABLE TO LIVE A

NORMAL LIFE. SO, YOU'LL BE SEEING THAT THE CHILDREN, WITHIN A FEW YEARS, THEY WILL BE CHANGING. IT TAKES TIME TO GET EVERYTHING OUT OF THEIR SYSTEM. BUT, YOU SEE THE CHANGE, BUT FOR THEM TO FEEL IT THEMSELVES, THAT'S WHAT TAKES LONGER, AND THAT'S WHAT TAKES THE ANTIDOTE. BUT THE NEXT LEVEL OF THEIR WELL-BEING AND THEIR HEALTH IS GOING TO BE WHERE THEY LOOK LIKE TO THE REST OF THE WORLD THAT THEY'RE OKAY, BUT INSIDE OF THEM, THEY ARE STILL GOING TO HAVE A FEELING OF SOME TYPE OF MISSING LINK, AND THAT'S WHAT NEEDS TO BE CURED."

"BECAUSE THEY NEED TO BE CURED 100%, NOT JUST TO WHERE IT'S SATISFACTORY TO THE PARENTS, OR SATISFACTORY TO THE EDUCATIONAL SYSTEM TO WHERE THEY CAN DEAL WITH THESE KIDS, AND NOT HAVE THEM IN SPECIAL CLASSES. IF THESE KIDS ARE NOT IN SPECIAL CLASSES NOW, THEY NEED TO BE IN SPECIAL CLASSES."

"YOUR SON (LAURA'S)...AND THIS IS JUST SO YOU CAN MAKE SOME CALCULATION...YOUR SON, BY THE TIME HE'S IN HIS 14TH YEAR... IN ALL YOUR NATURAL WAYS, YOU'LL

GET HIM TO THAT STATE, (WHERE HE LOOKS LIKE HE'S OKAY) BUT HE NEEDS CURE. THE BOTTOM LINE NEEDS TO HAPPEN. TAKE IT AS GOING TO THE GROCERY STORE AND GOING SHOPPING, AND THEN YOU DON'T GO TO THE CASHIER SO YOU CAN LEAVE. THERE NEEDS TO BE COMPLETION. YOU NEED TO REMEMBER THAT PART OF THE PROBLEM IS STILL THERE...SO YOU NEED TO STILL TAKE A LOT OF CARE WITH THAT WHOLE SITUATION. JUST BECAUSE WHAT'S HAPPENING TO HIM IS CONTROLLED, DOESN'T MEAN THE PROBLEM IS GONE."

"THEY ALSO WOULD BE GOOD TO BE AROUND PSYCHICS AND MEDIUMS THAT CAN READ BETWEEN THE LINES AND READ THEIR THOUGHTS BECAUSE THERE IS A LOT OF TRANSFERENCE IN THOUGHT. THAT'S THE TRUE COMMUNICATION WITH THESE KIDS."

"AND THEY'RE GOING INTO ADULTHOOD, THEY NEED HELP. DURING THE YOUNG ADULT STAGES, A LOT OF THEM WILL SEEM TO WANT TO GROW UP REALLY FAST. YOU THINK YOU HAVE A CHALLENGE WITH A YOUNG ADULT THAT DOESN'T HAVE THESE PROBLEMS GOING ON, YOU WAIT UNTIL YOU

ENCOUNTER THE YOUNG ADULT OF THE SO-CALLED 'CRYSTAL CHILD.' YOU NEED TO REMEMBER THAT THEY ARE INCORPORATING PSYCHIC, ALONG WITH THE DILEMMA THAT THEY'VE RUN INTO, THAT IS NONE OF THEIR FAULT. SO, NEVER BLAME THE CHILD FOR THE SITUATION THAT THEY'VE GOTTEN THEMSELVES INTO. WRONG PLACE AT THE WRONG TIME IS THE FACTOR OF THE SITUATION THAT IS AT HAND."

"THESE CHILDREN ARE NOT TO BE USED FOR THEIR PSYCHIC ABILITIES. YOU NEED TO KNOW THAT THESE CHILDREN ARE USING THEIR PSYCHIC ABILITIES. THE PSYCHIC ABILITY IS JUST AS A BLIND MAN WOULD USE HIS HEARING. SO, THEY'RE NOT AN OBJECT. THEY'RE NOT YOUR UTENSIL. THEY'RE SURVIVING WITH THEIR PSYCHIC. THAT'S HOW THEY GET ACROSS THAT THEY NEED TO GO TO THE BATHROOM, THAT THEY NEED TO EAT. IT'S THAT SENSE THAT'S HELPING THEM. AND ALL THESE PEOPLE ARE, 'OH, IT'S BAD TO BE PSYCHIC,' OR ANY OF THIS STUFF, AND THEY'RE JUST PUTTING THAT PART OF THEIR LIVES, THEIR EMOTIONS, THAT WHATEVER THEY WANT TO CALL IT, IN A NUTSHELL, AND SETTING IT ASIDE, THINKING THEY'RE

ALWAYS GOING TO USE IT FOR LATER. YOU HAVE TO CRACK THE NUT OPEN BEFORE YOU CAN EAT THE YUMMIES."

"HE'S PULLING ON HIS PANTS, HE'S PULLING ON HIS CLOTHES, TRYING TO STRAIGHTEN THEM OUT, AND HE'S MAKING THEM WORSE. IT'S LIKE, THEY WERE RIGHT, AND HE JUST PULLED HIS PANTS AND SHIRT AND COAT, AND NOW THEY ARE ALL CROOKED. AND HE'S LIKE, 'DID I DO THAT?' HE THOUGHT HE WAS STRAIGHTNEING THEM UP."

"THINGS HAPPENING ALL AT THE SAME TIME, AND THE FOCUS AS TO WHERE IT'S GIVEN. I'M VERY MUCH ALIVE. I AM VERY MUCH ALIVE. TO YOU, YOU MAY CALL ME IN A DIFFERENT VIBRATION, BUT I'M VERY MUCH ALIVE. I'M JUST IN A DIFFERENT SPACE."

"THERE'S A GENTLEMAN OUT THERE RIGHT NOW THAT IS WORKING ON SOME KIND OF CURE FOR ALL OF THIS. HE'S EXPLORING ALL OF IT, BUT RIGHT NOW, HE'S THROWING THINGS AROUND. HE'S A MAN WITH A VERY HOT, HOT TEMPER. THINGS DON'T GO RIGHT AND HE TRASHES EVERYTHING. HE PULLS OFF SHELVES AND HIS LITTLE

CONTAINERS AND TABLES, AND HE DESTROYS THEM FROM JUST THROWING THEM BECAUSE HE GETS ANGRY, AND HE KNOWS THAT HE'S NOT ON THE RIGHT TRACK. SO, HE DESTROYS EVERYTHING AND STARTS ALL OVER. SO, IT'S NOT LIKE HE'S STEMMING FROM ONE THING TO ANOTHER. BUT THERE IS A GENTLEMAN THAT IS WORKING ON ALL OF THIS, AND HE WILL HAVE A BREAKTHROUGH. OCTOBER WILL BE BIG FOR HIM. SOMETHING ABOUT BIRTH. SO HE'S SAYING SOMETHING ABOUT BIRTH OF OCTOBER."

"SOME OF THESE CHILDREN WILL HAVE SYMPTOMS OF ALLERGIC REACTIONS TO CERTAIN THINGS. THEY'RE NOT ON A REGULAR HEALTH PATTERN. SO A LOT OF THE THINGS THAT THEY ARE ALLERGIC TO NOW CAN BE INCORPORATED INTO THEIR SYSTEM LATER, BECAUSE THE REACTION IS GOING TO BE DIFFERENT. SO, THE ALLERGIES THAT THEY HAVE NOW ARE NOT ON A PERMANENT BASIS. AS YOU SEE THE ALLERGIES GOING AWAY, THAT WILL LET YOU KNOW THAT YOU'RE TAKING THAT CHILD IN THE RIGHT DIRECTION. THAT WILL BE YOUR CUE THAT THIS CHILD IS GETTING BETTER."

"BUT FOR YOU TO BE ABLE TO SEE IT, IT'S GOING TO TAKE A LITTLE LONGER, AND THEN WHEN YOU DO SEE IT, YOU NEED TO KNOW THAT YOU ARE NOT SEEING THAT CHILD WHOLE, YOU NEED TO KEEP WORKING WITH THAT CHILD, BECAUSE THERE HAS TO BE A SHOT THAT'S GOING TO BE GIVEN TO THIS CHILD AND THAT SERUM IS WHAT'S GOING TO BE THE BREAKTHROUGH. HE'S SAYING THE NUMBER 40 AGAIN."

Laura: "He keeps saying it will be when he's in his 40's."

MEDIUM: "AND IT'S A SHOT. AND THEN I SEE A TABLET. BUT THE SHOT IS THE QUICK... THE TABLET IS..."

"OH...YOU THINK YOUR CHILD IS BAD? YOUR CHILD IS NOT BAD. THERE ARE CHILDREN OUT THERE THAT YOU THINK ARE CRAZY. AND THEY ARE NOT BEING TAKEN CARE OF CORRECTLY. THEY THINK THAT THEY ARE CRAZY. AND THEY ARE LOUD, AND THEY ARE SCREAMING WITHIN THEMSELVES. THEY'RE INSANE ASSYLUM MATERIAL. YOUR CHILD IS NOT BAD COMPARED TO A LOT OF THE ONES OUT

THERE, AND IT IS THIS VERY THING THAT THEY HAVE THAT WE'RE TALKING ABOUT RIGHT NOW."

"SO ALL YOU PEOPLE WHO HAVE CHILDREN THAT YOU'VE COMMITTED, AND YOU'VE GOT THINGS BEING DONE TO THEM ON AN EXPERIMENTAL BASIS, AND MEDICATIONS BEING GIVEN TO THEM, YOU NEED TO TAKE A SECOND LOOK AND SEE IF YOUR CHILD WAS LIKE THAT ALL ALONG, OR IF IT HAPPENED DURING A CERTAIN STAGE IN THEIR LIFE, BECAUSE YOU HAVE YOUR CHILDREN IN THE WRONG PLACE. AND THESE CHILDREN, YOUR CHILDREN THAT YOU HAVE IN THESE PLACES ARE OF AGE 18, 19, 20 YEARS OF AGE. SO, REALLY PAY ATTENTION TO WHAT YOU ARE DOING TO YOUR CHILD. THESE ARE SOULS TRAPPED WITHING THEMSELVES. SO THESE CHILDREN ARE GOING TO BE COMING FROM MANY DIFFERENT PLACES. SOME WILL BE WITHIN THE HOUSEHOLD, SOME WILL BE IN INSANE ASSYLUMS, SOME WILL BE DISTURBING ALL OF YOU THAT THINK YOU'RE NORMAL."

"ONES FROM THE PLANETS UP ABOVE WILL BE COMING TO HELP IN PART OF THE SITUATION. BUT A LOT WILL DIE.

NOT OF THESE CHILDREN ONLY, BUT OF THE MASSES OF HUMANITY."

"YOU HAVE A QUESTION?"

<u>Laura:</u> "So is this just the REGRESSIVE type of autism? It's not the kids who never talked...it's the kids that regressed."

<u>MEDIUM:</u> "YOU HAVE TO DEFINE AUTISM. JUST BECAUSE YOU DON'T KNOW WHAT SOMETHING IS, YOU JUST DON'T THROW IT IN THERE. SO, AUTISM IS SOMETHING THAT HAPPENED TO THESE CHILDREN AFTER BIRTH."

"NOW IF YOU HAVE A CHILD, THAT WHEN YOU WERE PREGNANT, THEY TOLD YOU THIS CHILD HAD WATER ON THE BRAIN AND WAS GOING TO HAVE ALL KINDS OF PROBLEMS, THAT IS NOT THE CHILD THAT GOES IN THAT CATEGORY. THIS IS BEFORE BIRTH. THIS IS NOT A NEURO-WARFARE-CHEMICAL SUBSTANCE THAT HAS AFFECTED THIS CHILD. AND THAT IS WHAT WE ARE TALKING ABOUT HERE."

"THIS IS HAPPENING IN THE DRY LANDS OF NEVADA AND IT'S SPREADING TO THE SURROUNDING STATES. AND IT IS NOT CONTAGIOUS. AND IT'S NOT ADD, OR A HYPER CHILD. THOSE ARE ALL OTHER THINGS. WE ARE TALKING ABOUT ONE SUBJECT AND ONE SUBJECT ALONE. THAT'S WHY THIS IS THE MATERIAL THAT PEOPLE WILL SEEK OUT TO GET THEIR ANSWERS, AND THEY WILL GET THEIR ANSWERS."

"AND THE EQUATION THAT I LAY DOWN WILL BE THE FIX. THAT WILL BE THE SERUM; THAT WILL BE THE SHOT."

<u>Laura:</u> "Okay. Are you going to do that today?"

<u>MEDIUM:</u> "NO."

<u>Laura:</u> "So you're coming back?"

<u>MEDIUM:</u> "I'LL ALWAYS BE AROUND. THIS IS MY PET PROJECT, BUT THERE WILL BE OTHERS THAT WILL BE INTRODUCED. BUT I'LL BE AROUND THROUGHOUT THE WHOLE ENTIRETY OF EVERY SESSION BECAUSE I'M

PUTTING IT ALL INTO PERSPECTIVE. ALL THE OTHER PEOPLE ARE A PART OF IT, BUT I'M KEEPING IT IN PERSPECTIVE. THAT'S WHY I TELL YOU THIS IS MY MATERIAL, AND YOU'RE READING MY WORDS. IF YOU'RE NOT READING MY EXACT WORDS, YOU'RE READING OF WHAT I'VE ALLOWED TO COME IN FROM OTHER SOULS. ALL WE ARE DOING HERE IS HELPING EACH OTHER."

"THIS IS AN ACKNOWDEDGENT OF MY EXISTENCE AND A HELP FOR THE MESS THAT WE'VE CREATED. I FEEL THAT PART OF IT, I'M RESPONSIBLE FOR, AND I WANT TO MAKE THAT CORRECTION."

"AND YES, IT IS GOOD TO KNOW THE FUTURE, BUT SOMETIMES IT DOES GET MISHANDLED. IF YOU KNOW NO FUTURE, YOU HAVE NO IDEA OF FUTURE, YOU HAVE NO CREATIVITY, AND NOTHING IS EVOLVED. HUMANITY HAS TO BE EVOLVED."

"JUSTICE WILL BE SERVED. THERE WILL BE A GOVERNMENT THAT WILL TRY TO PAY THE PEOPLE. AS IN, IF YOU WERE INVOLVED IN THIS, CHECK HERE. A TAX RETURN

SITUATION. BUT THERE'S NO BUY OUT, BUT IT'S ACCEPTED, WHAT DO YOU DO? THE TRUE THING TO DO, THE BLESSED THING TO DO, IS TO MOVE ON AND CORRECT THE SITUATION. IT'S NOT ABOUT ATTACKING THOSE THAT ARE ON THE OTHER SIDE ANYHOW. BY THE TIME THE AWAKENING COMES, MOST OF THOSE PEOPLE INVOLVED WILL HAVE CROSSED OVER."

"YOUR PRESIDENT DOESN'T LIVE A LONG, LONG LIFE. AN ILLNESS IN THE CHEST AREA. HE JUST SHOWS ME GOING LIKE THAT (CHEST JERKS BACK AND FORTH). JOLTS, JOLTS. AND THIS IS BUSH."

"NIXON AND ALL THOSE PEOPLE, EITHER THEY ARE GONE, OR THEY MIGHT AS WELL BE, BECAUSE INSIDE THEY ARE. THE GROUP THAT SURROUNDS THEM...SOME OF THEM GOT KILLED. SOME OF THEM WERE LITERALLY HUNTED DOWN FOR THE PROJECTS THAT THEY WERE INVOLVED IN. AND THEY KNEW IT, AND THEY WERE FEARFUL, AND THEY DID IT ANYWAY. SO, SOME OF THEM ARE DEAD, WHICH HAVE BEEN ASSASSINATED. BUT THE REALITY OF WHY THEY

WERE ASSASSINATED VERSUS WHAT PEOPLE THINK IS NOT THE SAME."

"YOUR ARNOLD SCHWARZENEGGER HAS A LOT OF VISION. BUT HE MAY NOT DECIDE TO HOLD ONTO THE WORLD ON HIS SHOULDERS. IT'S JUST VERY HEAVY. HE LIKES THE IDEA, BUT HE'S A VERY EMOTIONAL MAN, NO MATTER HOW BIG HE IS. SOMETIMES HE GETS TOO CLOSE TO PEOPLE, AND HE'S MISUNDERSTOOD. HE'LL BE PULLING SOME STRINGS WITH SOME OF THE SITUATION THAT ALL THIS INVOLVES. HE HAS OR IS SURROUNDED BY A CHILD IN THE SAME PREDICAMENT AND IT MAKES HIM ANGRY, BECAUSE WHAT DO YOU DO? NO AMOUNT OF MONEY OR POWER CAN CHANGE WHAT'S GOING ON WITH THIS CHILD AT THE MOMENT."

"SO, NO ONE IS IN A BOAT ALL ALONE. ALL OF YOU NEED TO HOP ABOARD INSTEAD OF FEELING THAT YOU'RE ON THE BOAT AS A SINGLE. YOU NEED TO KNOW THAT A HAND IS REACHING OUT TO EACH AND EVERY ONE OF YOU. YOU HAVE THIS MATERIAL IN YOUR HANDS FOR A REASON.

INCORPORATE THE DIFFERENT PHASES, AND USE YOUR PATIENCE."

"YOU CAN'T CHANGE THE PLACE OF FOCUS UNTIL THAT PERSON IS AT THAT LEVEL TO CREATE THE SERUM. SOME OF THE INGREDIENTS ARE NOT RECOGNIZED TODAY. IT HAS TO DO WITH THE JUNGLES. SO IT WILL BE COMING FROM ANOTHER COUNTRY...PART OF THE INGREDIENT... ***AFRICA.*** IT HAS NOTHING TO DO WITH THE OTHER ILLNESSES AND DISEASES BROUGHT FROM THERE, BUT THERE'S SOME UNTOUCHED...AND IT'S ON THE FLOORS. IT'S NOT IN THE TREES; IT'S ON THE FLOORS...THE GROUND, WITH COVERINGS. AND IT'S SOMETHING THAT GROWS UNDER SOMETHING ELSE THAT HAS FALLEN. AND IT DOESN'T TAKE A LOT OF THE SUBSTANCE...IT'S NOT QUANTITIES, IT'S QUALITY. AND IT'S FRUITFUL, IT'S THERE. IT'S NOT A RARITY THAT WILL BE FOUGHT OVER. IT'S JUST THAT YOU DON'T KNOW RIGHT NOW."

Laura: "Is it a fungus, or lichen?"

<u>MEDIUM:</u> "IT'S DIFFERENT FROM A MUSHROOM. IT GROWS SQUASHED DOWN WITH STUFF ON TOP OF IT, IS WHAT HE'S SHOWING ME. YOU KNOW HOW A MUSHROOM HAS TO SPRING UP, AND HAVE A LITTLE ROOM TO BE ITS THING? THIS IS LIKE SOMETHING OVER IT, LIKE LEAVES AND THE TREES...YOU KNOW HOW THE TREES HAVE THE BARK AND THE OUTER PART, AND WITHIN THAT, CLOSE TO THE GROUND...AND ALL THAT STUFF IS OVER IT AND IT'S SQUASHED. IT'S NOT PRETTY; IT'S A GROWTH UNDER THERE. AND IT'S PLENTIFUL. SO IT'S NOT SOMETHING THAT'S SCARCE AND GOING TO BE VERY EXPENSIVE. AND IT DOESN'T TAKE A LOT. IT'S A SMALL AMOUNT."

"THE TABLET IS DIFFERENT. THE TABLET IS DRY AND IT LOOKS TO ME LIKE AN ASPRIN EXCEPT IT'S A LITTLE FATTER. YOU KNOW HOW ASPRIN IS JUST WHITE AND IT'S JUST KIND OF FLAT? THIS IS A LITTLE FATTER, BUT IT'S NOT ROUND. THE DRY PART OF THE OUTSIDE IS LIKE AN ASPRIN-LOOKING THING, BUT THE CENTER IS LIQUID. SO, SOMEHOW THEY FIGURE OUT HOW TO PUT THAT INSIDE OF IT IN ITS LIQUID FORM. AND THIS IS SOME TYPE OF MEDICATION THAT THEY'RE GOING TO BE COMING INTO

DEVELOPMENT. BUT THIS WILL BE HERE SOONER THAN THIS IS PUT INTO THIS FORM. BUT THERE IS A LIQUID CENTER TO THE PILL-TYPE ADMINISTRATION. AND OF COURSE THE SERUM IS LIQUID FOR THE SHOT. AND YEAH, WE STILL HAVE SHOTS. SO, YEARS DOWN THE ROAD, WE STILL HAVE THE NEEDLE AND THE SERUM. AND IT GOES IN THE LEG, RIGHT THERE (TOP OF THIGH) IS WHERE THEY ARE GOING TO BE INJECTING IT."

"THE DISCOVERY IS GOING TO BE MADE BY THIS GUY WITH THIS TEMPER. HE IS THE ONE. AND HE'S WORKING ON IT NOW. SO THERE'S A MAN OUT THERE TRYING TO FIGURE ALL THIS OUT. AND HE LOOKS LIKE HE'S BANGING POTS AND PANS. I JUST KEEP SEEING HIM AND HE'S GOT A TEMPER, OH! HE SAYS, 'THIS DOESN'T WORK' AND HE'S JUST SO INVOLVED AND IN DEEP THOUGHT."

Laura: "Is he an American?"

MEDIUM: "IT'S NOT FAIR TO ASK IF HE'S AMERICAN BECAUSE HE'S NOT NATIVE AMERICAN."

<u>Laura:</u> "I mean, does he live in America? Does he live in the United States?"

<u>MEDIUM:</u> "HE'S NOT TELLING... NOT SAYING RIGHT NOW. HE DEVELOPS IT FOR AMERICA. IT'S NOT YOUR JOB TO HUNT THIS PERSON DOWN."

<u>Laura:</u> (Laughs) "That's what I was thinking."

<u>MEDIUM:</u> "YOUR JOB IS TO GET THE MATERIAL OUT SO THAT THEY CAN HAVE THE CURE. SO IT CAN BE DISCOVERED, SO IT CAN BE INCORPORATED IN THESE LIVES TO MAKE THEM BETTER FOR NOW."

"I'M JUST GIVING THEM A LITTLE SKIP IN ALL THAT THEY HAVE TO GO THROUGH. BECAUSE WHEN YOU SEE BETTERMENT IN THERE, ALTHOUGH IT IS NOT 100%, IT'S STILL BETTER; FOR YOU AND FOR THEM. BUT YOU NEED TO REMEMBER THAT IT'S NOT COMPLETION. AND UNTIL COMPLETION IS AT HAND, THEN YOU KNOW YOU HAVE 100% OF YOUR CHILDREN BACK."

"AND THESE ARE YOUR LEADERS, YOUR GENERATIONS TO COME OF WHAT HAPPENS TO THE WORLD. DO YOU WANT TO TAKE CARE OF THIS WORLD, AND THEN THEY BLOW IT UP FOR YOU? THEN WHERE IS THE REST OF YOUR FAMILY? YOU NEED TO REMEMBER, ALL HAPPENS AT THE SAME TIME, AND YOUR FAMILY GOES FORWARDS AND BACKWARDS. SO THE CARE SHOULD BE THERE EVEN FOR THEM."

"AND NO, YOU'RE NOT DIRECTLY RELATED TO ME (THE WIRY ONE)...IT'S BECAUSE OF TRACING AND SEARCHING. AND HE WANTS THE FOCUS TO STAY IN THE DIRECTION THAT IT'S SUPPOSED TO BE. THAT WAY THE ANSWERS WILL BE THERE. THESE WORDS ARE FOR THE PERSON LOOKING FOR THE CURE."

"READING THIS FROM THE BEGINNING TO THE END WILL BRING YOU UNDERSTANDING. AND THIS IS WHAT YOU SHOULD EXPECT FROM THE MATERIAL THAT YOU'VE GOT YOUR EYES UPON."

"AND WHO CARES IF THIS JACKET WON'T SIT LIKE IT'S SUPPOSED TO. HE'S JOKING. HE'S TELLING ME HIS

SESSION IS UP. RIGHT NOW, HIS SESSION IS UP. IT'S LIKE HE'S...I DON'T KNOW WHAT HE'S DOING. HE'S RETIRING FOR THE MOMENT, FOR THIS FOCUSSING TIME RIGHT NOW."

"I KNOW HE CAN PUT HIS SOCKS ON CORRECTLY, AND I'M SEEING HIM FUMBLING AROUND WITH HIS SOCKS, AND THEY'RE WHITE. IT'S LIKE I HAVE A BIG OLD HOLE IN THE BACK OF MY SOCK AND MY HEEL IS COLD. I'M IN SPIRIT AND I KNOW I CAN PUT ALL OF THIS ON."

"I LOVE LIFE...I LOVE HERE, BUT I LOVE THERE AS WELL. SO MANY THINGS HAPPENED. MY BODY WAS HARD TO DEAL WITH. MY HEEL IS COLD. I'M LOOKING AT HIS HEEL, AND HE JUST DOESN'T HAVE HIS SOCK PULLED UP GOOD, AND HE THINKS THERE'S A HOLE IN IT, BECAUSE HE'S NOT LOOKING BACK THERE, AND IT'S THE RIGHT FOOT. ACTUALLY, HE DIDN'T PUT ON THAT SOCK, IT JUST WORKED ITSELF DOWN. YOU KNOW HOW..."

<u>Laura:</u> (Giggling) "Yeah."

<u>MEDIUM:</u> "I USED TO FORGET TO EAT, AND THEN WHEN I ATE; I ATE, AND ATE, AND ATE. SORT OF LIKE YOUR BEAR. I WOULD EAT, AND EAT, AND EAT, AND THEN I WOULDN'T EAT. BUT I WAS OKAY. SO, I HAD A FLUCTUATION IN MY BODY, BUT IT NEVER AFFECTED ME, BECAUSE I DIDN'T FOCUS ON IT."

"I WAS VERY MISUNDERSTOOD FOR A VERY LONG TIME. I GATHER MY THOUGHTS IN A DIFFERENT WAY NOW, AND THAT'S WHY I WANT MY HAND TO MOLD THE ENTIRETY OF THIS MATERIAL. AND ALL OF WHAT I WAS TELLING YOU ABOUT CHAPTER TWO, AND THREE, AND FOUR AND ALL OF THAT, THAT WAS MY WAY; MY MESSAGE IS TO YOU THAT I AM IN CONTROL."

(TO LAURA) "THE MATERIAL THAT YOU FIND WILL FALL AT YOUR FEET. SO, MARK DOWN YOUR TABS BECAUSE I ONLY DO IT ONCE, AND IT'S UP TO YOU TO REMEMBER THAT YOU'RE SUPPOSED TO LOOK THERE. CUZ THIS IS NOT ABOUT ME THROWING IT IN YOUR FACE OVER AND OVER. I'LL DO MY PART AND YOU HAVE TO DO YOURS."

"AND IT'S OKAY TO HAVE YOUR CHILD IN YOUR LAP. HIS HEAD LYING UPON YOU WHEN YOU'RE DOING SOME OF THIS WORK. IT'S ABOUT HIM ANYWAY. IT'S ABOUT ALL THE CHILDREN LIKE HIM. AND YOU NEED TO KNOW THAT IT'S ABOUT ALL THE CHILDREN THAT ARE FAR WORSE THAN THAT CHILD."

"KEEP IN TOUCH WITH YOUR GROUPS. MORE GROUPS NEED TO BE PUT TOGETHER ALL AROUND, SO THAT THESE CHILDREN CAN BE TAKEN CARE OF, AND THERE CAN BE RECOGNITION OF WHAT'S GOING ON WITH THEM."

"LAURA...YOU'LL BE TAKING THIS MATERIAL TO CLASSES THAT YOU'RE FORMING AROUND THE COUNTRY. YOU'LL CHOOSE DIFFERENT LEADERS IN DIFFERENT STATES, BUT YOU'LL BE OUTLINING HOW ALL OF THAT IS PUT TOGETHER. LATER IN YOUR LIFE, YOU'LL BE INCORPORATING IT IN A NONPROFIT ORGANIZATION FOR RESEARCH. BUT NO MATTER HOW MUCH YOU WANT TO TALK ABOUT IT, NO MATTER HOW MANY TIMES YOU WANT TO SAY IT, NO MATTER HOW YOU WANT TO FLIP IT, TURN IT, TWIST IT, WHIP IT UP...ALL YOUR ANSWERS ARE RIGHT

HERE. THIS IS YOUR ABS'S AND 123'S. AND IF YOU TRY TO CHANGE IT, FLUFF IT UP, ELABORATE IT, THEN YOU KNOW YOU'RE GOING IN THE WRONG DIRECTION. BUT THAT'S YOUR PART IN THIS SITUATION."

Laura: "I can do that."

MEDIUM: "THE MEDIUM'S PART IS THE ENLIGHTENMENT, THE INFORMATION, THE TOOLS THAT I'M BRINGING FORWARD. AND THERE'S A REASON THAT I CHOSE HER TO DO THIS CHANNELING. IT'S CLEAN. AND IT'S NOT CHANGED. SHE'S MORE OF A PERSON STEPPING BACK AND LOOKING AROUND THE WORLD. A TOOL. SHE UNDERSTANDS ME. AND IT'S BECAUSE OF HER FATHER. IT'S NOT WHAT YOU'RE LOOKING AT ON THE OUTSIDE, BUT THE BRAINS THAT ARE ON THE INSIDE; THE THOUGHT PATTERN AND HOW YOU USE IT. LOOK AT HITLER, THEN TURN AROUND AND LOOK AT JOHN OF GOD. SUCH AN ARRAY OF PEOPLE, OF MINDS."

"YOU NEED TO NOT BE FEARFUL OF CHILDREN WHO ARE STRICKEN, AND NOT EMPOWERED. JUST TRY TO UNDERSTAND THEM INSTEAD."

"DEVELOP YOUR PSYCHIC FOR PETE'S SAKE PEOPLE! IT'S THERE! IT IS PART OF WHO YOU ARE. IT'S LIKE A THUMB ON YOUR HAND. LOOK AT IT! NO THUMB? HOW DO YOU PICK THINGS UP? YOU MIGHT AS WELL WALK ON ALL FOURS, USE THEM FOR FEET. YOUR PSYCHIC IS YOUR THUMB. AND THAT'S THE DIFFERENCE...THAT'S HOW EVOLVED YOU BECOME WHEN YOU INCORPORATE IT IN ALL YOUR SENSES THAT ALREADY ARE. TO YOU IT WILL BE LIKE USING YOUR THUMB THAT YOU HAVE NOT EVER USED."

"THE REASON FOR THE HOLD UP HAS BEEN FEAR OF SOME PEOPLE SURPASSING OTHER PEOPLE. THE FEARFUL ONES WERE THE ONES WITH THE INTELLEGENCE FEELING AN UNFAIRNESS OF A PSYCHIC KIND OF AN INTELLEGENCE. AND TRYING TO PUT A CAP ON SUCH. THAT'S NOT THE ANSWER. BECAUSE THOSE WITH INTELLEGENCE CAN ALSO INCORPORATE THEIR PSYCHIC. BUT INSTEAD, THEY FOUND

IT FEARFUL, AND THEY FIND IT FEARFUL...SO THEY SAY IT'S BAD."

"AS LONG AS THEY SAY IT'S BAD, IT'S LIKE HUMANITY IS WALKING ON ALL FOURS...AND YES YOU DID...YOU DID WALK ON ALL FOURS IN THE BEGINNING. YOU WERE NOT EXACTLY THE APE, BUT ALONG THOSE LINES."

"THERE ARE A LOT OF THINGS THAT YOU USE NOW THAT YOU USE ON A PHYSICAL LEVEL, BUT YOU AREN'T GOING TO BE USING THEM AS THAT IN THE FUTURE. SO, YOU WON'T NEED SO MUCH STUFF AROUND YOU BECAUSE YOU WILL ACTUALLY BE ABLE TO INCORPORATE THAT INTO YOUR MIND AND INTO YOUR PHYSICAL BECAUSE THE TWO ARE COMING CLOSER AND CLOSER TOGETHER. SO, IT'S NOT A PHENOMENON. IT IS NATURAL."

(CD ENDS)

***

Later Discoveries

I tried not to say much during this reading because I didn't want to change the course of where the information was going. And I didn't want to be told that one of my ears was shutting down again. I just sat back and listened to most of it, unless I was asked something for the most part. And wow, did a lot of information come through. All of our roles were clearly defined in this project. How could I not continue at this point? I learned about the man who is looking for the cure, and about some of the missing ingredients for the serum. Also, more details about the serum and the new liquid tablet. Evidently, I needed to get my fingers moving and start transcribing. I was scolded by the spirit world. How funny.

I also found many validations from this reading about The Wiry One on a personal level from the descriptions he gave in the readings, but I had to take them out. I also found personal connections between The Wiry One and The President that came through in the readings, but I can't mention them either. The information is out there should you choose to discover it for yourself. The reason I am mentioning it at all is that I made many discoveries after the readings that validated the information given in them.

Personal Validations

One of the coolest things for me that came through was the knowledge that my son's allergies were not going to be permanent. He had been on a strict diet that is gluten-free, dairy-free, sometimes sugar-free (when he has yeast), since he was five. Let me tell you, it has been a struggle. I can't even imagine how it must make him feel, being so different. It breaks my heart.

Since these readings, I have changed some things in Trevor's treatment protocol based on the information I received in the readings. I am so happy to say that Trevor can now eat gluten and dairy again! On a rotation basis, but that's okay. Here's how it happened. He accidentally ate a regular cookie at school that had wheat in it, and his teacher called me, because his IEP (Individualized Education Plan) states that he can only eat foods from home. I told her to watch him for any behaviors or gastrointestinal problems, and she said that he seemed fine. I didn't notice anything at home either. Even over the next few days, he had no evident reactions to the cookie.

In this reading, it stated that the children will not have their food allergies forever, and that it will be a sign of how they are doing when they can incorporate these foods back in their diet. Now, since Trevor had his allergies eliminated with NAET, theoretically, he should be able to reintroduce those foods every 4 days. But, I wanted to let his gut heal for a while before I tried that. So, after the cookie incident, I decided to test this information. I brought Trevor to the doctor's office that did NAET on him and told them what had happened and we did Muscle Response Testing with me as the "surrogate" for gluten and dairy. He did not show an intolerance to them anymore. The doctor told me to go ahead and try to reintroduce them and see what happens.

I decided to add dairy back first. I gave him some digestive enzymes first that help break down foods. It was Mother's Day and he had his first real ice cream in 6 years! He literally inhaled it! It was the best Mother's Day gift ever! He showed no reaction to it, except he was happy! Not as happy as I was, though. This was huge progress for him. I decided to try gluten a few weeks later. It was my mom's birthday, and we got a real cake, chocolate with chocolate chips and cream cheese frosting. That's right, gluten and dairy at the same time. Normally, I'd be having a panic attack knowing he was eating these things. But I had to test it. He loved the cake, and again, as with the ice cream, he had no reaction to it physically or behaviorally.

Then, on his birthday a few months later, he had the same cake. It was the first birthday cake that I didn't have to make special for him in 6 years. I was a little teary-eyed when I went to pick it up. I actually felt normal for once. It was a great day! Now, don't think he eats cake and ice cream daily. These were special occasions; he is one of the healthiest eaters I know. I spend a small fortune on his diet. He eats lots of organic fruits and vegetables, free-range grass-fed meats, no artificial anything or Frankenfoods (genetically modified). Who knows what's safe now?

I also took all potato products out of his diet, or so I thought. I was a bit mad at myself because one of the foods he loved, and ate almost daily was Trader Joe's frozen gluten-free, dairy-free pancakes; and I didn't realize it until a year after the reading that it had potato flour in it! I thought I had it under control. Let me tell you, it wasn't easy. I never read the label for the pancakes because he had been eating them since before all of this, and who would think pancakes had a potato product in it? I figured it out when a friend of mine who has a son with autism asked me what was in them and I was horrified when I read her the ingredients on the box. Then I read all of the frozen pancake boxes and all the pancake mixes, and almost every one has either potato flour or potato starch in it, except Trader Joe's Gluten Free Pancake Mix. Not the frozen ones, the dry mix. I just make the whole package, freeze them and toast them.

I couldn't believe he could actually eat these forbidden foods again! He actually prefers some of his GF/CF favorites, and they are healthy, so I am not going to change his diet entirely. But it is so nice to be able to go to a restaurant and not have to bring special food, or to celebrate a special occasion and not have to make a separate item for Trevor so he can be included. It is another major milestone for him.

Grief

A few days after this reading, I was really struggling with processing all of this information, and I became quite angry. I was so mad about what had happened to my son, if the true cause of his regression was what was said in the readings. Was our government unknowingly causing our children to become "autistic," in an effort to create biological weapons to use on our enemies? Most parents, including myself, blamed our child's condition on vaccines, or specifically the mercury preservative, thimerosal, contained in a lot of the vaccines. I couldn't help but blame myself for vaccinating him, even when my intuition questioned it. We also were made to feel like autism was at least in some way genetic. It was clearly stated in the readings that regressive autism is ***NOT*** genetic. What a relief! Couples blame themselves or each other, which puts a rift between them, and most of them divorce.

What if this new information was true? I had to share it with other parents who have been blaming themselves as well. But I felt I would be ridiculed. All of my friends that I told a bit about it, either questioned my sanity or thought I was naive for believing it. I felt like I was the only one who understood the enormity and far reaching implications of this information. The fallout could be of epic proportions. I felt like I had to try to validate more of the information from the readings so it would be taken seriously. I believed it because I witnessed it, but I can understand other people doubting it. I probably would question it myself if I hadn't been in the room and experienced it personally. It does sound pretty unbelievable.

After my anger subsided some, I became depressed. Mainly for my son. I felt like his whole life had been stolen from him. The happy childhood that I so desperately wanted to provide for him had been replaced by pain and struggle. I cried like a baby thinking about what he went through when these two ingredients combined in his body and he couldn't tell me what was happening to him. I felt his pain. I was ashamed of myself for the frustration and anger that I had shown him over the years because I didn't know what he was going through, I just saw the screaming and bad behaviors. One night, I put him to bed and lay down next to him, and cried my eyes out and apologized for anything that I had done wrong, and for all of the trauma he's had to live with. I knew that on some level, he understood me. His big blue eyes said it all.

Learning about all of this was a grief process. I had gone through the classic stages: shock and denial, anger, and depression. Once I finally accepted it as truth, I knew I needed to take action. For now, that action was to finish the book; to get the information and put it out there to help others. I really wanted to go to the media and expose what I knew to save the children, but it wasn't the right time.

***

CHAPTER SIX

MEDIUM: "TODAY IS DECEMBER 17, 2007 AND THIS IS SESSION SIX FOR 'THE MUMMY.' IT'S A BOOK THAT WE'RE PUTTING TOGETHER. WE ARE LOOKING FOR SPIRIT TO BRING THE HIGHEST AND BEST INFORMATION, SO THAT'S WHAT WE'RE AFTER. LET'S SEE WHAT SPIRIT BRINGS. OKAY, BE WITH ME LAURA, LET'S MAKE A CONNECTION HERE. (SHE SAYS A PERSONAL PRAYER.) I ASK FOR THE HIGHEST AND BEST SPIRITS TO COME THROUGH NOW. MY SPIRIT CONTROL CAME THROUGH, AND HE'S VERY MUCH IN CONTROL TODAY. HE'S LIKE, 'NO' AND HE PUT HIS HAND UP LIKE IN A STOP POSITION TO STOP THOSE SPIRITS TRYING TO COME THROUGH WITHOUT HIS PERMISSION. SO, HE'S REALLY ON TOP OF IT, TO THE POINT WHERE I WAS ABLE TO SEE WHAT HE'S DOING."

"AND I DO HAVE THE WIRY ONE HERE...AND I HAVE MY BUDDY HERE, HE SAYS. HIS BUDDY IS JUST HERE WITH

HIM. HE'S NOT SO MUCH ABOUT GIVING INFORMATION; HE'S MORE OF A COMPANION PERSON HE'S SUPPOSED TO BE HANGING OUT WITH IN THE SPIRIT WORLD. SO, IT WENT BEYOND THEM BEING HERE TOGETHER ON THE PHYSICAL. SO THEY'RE TOGETHER THERE, STILL WORKING AND EVOLVING HUMANITY. THEY ARE STILL TRYING TO HELP. THE ONLY THING IS THAT THE WIRY ONE HAS DECIDED THAT WE NEED MORE HELP ON THE PHYSICAL LEVEL THAN THOSE ON THE SPIRITUAL LEVEL, BECAUSE THOSE ON THE SPIRITUAL LEVEL...THEIR TIMELINE AND OUR TIMELINE TO DEVASTATION IS ENTIRELY DIFFERENT. THERE'S HOPE AND A CHOICE OF SIMPLY CHOOSING JOY. HERE ON THE PHYSICAL LEVEL, WE HAVE TO CREATE IT. IT'S MORE OF A CREATION. IT'S MORE OF SOMETHING THAT HAS TO BE BUILT WITHIN US, AND THEN IT GOES ON THE OUTSIDE OF US."

"AND OUR FUTURE IS AT STAKE. NOT ONLY ON A WORLDLY LEVEL, THE EARTHLY LEVEL, THE DIRT THAT YOU WALK ON, THE BALL THAT SEEMS FLAT TO YOU. YOU LOOK AT A LITTLE PIECE, BUT WHEN YOU'RE STANDING ON THE DIRT, YOU'RE ACUALLY STANDING ON ONE HUGE, ROUND MASS.

AND YOU'RE ON TOP OF IT. AND IT NEEDS HELP AS WELL, BUT YOU THAT DRIVE IT, NEED TO BE HELPED FIRST SO THAT YOU CAN HELP THE EARTH. HOW DO YOU HELP THE EARTH IF YOU ARE NOT RIGHT?"

"AND YOUR FUTURE IS NOT RIGHT BECAUSE OF ALL THE CHILDREN COMING IN AND NOT STAYING IN A HIGH LEVEL PATTERN OF HEALTH. THEIR PATTERN STARTS DECLINING TOO SOON. AND THERE'S NOT GOING TO BE ENOUGH OF THOSE WHO DON'T HAVE THE PROBLEMS IN ORDER TO KEEP RHYTHM SMOOTH."

Laura: "What can we do?"

MEDIUM: "THERE NEEDS TO BE AN AWARENESS OF THE ROOT OF THE PROBLEM AND THERE NEEDS TO BE A SOLUTION. AND THE SOLUTION IS GOING TO HAVE TO BE PLAINLY PUT ON THE PHYSICAL LEVEL. AND THE REASON FOR ALL THE YADDA, YADDA, YADDA, INSTEAD OF JUST SAYING, 'HERE IT IS' IS ON THE PHYSICAL LEVEL IS IT'S A PLACE OF REASONING, OF MAKING SENSE OF MATTERS. IT'S NOT ABOUT JUST HAVING THE ANSWER."

"BECAUSE THE ANSWER HAS COME TO PEOPLE MANY, MANY TIMES AND THEY LOOK AT IT, AND STUPIDITY MAKES THEM THROW IT DOWN AND NOT UTILIZE IT. SO, THAT'S WHY YOUR EYES HAVE TO FLOW THROUGH THE ENTIRETY OF THE WORDS IN THIS BOOK."

"YOU NEED TO HAVE A REALIZATION THAT THE FUTURE IS AT STAKE, AND IT HAS TO DO WITH HUMANITY. AND YOU NEVER WOULD PUT THE EARTH SECOND, BUT IT'S A FACT THAT THAT'S WHAT NEEDS TO HAPPEN. THE EARTH NEEDS TO BE TAKEN CARE OF BY ALL MEANS, BUT IF THE EARTH IS TAKEN CARE OF, AND THEN YOU HAVE CHAOS RUNNING IT, IT WILL BE DESTROYED ANYWAY. IT'S THROWING DESTINY AFTER DESTINY IN ALIGNMENT WITH AN EXPLOSION OF THE WORLD. AND THEN WHERE DO YOU LIVE? THE FEW THAT ARE SET MINDED FLEE AND LEAVE THE REST? THAT'S NOT RIGHT. IS THAT RIGHT? THAT'S WHAT THEY WOULD DO. FAMILIES WOULD LEAVE PARTS OF THEIR FAMILY FEELING THAT THEY ARE NOT ABLE TO HELP THEM. THEY FEEL HELPLESS."

"AN EXPLANATION OF EVERY SINGLE THING THAT CAUSES A PROBLEM...YOU COULD GO FROM A CARROT, TO A POTATO, TO A BEET, AND ANALYZE EVERY ONE OF THEM AS TO THE LEVEL OF TOXICITY, BUT WHY? YOU KNOW IT'S IN THE EARTH, IN THE DIRT, THE TOPSOIL THAT GROWS THE CROP. SO, IT'S NOT ABOUT HAVING ALL OF THAT RIGHT HERE IN FRONT OF YOU, BECAUSE YOU COULD GO SEARCH OUT THAT INFORMATION AND KNOW THAT IT'S HAPPENING IN OTHER MATERIAL."

"SO YOU NEED TO KNOW AND PAY ATTENTION TO THESE ROOT VEGETABLES THAT YOU'RE CONSUMING, THINKING, 'I'M A VEGETARIAN, BE HAPPY FOR ME, I'M SO HEALTHY.' LOOK AT YOUR BODY...WHAT'S WRONG WITH IT?"

"AND IT'S NOT THE PESTICIDES; IT'S LITERALLY THE TOPSOIL THAT'S USED TO GROW YOUR FRUITS AND VEGETABLES. SO, START EATING DIFFERENTLY, START FEEDING YOUR CHILDREN DIFFERENTLY IN ORDER FOR YOU TO BE ABLE TO HANG ONTO THE WORLD. I DIDN'T SAY, 'CHANGE IT' I SAID, 'HANG ONTO IT.' AFTER YOU GET IT IN THE RIGHT DIRECTION, THEN YOU TRY TO MAKE CHANGES.

BUT FOR NOW, YOU NEED TO JUST SAVE YOURSELF FROM 'IT' BECAUSE IT IS...THE TOP PART OF IT IS CONTAMINATED."

"SO, IN REALITY IT'S A BLESSING WHERE THE EARTH TURNS AND HAS HAD DESTRUCTION, AND THE SOILS HAVE SWISHED AND FLIPPED. SEE, THE OCEANS AUTOMATICALLY DO THAT, AND THEY HAVE TIME TO HEAL. BUT THE EARTH...IT'S VERY DISTURBING WHEN IT TAKES A TOBBLE. THE EARTH WILL TAKE A TIP FROM ITS AXIS, BUT IT'S VERY MINUTE. EVERYONE HAS EXAGGERATED IT. IT WILL BE A TOBBLE, AND A SCARE, AND THEN IT STOPS. SO, IT'S FINE. AND IT IS BECAUSE THE ICE IS CHANGING. AND YOU NEED TO EAT FROM THE WATERS."

<u>Laura:</u> "Global warming?"

<u>MEDIUM:</u> "YES, GLOBAL WARMING. BUT IT'S NOT A DESTROYER. NO MATTER HOW MANY YEARS YOU GO FORWARD...50 YEARS, 100 YEARS; AND ALL OF THE RAMIFICATIONS THAT THEY'VE APPLIED TO ALL THEIR RESEARCH. BECAUSE THIS WILL KEEP GOING, AND THEN IT

WILL BALANCE OUT, AND IT STOPS. IT'S JUST TRYING TO BALANCE ITSELF RIGHT NOW."

"SO, PEOPLE NEED TO START FOCUSING ON...YOU PEOPLE, EVERY ONE OF YOU...NEED TO START FOCUSING ON YOURSELVES, YOUR OFFSPRING, YOUR CHILDREN, YOUR FRIEND'S CHILDREN. BECAUSE YOU ARE FROM EACH OTHER. YOU'RE ONE BIG UNIT AT THIS POINT."

"YOU'RE ALL GOING TO BE ALLOWED TO SPEAK THE SAME LANGUAGE. THERE MAY HAVE BEEN A DAY THAT THERE NEEDED TO BE A LOT OF SEPARATION, SO PEOPLE DIDN'T UNDERSTAND EACH OTHER. BUT RIGHT NOW IS A TIME OF NEEDING TO COMMUNICATE WITH ONE ANOTHER. SO THE WORLD AND COMMUNICATION HAS GOTTEN SMALLER, AND SMALLER, AND SMALLER OUT OF NEED. NOT BECAUSE YOU DECIDED THAT THAT'S WHAT IT WAS GOING TO BE."

"I'M PICKING UP A BEING; A REALLY TALL, SLENDER BEING. I FEEL LIKE...OKAY, THE WIRY ONE IS LAUGHING. HE SAYS THAT HE'S TALKED TO THIS FELLA BEFORE, SO IT'S MALE. AND HE SAYS THAT HE REFERRED TO THIS BEING AS A

FELLA, BUT IT'S MORE OF AN 'IT.' IT'S NOT A MALE OR FEMALE. IT'S A BEING THAT IS VERY MUCH IN LOOKING OVER US IN THE SOLAR SYSTEM; A MORE EXPANSIVE WAY OF TRAVEL. HE (THE BEING) WAS ACKNOWLEDGING THE INTRODUCTION THAT HE GOT FROM THE WIRY ONE, AND I WILL CALL HIM A 'HE' ALTHOUGH HE/SHE ISN'T. JUST FOR THE SAKE OF REFERENCE."

"ALDOLA, (THEN PRONOUNCES IT) ALDOOLA, IS THE NAME I'M SEEING. A CHAIN WENT AROUND THIS BEING'S NECK, AND THAT'S WHAT HE'S SAYING...THAT'S WHAT'S ON THE EMBLEM."

"HE IS OF A DIFFERENT SHADE, VERY TALL. I WOULD SAY EIGHT AND A HALF FEET AND SLENDER. BY LOOKING AT THIS BEING, YOU WOULD FEEL LIKE YOU ARE LOOKING AT ART. VERY FLOWY. FROM THE IMAGE THAT I'M SEEING, IT DOESN'T SEEM LIKE IT'S CLOTHED, BUT AT THE SAME TIME, IT DOESN'T LOOK NAKED. IT JUST LOOKS LIKE A FORM. THE HEAD IS NOT EXTRA BIG LIKE THEY SAY ALIENS HAVE OR ANYTHING LIKE THAT. THE HEAD IS IN

PROPORTION TO WHAT OUR EYE IS USED TO PERCEIVING. THERE'S NO HAIR. AND THE COLOR IS ODD."

Laura: "What color?"

MEDIUM: "IT GOES FROM A SILVERY...WE DON'T HAVE THAT COLOR...IT'S LIKE A SILVERY, ALMOST LIKE A CLOUD, TO A SILVERY, BUT ON A BEAUTIFUL DAY, NOT ON A CLOUDY DAY. THE COLOR IS...WE DON'T HAVE A COLOR THAT LOOKS LIKE THAT. BECAUSE IT'S LIKE A SATIN SHINE BEHIND THE COLOR OF...IT'S NOT EVEN A GOOD DESCRIPTION."

Laura: "What does he want to tell us? He/she..."

MEDIUM: "IT HAS A MOUTH (THE MEDIUM OPENS AND CLOSES HER MOUTH). I JUST SAW THE MOUTH. THE EYES LOOK...I JUST SEE THE MOUTH." LET ME SEE WHAT ELSE..."

(THE BEING TALKING) "HUMANITY IS GOING TO FEEL LIKE THERE IS A LOT OF DISCIPLINE GOING ON WITHIN THEMSELVES. THERE WILL BE MANY PEOPLE THAT WILL GAIN DISCIPLINE WITHIN THEMSELVES THAT HAVE NOT

BEEN ABLE TO DO IN DECADES. THEY HAVE GONE ALONG AND BEEN OUT OF CONTROL WITH THEMSELVES. THEY WANT TO DO THINGS, BUT DON'T. THEY TALK ABOUT IT, THEY SET THEMSELVES UP TO DO WHAT THEY PLANNED, BUT THEN IT DOESN'T HAPPEN. IT'S NON-DISCIPLINE WITHIN THEMSELVES. AND THE HAPPENINGS OF THE NEXT EIGHT YEARS, THERE'S GOING TO BE A LOT OF PEOPLE FINDING THEMSELVES BEING VERY DISCIPLINED. BUT THEY NEED TO KNOW IT'S NOT SOMETHING THAT THEY ARE DOING ON THEIR OWN, THEY ARE GETTING HELP FROM THIS BEING SO THAT THEY CAN FOLLOW THEIR PATH CORRECTLY AND GO FORWARD MORE ASSURED. THIS WILL BRING DISCIPLINE IN THEIR VERY OWN LIVES THAT THEY'VE BEEN TRYING TO INCORPORATE, BUT NEVER HAVE BEEN ABLE TO INSTILL IT."

"AND THESE ARE SOME OF THE PEOPLE THAT WILL BE HELPING THE REST OF HUMANITY. AND THERE ARE 90. THERE ARE 90 OF THESE PEOPLE. AND THEY WILL FIND EACH OTHER. AND THEY GO ACROSS THE WORLD. THEY ARE NOT ALL SET IN ONE AREA. SO THEY WILL BE TRAVELING, AND THERE WILL BE FINANCES, AND THERE WILL BE

EVERYTHING USED TO GETTING THIS CORRECTION DONE. SO, DON'T LOSE HOPE FOR YOUR CHILDREN."

"AND REMEMBER, IT'S NOT YOUR FAULT THAT OUR LEADERS ARE NOT OPENING LIKE THEY SHOULD. THEY ARE A CLOSED FLOWER. BUT YOU NEED TO REMEMBER THAT THEY ARE A FLOWER, AND THAT'S OF BEAUTY. HUMANITY IS BEAUTY. YOU RULE THIS PLANET BUT HAVE TAKEN IT FOR SUCH GRANTED; THIS GIFT THAT'S BEEN GIVEN TO YOU."

"MANY OF YOU ARE JUST LIVING DAY TO DAY. NOT LOOKING FOR JUST FIVE MINUTES OF YOUR TIME TO SPEND IN A GOOD WAY SHARING WITH SOMEONE THAT YOU DO SOMETHING FOR THEM, AND YOU GET NOTHING IN RETURN. YOU NEED TO STOP AND TAKE A LOOK AT YOURSELF. ALL OF YOU AS A WHOLE, AS A UNIT. AND AS YOU DO, YOU'LL HAVE YOUR ENCOUNTERS WITH THIS BEING BECAUSE YOU ARE SHOWING YOUR SELFLESSNESS."

"BUT THE 90 THAT WILL COME TOGETHER, THOSE ARE WITH INTENT. THAT IS NOT ABOUT GETTING BACK

BECAUSE OF GOOD KARMA GAINED OR ANY OF THOSE AREAS, DESCRIPTIONS THAT YOU WOULD LABEL OF DIFFERENT LEVELS OF THE HIGHER REALM."

"THOSE THAT ARE LETTING THEIR CHILDREN GROW UP WITHOUT THEM, THOSE CHILDREN THAT HAVE THIS PROBLEM...A LOT OF GUILT-DRIVEN AND FEAR OF LOOKING BACK. SO, INSTEAD OF TRYING TO JUDGE THEM, YOU MOVE FORWARD IN YOUR CORRECT DIRECTION. BECAUSE IF YOU JUDGE THEM, THEN YOU BEGIN TO FOLLOW. BECAUSE THEY ARE GOING TO TRY TO JUST SIMPLY GIVE YOU JUSTIFICATION, AND THERE ISN'T ANY. IT'S INEXCUSABLE. THERE ARE A LOT OF PEOPLE AROUND THE WORLD WHO ARE GOING TO HELP IN THIS SITUATION."

"HE (THE WIRY ONE) JUST WENT LIKE THIS..." (SHE PICKS UP THE CHALK, AND IN A DAZE, STARTS TO DRAW ON THE CHALKBOARD. IT LOOKS LIKE A NUMBER 5 THEN A SQUARE ROOT SIGN, AND ANOTHER 5 INSIDE OF IT WITH A 3 ABOVE IT, THE CUBED SYMBOL, AND THEN A LETTER S WITH A - SIGN IN FRONT OF IT, AND A SMALL "o" ABOVE THE LETTER S.) $5\sqrt{5^{3}}-S^{\circ}$

"HE SAID TO PUT IT DOWN...HE SAID TO PUT IT DOWN."

(MEDIUM'S WORDS) "MY ARM FEELS TINGLY FROM HERE TO HERE. I FEEL LIKE MY FACE IS SWOLLEN. IT'S JUST SWELLING. AND THIS ARM FEELS DIFFERENT FROM THIS ARM."

(HER VOICE GETS FASTER, 'S WORDS) "YOU KNOW, SOMETIMES I GO VERY FAST, AND SOMETIMES I GO VERY SLOW, SOMETIMES I GET VERY ANTSY, SOMETIMES I GET ALL THIS CONFUSION, AND THEN I NEED TO REST. I THINK I WAS DIABETIC AND I DIDN'T KNOW WHAT WAS WRONG WITH ME, CUZ I HAD TO EAT IN INTERVALS IN ORDER TO KEEP MY...WHAT I CALL SANITY. BUT YOU CALLED ME INSANE. UNTIL YOU SAW THAT YOU COULD DRAW FROM ME. SO IT'S OKAY TO LISTEN TO THE WILD ONE."

(MEDIUM IS SAYING WHAT SHE SEES) "EVERYTHING IS LOOKING MAJESTIC...EVERYTHING IS LOOKING MAJESTIC. THERE'S THE MOUNTAINS, AND YOU'LL SEE LOTS OF COLORS IN THE SKY AND LOOKING MAJESTIC."

"REMEMBER, THE COLOR IS POLLUTION. IT DOESN'T DO ANY GOOD TO RUN AWAY, AND MOVE HERE AND MOVE THERE, AND SCURRY AND BE SCARED. THE SOLUTION HAS TO BE MET AND PUT IN FORCE, AND THINGS HAVE TO CHANGE. RUNNING IS NOT THE ANSWER."

(THE WIRY ONE TO LAURA) "YOU ARE ASSISTING IN GETTING THIS PUT ON PAPER, BUT YOUR BIGGER PORTION, WHERE YOU'RE HEADED, HAS TO DO WITH THE ACTUAL HANDS-ON HELP FOR THESE CHILDREN. THE BOOK IS AN ANCHOR. THAT NEEDS TO BE PUT IN THE BOOK... THE BOOK IS AN ANCHOR... BUT IN TERMS OF ALL OF THE PEOPLE THAT ARE GOING TO GET INVOLVED. BECAUSE IT'S NOT SINGULAR, IT'S PLURAL."

"OKAY, LAURA, THIS IS FOR YOU. BECAUSE I SEE A ROPE, AND HE LASSOS YOU IN. IT'S LIKE HE GOT A ROPE AND HE'S LASSOING YOU IN. SO, THIS IS ALL FOR YOU. THIS HAS TO DO WITH YOU. YOU HAVE A LOT GOING ON. YOU HAVE THIS NEW BUSINESS AND YOUR KIDS."

(I did just take on a new business opportunity and it took up most of my time, along with taking care of my family.)

"ALL OF THIS HAS TO HAPPEN HERE (IN NEVADA). IT ALL HAS TO HAPPEN HERE BECAUSE THE PROBLEM IS HERE. SO IF YOU GO LIVE SOMEWHERE ELSE, HOW CAN YOU WORK ON THE PROBLEM? YOU CAN'T. BECAUSE THEN YOU'D HAVE TO TRAVEL HERE. HOW ARE YOU GOING TO TRAVEL AND LEAVE YOUR CHILDREN BEHIND? IT DOESN'T WORK, YOU'VE ALREADY EXPERIENCED THAT. EVERYTHING NEEDS TO COME TO YOU, SO THAT YOU CAN WORK WITH IT. YOU CANNOT GO TO IT. WHAT ARE YOU GOING TO DO, DRAG YOUR KIDS AROUND ALL OVER THE PLACE? IT HAS TO BE HERE. THE ROOT OF THE PROBLEM IS HERE, AND THAT'S WHERE THE CORRECTION STARTS."

(These readings really scared me and I had entertained the thought of moving somewhere else, far away.)

Laura: "How do I prove that there's biological warfare being created in Hawthorne, and do I even need to prove it? I mean, I just can't go making those kinds of accusations without proof."

<u>MEDIUM:</u> "THE PEOPLE KNOW IT. THE PEOPLE ALREADY KNOW IT. THIS ISN'T ANYTHING THAT YOU NEED TO PROVE. ALL I'M DOING FOR YOU IS PUTTING IT ALL TOGETHER."

"THE GUY THAT WROTE ABOUT AREA 51, DID HE PROVE EVERYTHING? BUT THEN IT CAME ABOUT. ALL THE CHANNELING THAT NOSTRADAMUS DID, IT CAME ABOUT LATER. ALL OF THIS IS LATER. THAT'S WHY THIS INFORMATION IS BEING CHANNELED. THAT'S WHY IT IS LIKE IT'S COMING THROUGH. THAT'S WHY YOU'RE HAVING TO...THESE ARE MY EXACT WORDS...BECAUSE IT IS CHANNELED. HAVE YOU READ THE JANE ROBERTS BOOKS? IT'S KIND OF THE FORMAT THAT THIS IS GOING END UP IN."

<u>Laura:</u> "No, I'm not familiar with her. Is it channeled?"

<u>MEDIUM:</u> "YES."

(Seth is a spirit who spoke through the author Jane Roberts, and is considered one of the greatest spiritual teachers of

our time. The Seth books were first published in the late 1960's.)

"I'M SEEING A MAN. I'M SEEING HIS OUTLINE. OKAY, NOW WHAT HE DID, HE JUST CAME OVER, AND YOU CAN PUT THIS IN THERE...HE JUST CAME OVER AND HIT MY TABLE, AND IT BOUNCED AND MY SAGE WENT ALL UP IN THE AIR. YOU KNOW HOW IT'S VERY POWDERY? IT'S JUST SAGE THAT I'VE BEEN USING FOR MANY SPIRIT CONNECTIONS, SO THIS IS LIKE CONNECTION AFTER CONNECTION, SO THE ENERGY IS IN THIS. AND HE HITS THIS AND IT PUFFED EVERYWHERE AND SAID, 'I'M GOING TO DO THIS!' WITH DETERMINATION. 'THE MAIN THING THAT NEEDS TO BE SUNK INTO EVERY SINGLE HUMAN BEING, IS THAT THIS IS NOT OKAY! NOT ON ANY LEVEL, NOT ON ANY LEVEL!'" (THE PRESIDENT)

(THE WIRY ONE) "I HAD ALL THE PROBLEMS THAT I HAD BECAUSE I AM VERY GIFTED. I DID WHAT I WAS SUPPOSED TO DO. I WASN'T SUPPOSED TO BE SPENDING A LOT OF TIME FOR MYSELF. AND I'M STILL THE SAME. I'M NOT SPENDING TIME FOR MYSELF. I WAS A PERSON WITH A

BODY THAT DIDN'T NEED A BODY. THE BODY, INSTEAD OF BEING HELPFUL TO ME, IT WAS A NUISANCE TO ME. I WAS MORE IN THE MIND IN CONNECTION. I ALWAYS SAW FUTURE. THAT WAS HOW I WAS ABLE TO INVENT."

"THAT'S WHAT I'M PUTTING OUT HERE FOR YOU TODAY, FOR THE WORLD TODAY. THIS IS NOT SOMETHING THAT I AM DOING FOR MYSELF. OR THAT I DON'T WANT TO DIE ON A PHYSICAL LEVEL. I COULD CARE LESS ABOUT THE EXISTENCE OF THAT AREA. I DON'T QUESTION IT. I KNOW THAT IT'S THERE AND I KNOW WHERE I'M GOING. SO THAT'S NOT AN ISSUE. I'M NOT IN THE PLACE THAT YOU ARE, TRYING TO LOOK FOR THE NEXT KISS, OR HOW MY STEP IS GOING TO BE STRIDE IN THE NEXT MOMENT, OR IF MY CHILD IS GOING TO LOVE ME, OR IF I'M EVEN GOING TO HAVE ONE. THOSE ARE THINGS THAT NEED TO BE CHANGED WITHIN EACH ONE OF YOU."

"AND WHEN YOU DO THIS, YOU'RE GOING TO SEE YOURSELF BLOOM INTO WHAT YOU WANTED ANYWAY. THE ONLY THING IS, YOU DO IT IN A SELFLESS WAY. BUT IT WILL HAPPEN. YOUR DESTINY IS ALREADY MAPPED OUT.

IT'S JUST HOW DEEP YOU WANT TO ENGRAVE IT, AS TO HOW IT'S ALL GOING TO PAN OUT."

"PRINCESS DI TRULY WANTED TO HELP THE WORLD. IN ALL HER GRACE, SHE TRULY WANTED TO HELP THE WORLD. THE CAR SHE WAS IN WAS MANIPULATED IN A WAY TO KILL HER. BUT IT WAS BECAUSE SHE WANTED TO HELP THE WORLD. AND AS SHE WANTED TO HELP THE WORLD, GREAT THINGS STARTED HAPPENING TO HER. THAT'S THE SAME THING I'M TALKING ABOUT WILL HAPPEN TO EACH AND EVERY ONE OF YOU. SHE DIDN'T GO DOING IT FOR THE REASON THAT IT TURNED OUT. SHE'S AN EXAMPLE OF WHAT I JUST EXPLAINED TO YOU...GO BACK AND READ IT AGAIN. IF YOUR HEART SO NEEDS, THAT YOUR HEAD AND YOUR MIND DIDN'T PUT IT INTO UNDERSTANDING."

"THERE'S A BOY. HE'S SHOWING ME A BOY. HE'S GOT HIS TROUBLES, AND IT'S OF THE SAME NATURE. SO IT HITS HIGHS AND LOWS. THIS IS GENERATIONS DOWN. SO IT'S IN YOUR '80'S, AND THIS WAS THE BEGINNING OF THE PROBLEMS. LATE '80'S, EARLY '90'S. IN THE LATE 80'S, YOU HEARD ABOUT IT. IN THE '90'S, EVERYBODY WAS LOOKING

AROUND. NOW EVERYBODY'S PULLING THEIR HAIR OUT. THEY'RE GOING TO LOOK LIKE ME IF THEY KEEP ON...A BUNCH OF WIRY ONES. WHEN HE SAID THAT, HIS EYES GOT REAL BIG, AND I FELT LIKE MY EYES WERE OUT OF SOCKET OR SOMETHING."

"HE'S SENDING A LOT OF PEACE AND JOY. NOT TO WORRY. AS THE WORDS GO ON THE PAPER AND THE WORDS PENETRATE THE EYES AND TOUCH THE BRAIN, THAT'S WHAT NEEDS TO BE."

"ALL OF YOU THAT ARE NOT AUTISTIC, YOU DO NEED TO DEVELOP YOUR PSYCHIC SO THAT YOU CAN TUNE IN TO YOUR CHILDREN, TAKE CARE OF THEM, CUZ THEY ARE YOUR FUTURE. IT'S GOING TO MULTIPLY. YOU THINK IT ALREADY HAS, AND IT WILL SOME MORE."

Laura: "How do we stop it?"

MEDIUM: "IT BEGINS WITH THIS MATERIAL, BECAUSE EVERYONE IS TAPPING INTO THE WRONG AREA."

"ORGANIC GROWN ON THE TOP SOIL, WITHOUT A BUG POISON? YOU THINK A BUG POISON IS GOING TO KILL YOU LIKE THIS OTHER STUFF IS GOING TO DAMAGE YOU? YOU'RE NOT A BUG. YOU ARE NOT AN INSECT. THINK PEOPLE!"

"HE'S SHOWING ME ALL THE DIFFERENT KINDS OF ANIMALS, LIKE COW, AND I SAW LAMB, AND LOOKING AT THE BEEF AND THE LAMB. IF IT'S GROWN ON HIGH GROUND, IT'S SAFER. THE HIGH GROUND BEEF. IF YOU HAVE A MOUNTAIN, AND YOU HAVE YOUR WINDS AND THE DUST, AND THEY DON'T HIT THE TOP OF THE MOUNTAIN, THOSE ANIMALS ARE EATING THE PURITY OF WHAT'S GROWING THERE. BECAUSE NOT ALL WIND HITS THE TOP OF EVERY MOUNTAIN AND CONTAMINATES IT. SO SEEKING TO RAISE ANIMALS ON HIGHER GROUND IS HELPFUL. BUT CHECK YOUR WINDS. THERE ARE MEASURES THAT ONE CAN TAKE TO NOT CONSUME CONTAMINATION. I'M NOT TALKING FOR INSECTS; I'M TALKING FOR HUMAN BEINGS. PAY ATTENTION PEOPLE!"

(TO LAURA) "WHAT DO YOU HAVE ON YOUR EAR? HE'S LOOKING AT YOUR EAR."

Laura: "My earrings? Fleur de lis."

MEDIUM: "HE WAS LOOKING AT YOUR EAR. HE'S LOOKING AT ALL OF YOUR...HE'S PAYING ATTENTION TO THIS ON AN ENERGETIC LEVEL. NOT AS LOOKING WITH HIS EYES. HE SAYS 'CUZ I HAVEN'T GOT A HOLD OF YOU' IS WHAT HE'S TELLING ME, LIKE GOTTEN IN TRANCE WITH ME TO USE MY EYES. SO HE'S LOOKING AT THE STONES ON AN ENERGY LEVEL. PEOPLE, YOU DO NEED TO KNOW THAT STONES DO MAKE A DIFFERENCE IN YOUR LIFE. IT'S A VIBRATION. YOU VIBRATE DIFFERENT IN DIFFERENT AREAS. PUTTING STONES AROUND YOU BRINGS THOSE AREAS TO YOU THAT YOU CAN'T GO TO, OR BE AT. SO LITTLE PIECES OF STONES ARE GOOD."

Laura: "Which ones?"

MEDIUM: "THOSE THAT YOU HAVE ARE GOOD FOR YOU. BUT THEY'RE BITS AND PIECES. YOU'RE NOT DRAGGING

YOURSELF DOWN, OR CHANGING YOUR ENERGY COMPLETELY. SO YOU'LL NOT WEAR THAT ALL THE TIME. YOU'LL FIND THEM AGAIN ON YOU AT EASTER. IT'S LIKE ON THE HOLIDAYS, YOU'RE ATTRACTED TO THEM. PUTS YOU IN A DIFFERENT VIBRATION."

"SOON I'LL BE PUTTING WORKERS WITH THE CHILDREN. THE SO-CALLED MUMMY CHILDREN. THE ONES WHO ARE LOCKED UP WITHIN THEMSELVES. WE'RE NOT TALKING ABOUT ALL THE CHILDREN THAT HAVE ALL THESE DIFFERENT THINGS. WE'RE TALKING ABOUT THE CHILDREN OF THE ERAS OF THE LATE 80'S... THE ONES NOW THROWN INTO THE CATEGORY OF AUTISM. BUT THE ONES IN REALITY ARE THE SO-CALLED AUTISTIC. AND WE'LL REFER TO IT AS THE SO-CALLED AUTISTIC BECAUSE SO MANY OF YOU ARE IN DENIAL THAT YOUR CHILD IS IN THAT GROUP. AND THEN OTHERS OF YOU JUST THROW YOUR CHILD INTO THE GROUP BECAUSE YOU DON'T WANT TO DEAL WITH IT. SO BEFORE ANY OF THIS IS APPLIED, THE DIAGNOSIS WILL HAVE TO BE MADE CORRECTLY."

<u>Laura:</u> "So 'autism' is the mummified children? The ones that were okay and now they're not okay."

<u>MEDIUM:</u> "THOSE ARE THE ONES THAT WE ARE TALKING ABOUT. SOLELY THE ONES. THE ONLY ONES."

<u>Laura:</u> "Regressive autism."

<u>MEDIUM:</u> "NONE OTHER...THIS IS NOT GOING TO HELP ANYONE ELSE. (POINTS TO THE SERUM ON THE BLACKBOARD) THIS IS VERY SPECIFIC. BUT THIS IS HITTING MULTITUDES, AND MULTITUDES, AND MULTITUDES OF HUMAN BEINGS, AND IT STARTS WITH LITTLE SOULS AT A VERY YOUNG LEVEL."

"YOU PEOPLE WERE SUPPOSED TO DEVELOP YOUR PSYCHIC, BUT NOT BE FORCED INTO IT THIS WAY. TALK TO THESE CHILDREN. DO DEVELOP; BE ABLE TO COMMUNICATE WITH THEM. SO THAT WHEN THEY'RE TAKING OVER, AND THEY'RE DOING WHAT THEY'RE DOING, THEY CAN APPLY THEMSELVES IN WHAT THEY DO. AND THEY WILL BE WAY

BEYOND WHEN THEY MANIFEST THEMSELVES IN THEIR TRUE BEING."

"WHEN THIS (THE DUST) ENTERED THE BODY, IT ENTERED THE NOSE, WENT TO THE BRAIN, DOWN THE BACK OF THE NECK...NEURO...AND THEN A WRAPPING, EMBRACING, LAYERS AND LAYERS AND LAYERS. AND THEN A LITTLE FIGHTING AGAINST IT...AND THEN A CLAIM OF NORMALCY. BUT IT'S NOT NORMAL. BUT THE YOUNG SOUL, HOW DOES IT KNOW? IT ACCEPTS, AND THEN IT'S AFRAID. IT LIVES IN FEAR. THE YOUNG CHILD LIVES IN FEAR. IT'S REACTING TO WHAT IT'S FEELING, BECAUSE THEN THE PARENT STARTS PROJECTING FEAR, AND THEN THE CHILD LIVES IN FEAR."

"AND 95% OF THE PARENTS SPLIT UP. SO THIS IS CAUSING A HIGH RATE OF DIVORCES. SO WHEN THE SOLUTION COMES TO THIS PROBLEM, IT'S GOING TO SOLVE OTHER AREAS. AND ALL THESE PEOPLE NEED TO TAKE A SECOND LOOK AT THEMSELVES; WHAT THEY HAVE DONE. WHAT THEY HAVE DONE TO THE CHILDREN AND THE ONES THAT THEY IN THEIR HEART LOVED, AND DO LOVE. AND WORE

OUT THE SOLE OF THEIR SHOE...AND THERE IS PHYSICAL RUNNING."

Laura: "Uh-huh."

(I was crying because I was divorced from my children's father at the time of this reading because of autism.)

"HE (THE PRESIDENT) JUST WENT LIKE THAT AGAIN (HIT THE TABLE), AND MY SAGE JUST POOFED ALL OVER THE PLACE. AND HE SAID, 'THIS WILL BE! THIS WILL CHANGE!'"

Laura: "God I hope so."

MEDIUM: "THERE'S ALSO ABANDONMENT... TOTAL ABANDONMENT BY BOTH PARENTS. BY ***BOTH*** PARENTS!"

"HOW ARE YOU DOING LAURA? DO YOU HAVE ANOTHER QUESTION?"

Laura: (Fighting back tears) "OK. How do I talk to my son if he just screams? How do I get in his head?"

<u>MEDIUM:</u> (HER VOICE CHANGES TONE AND CADENCE, IDENTIFIED LATER AS THE PRESIDENT) "HOW DO YOU TALK TO THESE CHILDREN IF THEY ARE SCREAMING? HOW DO YOU GET IN THEIR HEAD, YOU ASK?"

1. "YOU START PROJECTING LOVE. SIMPLY, MENTALLY. NO TOUCHING. LET THE CHILD EXIST IN THEIR COCCOON, IN THEIR MUMMIFIED BEING."

2. "OFFER A BATH. MAKE IT ALL SENSUOUS. BUT THIS IS JUST TO CALM. THE SMELLS...ALL OF THAT. BECAUSE THE COMMUNICATION PROCESS IS VERY DIFFERENT WITH THESE PEOPLE, WITH THESE CHILDREN, NO MATTER WHAT THEIR AGE IS."

3. "LISTEN, AND NOD YOUR HEAD. SPEAK SOFTLY WHAT YOU HAVE TO SAY. NO DIRECTION, NO DISCIPLINE. JUST BE. THEN YOU CAN START ALL OVER WITH THIS PERSON. WITH THIS CHILD. NO MATTER WHAT AGE THEY ARE. THOSE ARE YOUR STEPS IN ORDER TO START THEM ALL OVER AGAIN TO BE."

"MENTAL TELEPATHY AND YOUR PSYCHIC, THOSE ARE ALL THINGS THAT HAVE TO BE DEVELOPED. IT'S ANOTHER LANGUAGE. IT'S NOT ABOUT DEVELOPING IT, AND IT'S NOT SOME TYPE OF GIFT. IT'S JUST A LANGUAGE THAT YOU'RE LEARNING. AND YOU HAVE TO LEARN IT FOR THE SAKE OF COMMUNICATION."

Laura: "How does someone develop it that who has no clue? Where do you go?"

MEDIUM: "YOUR PSYCHIC IS ALREADY THERE. YOU JUST HAVE TO PAY ATTENTION TO IT AND TRUST. AND AS YOU PAY ATTENTION TO IT AND TRUST MORE AND MORE, YOU'LL SEE EXACTLY WHAT WORKS FOR YOU. YOU HAVE TO SEEK KNOWLEDGE. KNOWLEDGE IS NOT JUST GOING TO BE IMPLANTED IN YOUR HEAD. AND IT IS NOT A GOOD THING TO LIVE IN STUPIDITY. YOU HAVE TO SEEK KNOWLEDGE AND IT'S GOING TO BE THERE FOR YOU, BUT YOU HAVE TO SEEK IT OUT. YOU'VE GOT TO READ IT. THERE IS NO EXCUSE TO NOT HAVING KNOWLEDGE. THE VOLUMES ARE OUT THERE. IT'S INEXCUSABLE. AND DIFFERENT THINGS

ARE GOING TO WORK FOR DIFFERENT ONES OF YOU. SO YOU WILL FOLLOW YOUR PATH."

"AND WHEN YOU'RE DOING IT TO COMMUNICATE WITH THESE SOULS, THE MAJORITY OF THEM ARE EITHER YOUNG CHILDREN RIGHT NOW, OR YOUNG ADULTS. BECAUSE WE ARE TALKING ABOUT THE LATE 80'S...THERE ARE VERY FEW THAT ARE THE OLDER ONES. BUT IT WAS BECAUSE THEY HAD VERY LOW, LOW, LOW IMMUNE SYSTEMS. AND SOME OF THOSE THAT HAD THAT LOW IMMUNE SYSTEM, HAVE OTHER THINGS GOING ON TO WHERE THEY DON'T EVEN TRY TO TAP INTO THAT AREA OF THEIR LIFE. BUT TO TEAR IT DOWN, AND ATTACK IT? THAT'S NOT USING YOUR WISDOM."

"YOU'VE GOT TO PUT IT ALL TOGETHER PEOPLE! YOU HAVE TO PUT IT TOGETHER. YOU ARE GOING TO MAKE THE CHANGES. AND YOU START WITH YOURSELF AND YOUR LOVED ONES."

"TAKING ON A BIG BROTHER OR BIG SISTER POSITION SO THAT THEY CAN GO BACK TO THOSE PARENTS AND SEE

HOW HELPFUL IT HAS BEEN TO BE AROUND THE TYPE OF PEOPLE THAT ARE KNOWLEDGEABLE. AND WHEN THEY SEE CHANGE IN THEIR CHILDREN, THEN THEY'LL BE ADDED TO YOUR GROUP. SO THAT'S THE WAY TO REACH OUT AND SEND OUT THAT INVITATION, IS BY THOSE ORGANIZED PUTTING THEMSELVES OUT THERE AS BIG BROTHER AND BIG SISTER. AND THEN WHEN IT'S PROVEN TO THE PARENT OF THE CHILD, BECAUSE THEY SEE RESULTS, THEN THEY TOO WILL SEEK OUT TO BE A BIG BROTHER AND BIG SISTER. THEY TOO WILL SEEK OUT TO FUND AND SPREAD THE WAYS TO CHANGE AND HELP EACH OTHER."

"THERE'S TOO MANY. THERE'S TOO MANY THAT ARE BEING HARMED. YOU CAN NO LONGER SHUT YOUR EYES, BECAUSE NO MATTER IF YOU SHUT YOUR EYES, YOUR MIND KEEPS WORKING."

"SO YOU CAN'T TURN YOUR BACK TO THESE PEOPLE. ESPECIALLY THOSE THAT ARE NOT PUT INTO OFFICE BY THE PEOPLE. WHAT WOULD HAPPEN TO PLACES THAT ARE RULED BY HEIRS? SOME CONTROLLING MANIAC

CONTROLLING THE CHILD THAT CAN'T BE STILL. THAT CANNOT RULE. WHAT WILL HAPPEN TO COUNTRIES?"

"HE'S SAYING DO NOT ALLOW TO BE STUDIED BY GARY SCHWARTZ. NEITHER OF YOU."

Laura: "Why not?"

MEDIUM: "THIS IS NOT SOMETHING THAT HE NEEDS TO PROVE. THIS IS NOT SOMETHING THAT NEEDS TO BE WRITTEN ABOUT BY HIM. CAN YOU IMAGINE GOING OUT AND FINDING PEOPLE WHO ALREADY ARE DOING THE RIGHT WORK; AND THEN HE CHOOSES TO TEST THEM, AND GLORIFY HIMSELF? AND THAT'S WHAT THIS IS ABOUT FOR HIM. HE WILL BE COMING TO YOU AND DO NOT ACCEPT BECAUSE THAT LOSES FOCUS ON WHAT YOU'RE DOING."

(MEDIUM'S WORDS) "THAT WASN'T THE WIRY ONE. I DON'T KNOW WHAT THE HECK WAS GOING ON."

Laura: "Gary Schwartz studies mediums, he wrote *The Afterlife Experiments.*"

MEDIUM: (MEDIUM'S WORDS) "I KNOW HE DOES. OK, BACK INTO IT."

(THE PRESIDENT) "SO, THIS GROUP...THE BIG SISTER, BIG BROTHER GROUP THAT IS GOING TO BE THE TECHNIQUE TO DRAW MORE TO THE GROUP...AND THESE CAN BE SET UP THROUGHOUT THE WORLD SO THAT THERE CAN BE PROOF OF THE CHANGES OF THESE CHILDREN. THE TECHNIQUE OF USING PSYCHIC FOR COMMUNICATION. THIS IS AN OUTREACH PROGRAM, AND THE STEPS, GOING THROUGH THE LITERATURE, AND GOING THROUGH THE WORDS, AND INFORMING YOURSELF AS TO WHAT'S GOING ON HERE WILL BE YOUR BASIS OF YOUR BEGINNINGS. AND THIS IS SO THAT THOSE CHILDREN CAN BE REACHED OUT TO BECAUSE MANY DON'T EVEN GET THE SIMPLE ACKNOWLEDGEMENT OF WHAT'S GOING ON WITH THEM. THAT WAY, IF THERE'S AT LEAST ONE PARENT LEFT IN THE SITUATION, THAT PARENT CAN BE HELD ONTO."

"THEY'LL FEEL A LITTLE HEAVENLY ABOUT IT BECAUSE THEY WILL BE EXERCISING THEIR PSYCHIC ABILITIES AND

FEEL LIKE IT'S A GIFT. BUT OUR OBJECTIVE HERE IS TO HELP THOSE CHILDREN, TO HELP OUR FUTURE. IT'S NOT ABOUT THE BIG HEAD THAT'S ACQUIRED. BUT WE'LL NOT CARE ABOUT THAT. JUST SO THAT WE DO OUR PART. RECOMMENDING THE PEOPLE THAT ARE DOING IT FROM KNOWLEDGE INSTEAD OF FROM CIRCUMSTANCE. AND THAT'S WHAT YOU CAN INCORPORATE FROM USING ALL THE DETAIL. GO BACK AND READ AGAIN IF YOU HAVE TO. BUT YOU CAN INCORPORATE ALL OF THESE THINGS AND THEN DRAW IN THE PARENTS, AND SAVE FAMILIES. IT DOES NOT MATTER IF THEY FEEL THAT THEY ARE DOING IT FOR THEMSELVES, BECAUSE IN THE LONG RUN, IT'S ABOUT OUR FUTURE."

"THE SELFLESS ONES ARE THE ONES THAT ARE SETTING UP THE BEGINNING. THE ONES THAT ARE STAGING THIS. IT IS YOU, IT IS YOU."

Laura: "Me?"

MEDIUM: "EVERYONE READING THE BOOK. EVERYONE THAT IS INCORPORATING THESE TECHNIQUES. EVERYONE THAT

IS GOING THE MEASURE. EVERYONE THAT IS COMING TO THE ORGANIZATIONS THAT ARE GOING TO BE SET UP. AND YEAH, YOU'LL BE SETTING ONE UP. ALL THE WORDS THAT ARE COMING THROUGH ARE FOR THE READER. SO IF YOU READ THE BOOK...YES, YOU! AND GOOD QUESTION. YOU PUT IT DOWN JUST LIKE THAT; ALL OF IT."

(MEDIUM'S THOUGHTS) "I FEEL THE PRESIDENT...I SAW THE CHAIR...I FEEL THE PRESIDENT. HE'S SAYING, 'YEAH, IT'S ME.'"

Laura: "Welcome back."

MEDIUM: (MEDIUM'S WORDS) "I FEEL LIKE ALL THAT WAS THE PRESIDENT. THAT WAS THE PRESIDENT FROM...REMEMBER WHEN I TOLD YOU THERE WAS SOME KIND OF CHANGE, AND I THOUGHT THAT MAYBE IT WASN'T THE WIRY ONE? THAT WAS THE PRESIDENT. CUZ IT SWITCHED OVER AT SOME POINT, AT SOME POINT THERE WAS A SWITCH."

"I FEEL A PUSHING OVER HERE. I JUST FEEL A PUSHING (TO HER SIDE). I JUST FEEL ENERGY RIGHT HERE. THE ENERGY THAT I FEEL WITH THE PRESIDENT, THE WAY THAT HE IS...IT'S LIKE HE DOESN'T LIKE TO TOLERATE THINGS. I HAVE A MAN OF ACTION HERE. I HAVE SOMEONE THAT DOESN'T LIKE IGNORANCE. THAT WILL GET IN YOUR FACE. THAT WILL GO DOWN, AND THEN HE'LL SLAP HIMSELF FOR DOING SOMETHING WRONG. SO, HE'S VERY...HE WILL JUDGE HIMSELF, BUT HE WON'T JUDGE OTHERS. HE'LL PUT HIMSELF RIGHT OUT THERE. SOMETIMES HE DOES NEED A NUDGE OR TWO. STRONG, STRONG PERSONALITY, VERY STRONG-WILLED. A MAN OF ACCOMLISHMENT. INTOLLERANT. IT MAKES ME ANGRY WHEN PEOPLE DON'T TRY TO DO THEIR BEST. IT'S JUST HARD TO UNDERSTAND WHEN PEOPLE ARE JUST SITTING THERE WASTING LIFE...LIKE THEY'RE JUST GOING TO LOOK AT A BUTTERFLY? WHAT ARE THEY DOING? THERE IS SO MUCH OUT THERE. HOW CAN SOMEBODY SIT WITHIN THEIR FOUR WALLS AND NOT...HE SAYS, 'I'LL BE BACK, I'LL BE RIGHT BACK.' HE JUST LEFT."

(MEDIUM'S WORDS) "I JUST DON'T GET ANYTHING. OH, THAT WAS WEIRD. I DON'T GET ANYTHING. HOLD ON, LET ME SEE. I JUST FELT LIKE, LAURA, I'M ME...I'M JUST HERE."

(CD ends)

***

Later Discoveries

The Wiry One had mentioned in one of the readings that he would be the main one with us for the first five readings, and then someone else would step in. This was the sixth reading, and it was The President that stepped in more. I also believe that it was The President that hit the medium's table twice and said with determination "I'm going to do this! This is not okay on any level!" The second time he said "This will be! This will change!" The voice and demeanor were different from The Wiry One. The being from another planet also stepped in, which was strange, but I am not questioning it. It was sometimes confusing to know who was delivering the messages.

One morning, just as I was waking up, the idea popped in my head to look into the Big Brothers, Big Sisters program and The President from the readings. This happens to me a lot, even in the middle of the night. I get prompted or inspired, and I keep a notebook by my bedside to write these thoughts down. It is a form of automatic writing. I did a little research on it, and I found out on their website that in 1934, The President and his wife became patrons of Big Brothers and Big Sisters Federation. Wow! It was told in the readings that there would be a program like this started for children with autism, incorporating elements from this material. Now this reference made sense.

I also found out that there is an Institute bearing his name. On its website, it told his life story, and not surprisingly, he was a disability advocate because of his struggle with polio. He created what became the March of Dimes, which "provided the millions of dollars needed to fund the long, difficult, and ultimately successful search for a polio cure. On April 12, 1955, on the tenth anniversary of (The President's) death, Dr. Jonas Salk announced that a polio vaccine he had developed was now ready for use by the general public. Five years later, Dr. Albert Sabin announced the development of the oral vaccine."[49] No wonder he came through and talked about the polio vaccine and its involvement in causing Multiple Sclerosis! I saw a lot of parallels with this book and The President's legacy: looking for a cure for a disease, advocating for the disabled, his history with The Wiry One, and his involvement with biological warfare during his Presidency. Now I understood even more why he was coming through in the readings to help in this situation.

Personal Discoveries

After this reading I decided to look at Trevor's vaccination history, and was mortified! I discovered that not only did Trevor have the MMR vaccination at age one, he had a SECOND one at age four; four months after we had moved to Reno, NV. We were right in the epicenter of the creation of the biological warfare when he received his second MMR. It was given to him on September 5, 2002. It was still production time then according to the information given during the readings. Production didn't stop until October and throughout the winter months. I always

[49] http://feri.publishpath.com/disability-advocate

thought that Trevor got worse after we moved to Nevada. He talked less, and screamed more, and was sick all the time. I wondered if that second MMR shot made it worse, even though he was already "contaminated."

Next, I looked at Trevor's baby book, which I stopped writing in because it got to be too depressing. It is a five-year record of early childhood. The saddest part was what I had written in the "sayings" part for each year. My First Birthday sayings were: "mama, dada, car, dog, what's that? (While pointing)." He started walking and talking at nine-months-old. He pointed to Sesame Street characters and named them; he also pointed to colored crayon stickers on his wall and named them. My Second Birthday sayings read: "not much- you do everything you can to not talk, like opening the refrigerator yourself, and then tagging someone until they follow you. He said less at two than at one! My Third Birthday sayings read: "Very little decipherable, cho-ah-ooh, cha-whey-whey. You count to 20 a lot and say some of the alphabet. You have your own language that you babble all day. My Fourth Birthday sayings was left blank. It must have been too hard for me to face, watching my once-happy, bright baby regress before my eyes.

Thimerosal

Shortly after this reading, January 8, 2008, there was an article in the LA Times that caught my eye. The headline was "Mercury's removal doesn't stop autism's rise, study shows." I read on: "The prevalence of autism in California children continued to rise after most vaccine manufacturers started to remove the mercury-based preservative thimerosal in 1999, suggesting that the chemical was not a primary cause of the disorder, according to a study released Monday." The analysis found that from 2004 to 2007, when exposure to thimerosal dropped significantly from three to five year olds, the autism rate continued to increase in that group from 3.0 to 4.1 per 1,000 children.[50]

It was all coming together, like the pieces of a puzzle. There was a link to a vaccine, but it was not the preservative (thimerosal) that was causing autism, as the message in the reading clearly stated. No one was seeing the whole picture here. The truth needed to be told.

---

[50]Chong, Jia-Rui, "Mercury's removal doesn't stop rise autism's, study shows," *Los Angeles Times,* (January 8, 2008).

If you notice, there is a six month gap between this reading on Dec. 17, 2007 and the next one, June 5, 2008. The main reason for that is that the medium was getting scared. She thought that someone was going to come after her for exposing the truth. I was scared as well, but I had a living reason to continue to seek more information; my son. I contacted her numerous times to get together. Finally, she agreed to get together again.

***

CHAPTER SEVEN

MEDIUM: "OKAY, TODAY IS JUNE 5, 2008, AND LAURA AND I ARE HERE TO MAKE A CONNECTION FOR THE BOOK. RIGHT NOW, WE ARE JUST CALLING IT 'THE MUMMY' AND WE ARE TAKING UP FROM WHERE WE PREVIOUSLY LEFT OFF. HERE WE GO LAURA, LET'S SAY A PRAYER AND GET STARTED. WE ARE SEEKING ASSISTANCE, CHANNELED THROUGH ME."

"HERE WE GO. (SHE SAYS A PERSONAL PRAYER.) I ASK FOR THE HIGHEST AND BEST SPIRITS TO COME THROUGH NOW. WOW...OKAY...RIGHT NOW I'M FEELING...INSTEAD OF MY SPIRIT CONTROL COMING THROUGH, I ALWAYS FEEL LIKE HE'S HERE, BUT I FELT ALL THESE OTHER ENERGIES. AND I HAVE NOT FELT THEM SINCE THE LAST TIME THAT WE MET TO PUT THIS BOOK TOGETHER (SIX MONTHS AGO)."

"I KNOW THE WIRY ONE IS HERE, AND I WANT TO SAY THE PRESIDENT, BUT I ALSO SAW SOME OTHER PEOPLE. THERE

ARE SOME OTHER MEN. I DON'T SEE FEMALES, WHAT I AM SEEING ARE MEN. I SEE MALES."

"AND ALL OF THE SUDDEN, I SAW SOME WRITING ON THE CHALKBOARD. HE JUST WENT (MAKES A SCRIBBLING MOTION WITH HER HAND). HE JUST WENT (PICKS UP CHALK AND SCRIBBLES ON OUR CHALKBOARD) JUST REAL QUICK; HE JUST DID SOME WRITING ON THE CHALKBOARD. I JUST SAW THE VISION OF THAT."

"I LIKE TO CALL HIM 'THE WIRY ONE' AND FOR SOME REASON, HE LIKES TO BE CALLED THAT. 'IT'S ME' HE SAYS, 'IT'S ME. IT'S WHO I AM. BECAUSE I LET GO OF MYSELF, I WAS ABLE TO DO ALL THAT...I AM GENIOUS, I AM GENIOUS.' HE FEELS LIKE HE HAS EVERY RIGHT TO, AND HE DOES. HE DOES, BECAUSE IN THE EYES OF HUMANITY, THEY'VE SHOWN HIM THAT. AND SINCE HE'S BEEN IN SPIRIT, HE KNOWS OF THIS. ONLY THEY STILL NEED ME, AND THAT'S WHY I AM TRYING TO HELP AGAIN. BUT I ALWAYS COME IN BIG SPURTS IN THE HELP THAT I GIVE HUMANITY. IT'S IN THINGS THAT REALLY MAKE A DIFFERENCE."

"AND HE'S SAYING THAT ALL HIS HELP WITH AUTISM IS GOING TO MAKE A DIFFERENCE BECAUSE IT'S HITTING IN A BIG WAY. PEOPLE DON'T KNOW WHAT TO DO ABOUT IT. SOME PEOPLE THINK THAT THEY CAN'T DO ANYTHING ABOUT IT. BUT YOU HAVE TO GET TO THE CENTER OF IT, TO THE NUCLEUS, TO ITS ORIGIN. THAT WAY YOU CAN SUPPRESS THE ATOMIC EXPLOSION THAT CAN COME WITH IT. AND IT'S NOT IN A WAY OF BATTLE. BECAUSE IT COULD BE WORSE. BUT WE ARE GOING TO TURN THAT OFF. WE ARE GOING TO TURN THAT LIGHT OFF. WHEN YOU GIVE SOMETHING LIGHT, IT HAS LIFE, AND THAT'S WHY HE'S SAYING HE'S GOING TO TURN THE LIGHT OFF, BECAUSE HE'S GOING TO TAKE THE LIFE OUT OF THAT. WHAT'S GOING TO HAPPEN WITH AUTISM IS NOT ABOUT A CURE; IT'S ABOUT ELIMINATION, STOPPING IT COMPLETELY. KILLING IT. TURNING THE LIGHT OFF, SO IT HAS NO LIFE. I (THE MEDIUM) ASKED, 'SO HOW DO YOU DO THAT?' AND HE SAID, 'YOU'LL SEE.'"

"I (THE MEDIUM) ASKED HIM WHY WE SKIPPED FOR SO LONG, AS TO DOING THIS WORK, COMMUNICATING, AND

PUTTING ALL OF THIS TOGETHER, AND I JUST SAW HIM STUMBLING AND TRIPPING. AND I ALSO FELT A SENSE OF HIM PREPARING. SO I DON'T KNOW IF HE'S REALLY PREPARING HIMSELF, OR HE'S PREPARING THE SCIENTISTS, THE WIRY ONES."

"OKAY, HE SAYS HE'S PREPARING AND I SAID TO HIM, 'ARE ALL OF YOU SCIENTISTS WIRY LOOKING LIKE THAT?' AND HE SAYS THAT THEY GET SO INVOLVED WITH WHAT IT IS THAT THEY'RE DOING THAT THEY DON'T FEEL LIKE SPENDING TIME ON THEMSELVES. THEIR TIME IS SO VALUABLE THAT THEY DON'T INVEST IN THEMSELVES AS FAR AS WHAT THEY LOOK LIKE. THERE WASN'T AN INTEREST THERE. IT'S JUST THAT TIME IS SO VALUABLE THAT IF YOU ADD UP ALL OF THE MOMENTS THAT YOU TAKE FOR YOU TO LOOK LIKE YOU DO; IT'S JUST TOO MUCH VALUE IN TIME TO A SCIENTIST. THEY BECOME THAT WAY IS WHAT HE'S SAYING. AND THAT'S WHAT HAPPENED TO HIM. SO YES, A LOT OF VERY GOOD SCIENTISTS OUT THERE...THE ONES THAT LOOK LIKE THAT, THOSE ARE THE ONES THAT ARE GOOD, IS WHAT HE'S SAYING. BECAUSE

THEY VALUE THEIR TIME SO GREATLY THAT IT'S NOT IN THEMSELVES."

"I (THE MEDIUM) JUST FEEL MY HEART POUNDING. I JUST FEEL LIKE I'M GOING BIG AND LITTLE, BIG AND LITTLE. I JUST FEEL THE ENERGY OF...THIS IS A DIFFERENT PERSON. MY TEETH DOWN AT THE BOTTOM FEEL LIKE THEY ARE BARELY ATTACHED. YOU KNOW, THEY'RE VERY SEPARATED, AND THE ATTACHMENTS ARE LIKE MAYBE REMOVING A COUPLE OF TEETH, AND SPREADING THE REST OF THEM OUT. AND YOU KNOW HOW YOU WOULD HAVE GAPS? AND I JUST FEEL LIKE MY TEETH ARE NOT VERY STRONG, AND IT IS ON THE BOTTOM. AND I FEEL LIKE THE PERSON HAS COLOR, DARK COLOR. SO EITHER THEY'RE SOME KIND OF AFRICAN, I DON'T KNOW, THEY'RE BLACK, BECAUSE I AM SEEING THE EYEBROWS NOW, AND THEY'RE NAPPY. YOU KNOW THE NAPPY HAIR. WHAT I'M PICKING UP HERE IS, THERE'S THIS MAN, HE IS BLACK, OR AFRICAN, THAT SORT OF LOOKING TYPE OF AN INDIVIDUAL."

"AND THIS MAN, I DON'T FEEL CAME TO FAME, BUT HE WAS CONSULTED WITH BY SOME WELL KNOWN INDIVIDUALS

THAT HAD TO DO WITH SCIENCE. SO, THIS MAN IS VERY SAVVY, BUT HE DIDN'T GET TO BE KNOWN BECAUSE OF HIS ORIGIN. AND GOING BACK INTO THAT TIME, HE WOULD BE SOMEONE THAT SOMEHOW GOT INVOLVED AS A HELPER. HE HAS A VERY STRONG MIND, SO HE GOT INVOLVED FURTHER, THE ONLY THING WAS, HE COULDN'T...IT WAS LIKE HE WAS SUPPRESSED AS FAR AS...HOW COULD HE KNOW ANYTHING? HE'S THE WRONG COLOR. BUT HE'S HERE TO HELP US WITH ALL THIS."

"OH, HE (THE WIRY ONE) WROTE SOME MORE STUFF. IT LOOKED LIKE ONE OF THOSE...HE DID THAT REAL QUICK. IT ALMOST LOOKED LIKE A MUSIC NOTE. LIKE A...YOU KNOW HOW... (DRAWS A SQUIGGLE MARK ON THE CHALKBOARD) BUT IT'S THIS, MORE OF THAT. I AM GOING TO KEEP THIS CHALK IN MY HAND, BECAUSE HE DID IT SO FAST."

"HE NEEDS TO...(ADDRESSES HIM) 'OKAY, IF YOU ARE GOING TO SEND ME IMAGES ON THE BOARD, YOU'RE EITHER GOING TO HAVE TO MAKE MY HAND WRITE THEM, OR YOU'RE GOING TO HAVE TO LET ME SEE THEM LONGER.' IT WAS A FLASH, LIKE A FLASH THAT HE JUST DID."

(LAURA BROUGHT HER VIDEO CAMERA ALONG THAT DAY, AND SHE TURNS IT ON AND VIDEOTAPES WHAT HAD BEEN WRITTEN ON THE CHALKBOARD.)

"THE REASON THAT HE DID THAT...HE SAYS THAT HE WAS HAVING ME TALK TO THIS OTHER FELLA AND THEN HE JUST SLIPPED RIGHT ON IN THERE BECAUSE IF HE DOES THAT TO ME, HE'S SAYING IT IS GOING TO BE CLEARER, BECAUSE I DON'T HAVE TIME TO THINK ABOUT IT, AND THAT'S WHAT HE WANTS. VERY, VERY CLEAR. HE DOES NOT WANT ME IN ANY WAY TO BE ANALYTICAL OF WHAT'S TRANSPIRING IN THIS WHOLE SITUATION."

(THE WIRY ONE) "YOU KNOW, I USED TO JUST GO TO SLEEP AT TIMES. AND THEN I'D HAVE A WAKING MOMENT, AND I HAD ASTONISHING IDEAS. AND IF I FOLLOWED EVERY ONE OF THEM, I'D FINISH NOTHING. SO WHAT I STARTED DOING WAS ATTACHING MYSELF TO DIFFERENT PEOPLE SO THAT THEY KEPT COMING BACK TO ME, AND I'D GET COMPLETION OF WHAT I'D STARTED. OTHERWISE, I'D BE ALL OVER THE PLACE. NOT THAT I WOULD BE...I WAS. AND

THERE'S SO MANY THINGS THAT I STILL HAVE TO EARTH WITH WHAT'S COMING. (THE MEDIUM SAYS, I WAS ASKING HIM, 'WHAT DO YOU MEAN, TO EARTH?') AND HE SAYS, 'WHAT DO YOU WANT ME TO DO? TO HEAVEN IT?' I WAS LIKE, 'IT KIND OF DOESN'T MAKE SENSE.' AND HE SAYS A LOT OF IT DOESN'T MAKE SENSE BECAUSE IT IS NOT UNDERSTOOD."

"IT'S LIKE US GETTING USED TO THAT, SO THAT WE CAN DECIPHER WHAT HE'S TRYING TO...IF I DON'T BRING YOU ALL THE INFORMATION THAT I HAVE ATTACHED WITH ALL OF THIS, IT WILL BE WORSE. YOU WON'T MAKE SENSE OF IT AT ALL. AND IT'S GOT TO HAVE ENOUGH IN ORDER FOR YOU TO HAVE UNDERSTANDING. WHAT I AM DOING IS LEADING UP TO WHAT YOU NEED."

"HE DID THIS... (DRAWS 3 VERTICAL MARKS ON THE CHALKBOARD CLOSE TOGETHER WITH A DIAGONAL LINE ACROSS IT) AND HE SAID 'TREE', HE SAID 'TREE.' AND I SAID IT DOESN'T LOOK LIKE A TREE, AND IT'S NOT THREE. (VIDEO CAMERA TURNS ON). AND HE JUST WROTE 3 LINES

AND PUT A LINE ACROSS IT. SO, TREE, TREE IS WHAT HE WAS SAYING."

"THIS IS NOT A NUMBER; THIS IS SOME KIND OF SYMBOL THING. THIS IS NOT A NUMBER; THIS IS A 2, 8, AND A CIRCLE AND SOME KIND OF SYMBOLISM. THIS DOESN'T GO THERE." (ERASES SOMETHING AND DRAWS MORE ON THE BOARD.)

"HE'S SAYING, 'I'M ALRIGHT, I'M ALRIGHT, I'M ALRIGHT.' BECAUSE ALL OF THE SUDDEN HE JUST FELT VERY STRANGE, AND I WAS ASKING HIM 'WHAT'S UP WITH YOU, WHAT'S GOING ON?' AND IT'S JUST, 'I'M ALRIGHT, I'M ALRIGHT.' I FEEL LIKE HE'S REALLY EXERTING HIMSELF TO MAKE ME MOVE, SO YOU KNOW HE SAYS IT'S NOT THE SAME WHEN SOMEBODY STARTS...THAT I'M SAYING WHAT I'M HEARING...BECAUSE WHAT THEY'RE DOING, THEY'RE MAKING ME HEAR, BUT WHAT HE'S DOING IS MAKING ME HAVE MOVEMENT, SO THAT'S TAKING A DIFFERENT APPROACH, IT'S A DIFFERENT THING THAT HE'S DOING. HE SAYS HE'S OKAY. HE SAYS, 'I'M OKAY' (SHE IMITATES HIM

FALLING OVER DIZZY AS HE SAYS IT) THE MEDIUM LAUGHS AND SAYS, 'HE DOESN'T LOOK TOO GOOD.'"

(THE MEDIUM SAYS TO THE WIRY ONE) "OK, WELL, WE DON'T HAVE TO WRITE SO MUCH, JUST TALK TO ME."

"HE SAYS THE WRITING IS VERY IMPORTANT. HE SAYS THAT THE WRITING IS VERY IMPORTANT, AND HE'S ALSO TELLING ME THAT ALL OF THIS (WHAT'S WRITTEN ON THE BOARD) IS IN THE MIDDLE OF WHAT'S NOT FILLED IN. (CAMERA TURNS BACK ON) HE SAYS THAT WHEN THIS IS A FINAL THING, THIS IS GOING TO HAVE THINGS THAT GO HERE (POINTS IN BETWEEN THE WRITTEN ITEMS) AND THINGS THAT GO HERE (POINTS LOWER ON THE BOARD). IT WILL BE SEVERAL THINGS THAT GO...BUT THESE ARE FILLERS. IT'S LIKE PUTTING A PUZZLE TOGETHER BUT WE'RE PUTTING THINGS IN THAT...HE ALREADY KNOWS THE WHOLE THING, IT'S JUST LIKE GIVING US A PIECE OF THE PUZZLE AND STICKING IT THERE, STICKING IT HERE, STICKING IT THERE; BUT IT WILL ALL BE PART OF A WHOLE. A WHOLE THING. AND HE'LL HAVE HIS SIGNATURE, OKAY. (SHE DRAWS A DIAGONAL SIGNATURE AT THE

BOTTOM RIGHT CORNER OF THE CHALKBOARD). HE'S SHOWING ME A BUNCH OF BUBBLES AND AS WE ARE DOING ALL OF THIS, THIS IS LIKE A POPPING, A POPPING OF BUBBLES. SO THIS IS JUST A LOT OF PIECES."

"YOU KNOW THE WIRY ONE WAS KIND OF A FUN PERSON ON HIS OWN, BECAUSE HE DOES HIS LITTLE DANCE. HE DOES HIS LITTLE DANCE. IT JUST FELT GOOD ALL OF A SUDDEN. I FEEL LIKE HE'S RECOUPING FROM...IT'S NOT THAT I'M RECOUPING, IT'S THAT I'M FIGURING IT OUT, HOW IT IS TO DO WHAT I NEED TO DO WITHOUT DEPLETING MY ENERGY. SO I'M GETTING HELP FROM OTHERS HERE SO THAT I CAN BECAUSE THERE'S MORE THAN ME THAT WANT TO DO THIS PROCESS."

"SO, LAURA WHAT I'M PICKING UP FROM THIS, IS WHEN HE SAID THAT, IS THAT HE'S DRAWING SOME KIND OF ENERGY FROM OTHERS SO THAT HE DOESN'T HAVE THIS 'I'M ALRIGHT, I'M ALRIGHT,' AND IT LOOKS LIKE HE'S ALMOST GOING TO PASS OUT. WHAT HE'S GOT GOING ON HERE IS PHYSICAL PHENOMENON, AND THAT IS WHY YOU'RE HERE WITH THAT CAMERA. BECAUSE OF THE

PHYSICAL PHENOMENA THAT IS COMING TO PASS THAT YOU'RE SUPPOSED TO BE CAPTURING."

<u>Laura:</u> "I knew that I had to bring this today."
(I woke up the night before with an "inspired" thought to charge and bring the video camera, and brought it just in case.)

<u>MEDIUM:</u> "HE'S ACKNOWLEDGING THE CHAIR (A SWIVELING CHAIR THAT THE MEDIUM WAS SITTING ON) AND THE MOVEMENT, HE LIKES IT. I FELT LIKE HE WAS IN MY BODY, AND HE WAS JUST MOVING THE CHAIR AROUND, AND I SEE IT FLIPPING UPSIDE DOWN. SO, HE'S FLIPPING IT UPSIDE DOWN TO LOOK AT THE CONSTRUCTION. (THE MEDIUM ASKS HIM, 'SO DO YOU NOT SEE ALL OF THIS STUFF WHILE YOU'RE OVER THERE?') HE SAYS HE DOES, BUT NOT LIKE WHAT HE HAS BEEN."

"AND YOUR KIDS ARE GOING TO BE OKAY! IT'S JUST TAKING SOME PERSISTENCE ON THE PARTS OF EACH ONE OF US. AND I'VE GOT THE PERSISTENCE, AND I KNOW THAT YOU DO AS WELL. BECAUSE OF THE VALUE OF WHAT'S IN

IT FOR EACH INDIVIDUAL THAT EMBRACES THIS INFORMATION."

"HE'S SHOWING ME VISIONS OF THE EARTH. I'M SEEING THE GROUND AND I'M SEEING THE TOPSOIL, AND ALL THAT HE'S TALKED ABOUT BEFORE, WHAT I'VE TOLD YOU...THE CONTAMINATION. AND GETTING IT IN THE HANDS, AND IT PENETRATING THROUGH THE SKIN, AND EVEN THROUGH THE OPEN AREAS LIKE THE NOSE AND THE MOUTH. BUT YOU NEED TO KNOW THAT IT'S EVEN THROUGH THE SKIN. AND THESE CHILDREN NEED TO GET WASHED!"

"THERE ARE PREGNANCIES...THERE ARE PREGNANT WOMEN WORKING OUT THERE."

Laura: "Where they're making it?"

MEDIUM: "MMM-HMMM. THAT HAVE NOT BEEN SENT HOME YET."

Laura: "Will that affect their babies in utero?"

<u>MEDIUM:</u> "IN A WORSE WAY. SO THAT WILL ALL BE INCORPORATED, BUT THOSE, I WILL NOT BE ABLE TO REPAIR BECAUSE THAT'S GOING TO BE PHYSICAL, PERMANENT PROBLEMS THAT THEY WILL HAVE TO BE CHALLENGED WITH THROUGHOUT THEIR WHOLE LIFE. I FEEL GREAT PAIN IN THE JOINTS. MY FINGERS ARE THROBBING. THROBBING PAIN OF THE JOINTS, AND HE STOPPED...NOW HE DID IT AGAIN. EACH FINGER, THE ATTACHMENT IS THROBBING. ALONG WITH THE WHOLE MIND, IT SPARKS, BUT IT'S SPARKING...THE WAY THE BRAIN IS WORKING, IT'S SPARKING, PROCESSING, BUT IT'S ALL OVER THE PLACE. IT'S LIKE IT'S NOT CONNECTING WITH THE RIGHT LITTLE CONNECTORS FOR YOU TO BE ABLE TO UNDERSTAND. IF THEIR LEFT BRAIN, RIGHT BRAIN...IT MAKES A DIFFERENCE ON THE HAND THAT THEY ARE HAVING THE JOINT ISSUES WITH. AND IT'S NOT DOWN HERE (POINTS TO WHERE THE PALM MEETS THE FINGERS), IT'S THESE, THE TOP (POINTS TO FINGERTIPS) THE TOP JOINTS, IT'S NOT THESE JOINTS (THE LOWER ONES)."

"AND SO THAT YOU CAN UNDERSTAND WHAT WE'RE TALKING ABOUT HERE, PUT YOURSELF IN THE DENTIST'S CHAIR. AND THEY GIVE YOU A SHOT, AND THEY NUMB HALF OF YOUR MOUTH, AND IT'S EXACTLY....AND HOW DO THEY DO THAT? OKAY, THAT SIDE GETS NUMB, THEN IT'S EXACTLY...AND IT WILL BE RIGHT DOWN SMACK IN THE MIDDLE OF YOUR TONGUE. SAME THING WITH YOUR FINGERS. THAT'S WHY IT'S THIS JOINT ONLY (FINGERTIPS) AND NOT DOWN HERE (LOWER JOINTS). YOU WOULD THINK THAT IT WOULD BE EVERY BONE, EVERY JOINT, BUT IT HAS TO DO WITH THOSE TOP ONES."

"HE'S TALKING ABOUT PECANS? PECANS, PECAANS (PRONOUNCES IT TWO DIFFERENT WAYS). IT'S A THEORY OF SOMEBODY WHO SOUNDS LIKE A PECAN...PECAAN. I DON'T KNOW, IT HAS TO DO WITH THEORY, AND HAS TO DO WITH PECAN. THE WIRY ONE IS GIVING YOU A JOB. HE'S TELLING YOU SOMETHING ABOUT PECAN, OR PECAAN, AND I THINK JOHN. I SAW JOHN. AND IT HAS TO DO WITH THEORY. I HEAR 'MASTERMIND.' BUT IT ALL FITS TOGETHER. IT'S LIKE, YOU TAKE THIS (POINTS TO THE CHALKBOARD), AND YOU TAKE THAT THEORY, CUZ YOU

HAVE TO BRIDGE IT, YOU HAVE TO DECIPHER WHAT I'M DOING. THIS IS FAR MORE ADVANCED. BUT THIS IS WHAT YOU NEED TO GET TO, BUT YOU HAVE TO BUILD A FOUNDATION OR YOUR HOUSE FALLS DOWN."

"I'M NOT GIVING YOU THE FOUNDATION; I'M GIVING YOU THE ANSWER. SO, THE FOUNDATION, YOU CAN PRODUCE IT...YOU'RE AT THAT LEVEL...THIS IS THE PART YOU'RE GOING TO NEED (POINTS TO THE CHALKBOARD). AND THIS IS WHAT THIS IS ALL ABOUT, BECAUSE THIS IS THE PART THAT YOU PEOPLE CANNOT FIGURE OUT."

<u>Laura:</u> "Is he alive or deceased...Pecan?"

<u>MEDIUM:</u> "I SEE HIM WALKING ON THE EARTH, BUT I'M NOT SURE, OKAY? I SAW THE WORLD AND I SAW HIM WALKING."

"OKAY, LAURA, THIS IS FOR YOU...HE SAYS DON'T GET BEHIND ON YOUR TRANSCRIBING. AND I SAID TO HIM, 'WELL, IT'S NOT LIKE WE'RE IN A BIG HURRY TO DO THIS' AND HE SAID, 'YES, YOU ARE! TELL HER NOT TO GET

BEHIND ON THE TRANSCRIBING!' BECAUSE I SAID TO HIM, 'I'M STILL WORKING ON THIS OTHER THING, AND HE TOLD ME (SHAKING A FINGER AT ME) 'DON'T GET BEHIND ON THE TRANSCRIBING.' BUT I WAS KIND OF REJECTING AND SAYING, 'BUT...BUT...BUT' AND HE SAYS, 'NO BUTS.'"

Laura: "It's done so far."

MEDIUM: "DIFFERENCE....DIFFERENCE...ALL OF THIS IS MAKING A BIG DIFFERENCE...IS, IS, IT IS. WE'RE NOT ***TRYING*** TO DO SOMETHING. WE ***ARE*** DOING SOMETHING. THERE IS NO TRY HERE. YOU DON'T UNDERSTAND, THIS ***IS*** WHAT'S HAPPENING."

"AND HE'S SAYING THAT IT'S GOING TO BE INDIVIDUALS THAT ARE GOING TO BE BACKING THIS THING UP THAT ARE GOING TO BE EXPOSING DIFFERENT AVENUES IN DIFFERENT AREAS OF WHAT'S BEEN GOING ON BECAUSE OF THE EFFECT THAT IT'S HAVING ON THEM AND THEIR OFFSPRING...OR FRIENDS OR FAMILY'S CHILDREN."

(MEDIUM'S WORDS) "I WAS ASKING HIM IF THIS WHOLE THING HAS TO DO WITH...OKAY, YOU KNOW THE PERSON THAT WE SAW ACTUALLY WORKING WITH THIS, A FEMALE THAT WAS PREGNANT, AND THE SEVERITY OF WHAT'S GOING ON WITH THE MUMMY THAT'S BEING CREATED WITHIN HER. AND SO I ASKED IF THIS SOMETHING THAT'S INCORPORATED IN THESE PEOPLE'S BODIES AFTERWARDS THAT THEY GET OUT OF THAT ENVIRONMENT AND THEY GO OFF TO OTHER PLACES AND HAVE CHILDREN, IS IT GOING TO AFFECT THE CHILDREN THAT THEY HAVE?"

"AND THE ANSWER TO THAT IS THAT IF THEY EXTERNALLY CLEAN, THERE WON'T BE A PROBLEM. BUT IF THEY DO NOT EXTERNALLY CLEAN, THEN THE PROBLEM OCCURS, BECAUSE IT HAS TO DO WITH CONTAMINATION."

"SO, LET'S SAY THAT YOU HAVE A CHILD, AND YOU GET THEM VACCINATED OR THEY COME DOWN WITH A HIGH FEVER BECAUSE OF A COLD, OR ANYTHING THAT DROPS THEIR IMMUNE SYSTEM DOWN WITH FEVER. THEN, LET'S SAY YOU HAVE A JACKET THAT WAS CONTAMINATED, AND

YOU HAVE IT THERE, AND YOU PLACE THE CHILD THERE ON THE JACKET...THERE YOU HAVE IT (AUTISM). SO IT DOESN'T TAKE A LARGE AMOUNT OF THIS CONTAMINATION."

"SO IT IS NOT SOMETHING THAT IS GROWING AND EXISTING WITHIN A BODY. IT IS NOT SOMETHING THAT A CHILD THAT IS AUTISTIC IS GOING TO HAVE ONE. IT'S NOT ABOUT THAT; IT'S ABOUT CONTAMINATION THAT ATTACKS WHEN THE IMMUNE SYSTEM IS DROPPED WITH FEVER."

"AND THE THING ABOUT IT IS THAT PEOPLE KEEP THINGS. THEY'LL KEEP BAYONETS, THEY KEEP THINGS THAT THEY BRING BACK THAT THEY HAD IN THE MILITARY AND THEY DON'T SANITIZE THEM. SO THEN YOU HAVE A CONTAMINATED OBJECT, AND KIDS LOVE TO TOUCH EVERYTHING. SO IF IT'S LOW DOWN...YOU HAVE THAT ITEM OF REMEMBERANCE OR WHATEVER IT IS, YOU NEED TO HAVE THAT AWAY FROM THE YOUNG ONES. FROM ONE END OF THE SPECTRUM TO THE OTHER. SO WE'RE NOT

JUST SAYING THAT ONLY PART OF A SECTION HAS TO DEAL WITH THIS. BUT IT'S ALL BECAUSE OF MILITARY."

"BUSH KNOWS...HE KNOWS...AND KEEPS GOING, AND DOESN'T BLINK AN EYE...HE KNOWS."

"THIS IS WHAT HE (THE WIRY ONE) DID...I (THE MEDIUM) SAID, 'YEAH, BUT HE'S FROM TEXAS (BUSH) AND I'M FROM TEXAS, SO I ASKED, WHAT ARE YOU DOING?' AND HE (THE WIRY ONE) JUST SHOOK HIS HAIR, AND HE HAD HIS HANDS ALL OVER IT AND HE JUST WENT INTO SOME KIND OF TIZZY. I THINK HE WAS GOING TO THROW A FIT...I DON'T THINK HE LIKES TO BE QUESTIONED. THE WHOLE ANXIETY THING THAT JUST HAPPENED WITH HIM, THAT HE MADE ME FEEL...HE JUST DID THIS (SHE PUTS THE CHALK DOWN AT THE BOTTOM OF THE BOARD) HE JUST DID THIS...I WANT TO STOP, IS WHAT HE DID, AND HE SAID I WANT TO STOP. I JUST SAW A VISION OF HIM, AND HE JUST PUT THE CHALK DOWN, AND HE SAID I WANT TO STOP. I WANT TO STOP."

(THE WIRY ONE) "I HAVE A LOT OF HELP HERE IN SPIRIT, I HAVE ALL MY FRIENDS, AND I HAVE A LOT OF PEOPLE THAT HAVE THE SAME INTERESTS. A LOT OF THE PEOPLE HERE WITH ME HAVE TO DO WITH THESE CHILDREN. A LOT OF THEM, IT'S THEIR FAMILY. THEY'RE JUST, PER SE, AN AUDIENCE, BUT I HAVE UTILIZED ALL OF THAT TO BE ABLE TO KEEP MY ABILITY TO CREATE MOVEMENT. THIS IS THE FIRST DAY THAT HE'S DONE THIS."

"I JUST FEEL HIM GOING LIKE THIS, JUST GOING LIKE THAT, (MESSES UP HER HAIR) A LOT OF...HE DOESN'T KNOW, HE'S JUST MESSING WITH HIS HAIR. I'M PICKING UP THAT THAT'S SOMETHING THAT HAPPENED TO HIM BEFORE HE GOT GREAT INSIGHTS...BECAUSE HE WAS PUTTING HIMSELF INTO SOME KIND OF ZEN STATE...A PROCESS OF CLARITY. HE SAYS, 'IT'S WHAT I DID...IT'S WHAT I DID...SO ALL THE THINGS THAT YOU CALL REMARKABLE IN MY WORK...I INDUCED IT IN THAT WAY. BUT AT TIMES, PEOPLE FOUND ME CRAZY...BUT WHO'S TO SAY THAT ALL OF YOU ARE NOT THE CRAZY ONES?'"

"HE LIFTS HIS LEGS UP (SHE IS SITTING DOWN, AND ELEVATES AND CROSSES HER LEGS), AND HE TALKS ABOUT HOW HE LOVED LIFE, HE LOVED LIFE...MY LIFE...AND I CREATED FRIENDS THAT WERE SPECIAL TO ME."

"I JUST SEE HIM GO LIKE THAT...AND HE GOES LIKE THIS TO THE CHALK (PUSHES IT AWAY), SO HE'S LEAVING IT, BUT HE JUST TOUCHES THE BOARD...AND HE'S DOING A LITTLE DANCE. I CAN NOT EVEN MIMIC HIM. HE'S JUST DOING THIS... AND IT'S HIS DANCE, HIS LITTLE DANCE."

"HE JUST TOLD ME TO GET UP. OKAY, LAURA, THIS IS FOR US. HE SAYS THAT HE'S VERY APPRECIATIVE ABOUT WHAT IT IS THAT WE'RE DOING. THIS IS OF GREAT VALUE. THIS PART OF IT (THE CHALKBOARD) IS NOT FOR US, IT'S FOR THE WORLD. IT IS OF GREAT VALUE, AND THERE ARE MORE SOULS THAT ARE GOING TO BE INVOLVED IN THIS WHOLE SITUATION."

"AND HE'S SHOWING ME LIKE YOU WOULD SEE AN EXPLOSION, BUT NOT THE EXPLOSION ITSELF, BUT THE PART WHERE IT'S ONLY MOVEMENT IN THE ENERGY, WHERE

IT LOOKS INVISIBLE. HE'S NOT SHOWING ME THE EXPLOSION; HE'S SHOWING ME THAT ENERGY, THAT VIBRATION MOVING SO FAST THAT IT MOVES ENERGY. IT'S MOVING THE VIBRATION DIFFERENTLY TO WHERE WE SEE IT WITH THE NAKED EYE, AND THEN THAT WILL BE CAPTURED."

"I (THE MEDIUM) SAID, 'I THOUGHT YOU WERE DONE? BUT I DON'T FEEL HIM LEAVE. I FEEL THAT ENERGY.' I SEE HIM LIKE THIS, BUT HE'S GOT SOMETHING HOLDING HIM UP. HE'S TELLING ME HE'S NOT WRITING ANYTHING DOWN, AND FOR ME NOT TO LET ANY OF THAT GET ERASED. YOU KNOW HOW BEFORE WE ERASED THAT CORNER? OR TRIED TO, AND HE'S WRITTEN SOMETHING ELSE THERE?"

Laura: "Yeah."

MEDIUM: "HE SAID, 'DON'T LET THAT GET ERASED.' SO, THIS IS PART OF THE MIDDLE OF..."

Laura: "You just re-wrote everything that was there before."

<u>MEDIUM:</u> "I DON'T KNOW..."

<u>Laura:</u> "It looked just like that. You erased it last time, and drew it back on."

<u>MEDIUM:</u> "HE SAYS, 'THAT'S NOT TO BE ERASED.' SO IT'S WHAT IT IS RIGHT NOW, BUT IT'S LIKE A PUZZLE BECAUSE THIS IS NOT FILLED IN...THIS IS NOT FILLED IN (IN BETWEEN THE SYMBOLS). AND I STARTED TO PUT MY HAND ON THE (CHALK)...AND HE SAID, 'NO.' THERE ARE SOME OTHER THINGS THAT YOU NEED TO KNOW BEFORE I KEEP WRITING. BECAUSE ALL OF THIS IS GOING TO BE SIGNIFICANT AS TO THE INFORMATION THAT'S COMING THROUGH VERSUS WHAT INFORMATION YOU HAVE HERE."

"SO THIS (VIDEO) RECORDING IS GOOD, BECAUSE IT WILL BE EASIER TO PUT TOGETHER. THIS DOESN'T HAVE TO DO WITH THE BOOK, BUT IT MAY HAVE TO DO WITH...NOT MAY...IT HAS TO DO WITH THE PERSON THAT WORKS ON IT, TO WHERE, WHEN THEY COME FOR MORE INFORMATION, THEY'LL WANT THE ORIGINAL, BECAUSE THEY'LL BE ABLE TO PIECE IT."

(THE DVD ENDED ON THE VIDEOCAMERA LAURA WAS USING)

Laura: "Hold that thought."

MEDIUM: (MEDIUM'S WORDS) "I AM NOT HOLDING A THOUGHT...I AM OUT OF IT...I DON'T FEEL ANYTHING, LAURA."

Laura: "He's waiting for me to open this...I need to get longer ones."

MEDIUM: "NO, I THINK WE'RE DONE. I THINK WE'RE DONE. THE THING (TIMER) SAYS WE HAVE 15 MORE MINUTES, BUT I THINK WE'RE DONE. I AM NOT CONNECTED. 'YOU'RE NOT GOING TO FIX IT' IS WHAT I HEARD."

(CD ends)

***

We talked for a while after the session about the significance of the video recordings, and the medium voice recorded this following bit of clarifying information that she felt during the session:

<u>MEDIUM:</u> "OKAY NOW, YOU KNOW HOW I WAS WRITING SOME THINGS, AND THEN THINGS THAT WERE BEING SAID HAD TO DO WITH WHAT WAS BEING WRITTEN, SO THAT THERE WOULD BE AN UNDERSTANDING OF THAT. AS FAR AS HAVING THAT WHOLE THING THERE, WHAT I WAS PICKING UP WAS THAT THE WHOLE THING WILL BE IT, BUT IN ORDER FOR THEM TO FIGURE OUT WHAT IT IS...OKAY, THEY ARE GOING TO SEE THIS (THE CHALKBOARD), AND THEY ARE GOING TO READ IN THE BOOK, AND SEE THIS (THE CHALKBOARD), AND READ IN THE BOOK. WHAT'S GOING TO BE HAPPENING TO THEM, FROM WHAT I WAS FEELING IS THEY ARE GOING TO HAVE TO PLAY IT, AND LOOK AT THIS AND SEE HOW IT WORKS. AND ALL THEY ARE GOING TO HAVE ARE THE WORDS IN A BOOK AND THIS, AND THEY ARE GOING TO HAVE TO READ, AND

FIGURE OUT WHERE WHAT PART OF THIS GOES. SO, YOU VIDEOTAPING SOME OF THIS...THE PERSON ACTUALLY WORKING WITH THIS...THIS WILL DO THEM GOOD. THE OTHER PEOPLE READING ABOUT IT...YOU KNOW, THEY SEE IT, AND THEY ARE..."

Laura: "It's not for them"

MEDIUM: "YOU'RE RIGHT, IT'S NOT FOR THEM."

Laura: "It's for the scientists."

MEDIUM: "AS FAR AS PUTTING IT TOGETHER, BECAUSE THAT'S WHAT'S GOING TO HAPPEN TO THEM, THEY'RE GOING TO BE READING THE BOOK, AND LOOKING AT THIS, AND IT'S GOING TO BE LIKE HAVING TO MATCH WHERE IT ALL FITS TOGETHER. AND THAT CAME TO ME IN THAT WHOLE THING, BUT I DON'T THINK THAT I EXPRESSED MY OWN UNDERSTANDING OF WHAT I WAS HEARING."

***

Later Discoveries

The medium made copies of both the audio CD and DVD recordings for me, and I picked them up from her house a few days later. I took them home and watched the video. The most amazing thing, aside from the obvious; was that the chalkboard doodles from six months earlier looked exactly the same as what the medium drew in its place this time! I was taking notes during our earlier session, and had drawn a picture in my notes of what the medium had drawn on the chalkboard. So even though she erased it, I had a picture of it in my notes. When I got to the part in the DVD of the new chalkboard drawing, I paused it and went to get my notes from my bedroom. I was absolutely floored! They were identical!

For the medium to draw the same sequence, including unfamiliar mathematical symbols six months later, was proof to me that something phenomenal was happening. Plus, the medium is in a trance-like state during this whole process and doesn't really remember much afterward. It's not like she memorized the sequence of numbers and symbols before erasing it to prove to me later that she was really getting this information from spirit. I already trusted that. It was just pretty amazing for me to see it in person.

Underground Proof

As I was watching the video, I received a text message from a friend and he asked me what I was doing that night. I said I was staying in because I had to work the next morning. (I was single at this time.) He said that if I wanted to meet him to watch a band, he'd send a limo to my house to pick me up and take me back home. I thought he was kidding, and texted him back to say I was ready and gave him my address. Then I didn't hear from him. Half an hour later, a limo was at my house. I told him to give me ten minutes to change, asked my mom if she would watch the boys, and we were off. There had to be a reason this was happening, I reasoned. I never had a limo pick me up at home before.

The limo driver walked me in to where my friend was, at a club inside a big casino in downtown Reno. He introduced me to the two people he was with, a younger girl and a man who appeared to be in his upper 40's. My friend told me that the man was a retired senator or congressman, I don't remember which, and that it was his limo that picked me up. I don't want to give his name and put him in any danger. There was a fun band playing 80's rock in the bar. The guy in his 40's asked me to go dance with him to "Pour Some Sugar on Me" by Def Leppard.

After dancing, we went back to the bar where the other two were, ordered a drink and started chatting. I asked him what he did for a living. He said that he was retired. He seemed so young to be retired, so I asked him what he did with all of his free time. He said that he traveled a lot. I asked him what his favorite place was that he's ever been, expecting him to name some exotic island. He answered, "Hawthorne." I almost spit out my drink, and asked, "Hawthorne, Nevada?" "Yes," he replied. "Why Hawthorne?" I asked. "A relative of mine lived there when I grew up; I love that place and I used to go there a lot." I asked him if he had ever been on the military base. He said, "Yes." Fishing for information, I asked if he had ever been in the underground part, and he replied, "Yes." I fished some more, "Really? In the ammunition bunkers or in the underground city part?" He replied, "I was in the underground city; I was taken on a tour down there years ago when I worked for the government."

I couldn't believe it! I just received validation that the underground city existed, and that this former high-ranking government employee had been taken on a tour there for some reason! Not wanting him to be suspicious of my odd line of questioning, I said, "I just can't believe that Hawthorne is your favorite place. That town gives me the creeps when I drive through there." Then, like a phantom, he disappeared. He must have had the limo take him home. I ended staying with the other two for a few hours and then took a cab home because we couldn't find the limo. It was well worth the $40 cab fare. That was definitely the reason I was there that night. I documented it when I got home so I wouldn't forget.

Underground Bases

I still felt that I needed more information about the underground base in Hawthorne, NV; the place where all of this was supposedly being made and decided to do some research. Now, I was never a conspiracy theorist, but let me tell you, after a little research, I am quickly becoming one. I used to roll my eyes at people who thought our government was doing all these secret things behind our backs. I had more important things to spend my energy on, like taking care of two children, for instance.

But, I did find some very convincing things that backed up a lot of what was brought through in these readings. Bear down.

Since I didn't personally know anyone who worked in the alleged underground base in Hawthorne, I tried to find people online who had. The most incredible story has to be that of the late Phil Schneider. He was a former government geologist and structural engineer with 17 years experience working in government "Black Projects." He claims that he helped build deep underground military bases or as he called them D.U.M.B. bases, both in the U.S. and worldwide, and that he co-invented methods used in shaped charge explosives to facilitate the building of the underground bases as well as submarine bases. He worked in the underground bases at Area 51, S-4, and Los Alamos. He had a level 3 security clearance (Rhyolite 38). In 1995, after he quit his job, he broke his military security oaths and went on a lecture tour, exposing what the U.S. Government was hiding.

Phil Schneider claimed that there were 131 underground bases in the U.S., 129 of them fully operational, and 1200 underground bases worldwide. They are an average of a mile deep, and they are about the size of a medium-sized city. He said that in 1995, 28%

of the Gross National Product of the U.S. was spent building them, financed through the "Black Budget," which is hidden from Congressional view and oversight, and can't be audited by the U.S. Treasury System. It is totally illegal. He also said that he helped build the tunnels for the magnetic levitation (maglev) train system that connected the bases underground, and reached speeds up to mach two. (There has been an above ground maglev train in operation in Japan since 2003.)

Now, this next part gets a little weird, but there's a reason I've included it. He talked about a lot of government cover-ups, including the "alien agenda." He was one of only 3 survivors of the infamous alien/human war at the Dulce, NM underground base where 66 government agents and workers lost their lives in Aug. 1979. He is missing 3 fingers on his left hand from this encounter, clearly visible if you watch his lectures.

Thirteen attempts were made on his life in 1995 as he was lecturing about the subjects. He promised in his last lecture in Nov. 1995 that his soon to be released book would contain the latitude and longitude for each of the 131 underground bases. Phil Schneider died in Jan. 1996, found in his apartment, strangled to death by some type of cord. It was called a "suicide." Kind of hard for a guy missing three fingers on one hand, and limited shoulder mobility, dying of cancer. He had told friends and relatives that if he ever "committed suicide" they would know he had been murdered. According to his ex-wife, all of his lecture materials, photographs, alien metals, and notes for his book were missing from his apartment, while everything else of value was still there. Yet, his death was never investigated and his blood and urine samples from the autopsy were "missing." Very suspicious. You can see some of his lectures and more on his memorial site, www.philschneider.org. Shocking, to say the least. I lost a lot of sleep around this time researching all of this.

Phil Schneider's story was of particular interest to me because he helped build the underground bases. He described how they were built with great detail. He said that to create the D.U.M.B. bases, they use explosives to hollow out the base, then a plasmic laser machine melts or defragulates the rock to an extremely fine powder, melts it, and then sticks it on the walls as a coating. There is nothing to take out, it is vaporized. They have been building them day and night unceasingly since 1940. They used to use boring machines and drill down, during WWI, and

WWII, those machines are now obsolete. The new machines have been around for 25 years (in 1995) and drill up to 7 miles a day.

He said that initially, underground facilities were built in case of nuclear attack so that the President and other government officials could go down there and survive. Now, there is a different agenda for them. He said that the bases are used strategically by different military organizations; the Army, Navy and Air force. Half of them are used as research and development labs, and the other half, he claimed, are used to house aliens. I don't know if I believe all of that or not, but one thing he said was of interest to me. He said in one of his lectures that "the military is involved in building biological weapons out of alien body byproducts." Creepy, yes; true, who knows?

I also heard him talk about the ventilation systems in the underground bases in one of his speeches. He said that there are air vents coming from the base that are sometimes visible outside on the side of the mountain that the base is build under. This was of interest to me because they said in the readings that the biological warfare "dust" that they are creating in Hawthorne is getting into the air and is blowing around the country, and that they are being sloppy. So my guess is that the dust is coming out through the ventilation system, as it did in the Sverdlovsk anthrax leak in the Soviet Union in 1979.

Since Phil Schneider died in 1996, and had already retired from the military, he may not have known about what was supposedly going on in Hawthorne, NV. In the readings, it was stated that the biological weapons associated with autism had been in production there for the past 11 years (in 1997). Which means it began in 1996, the year Phil died. In his lectures Phil mentions a book that came out that year by Richard Sauder, PhD, called *Underground Bases and Tunnels: What is the Government Trying to Hide?* He said it would back up what he's saying.

I started to look up information on Richard Sauder. Since then, he wrote another interesting book called *"Underwater and Underground Bases."* He's really done his homework and is the leading researcher in this area. I urge you to look at the information and decide for yourself. You can watch his You Tube presentation from the first X-Conference in 2004, and listen to interviews with him on Coast to Coast radio with George Noory. He has lots of documents that are in the public domain, such as patents and military contracts. He also claims there are over 131 underground military bases in the U.S.

He talks about the underground maglev trains, connecting the bases and knows people who claim to have been on them. He discusses the compartmentalization of the military and the "need to know" basis of information, security clearances and oaths, and how information is concealed from anyone who doesn't "need to know." He calls them clandestine operations and talks about a "black world" in which trillions of U.S. taxpayer dollars are unaccounted for and can be used for these types of operations. It all matches the description given in our readings of how the military people in Hawthorne don't always know what they are doing, they are just following orders. The truth, as they say, is out there, it is just piecing it all together.

Another interesting person I found was John Lear, the son of the Lear Jet creator. He is a former CIA pilot, with more accomplishments and accolades than I can name. According to Mr. Lear, there is an underground U.S. Navy submarine base in the Nevada desert, at the Hawthorne Army Depot to be exact. There is even a sign posted on the base that reads "Naval Undersea

Warfare Center." He claims that there are deep underground tunnels that lead to and from the Pacific Ocean from Hawthorne. There is an eye-opening thread on the Above Top Secret website about it. You can also go to You Tube and watch the numerous interviews with John Lear. There is too much information to include here. He seemed credible to me and is another person who worked for the government and is coming forward to expose things that the government is hiding.

You can also see pictures from inside some of the underground bases on You Tube if you look up D.U.M.B., or Deep Underground Military Bases. John Lear also discusses the existence of the maglev trains connecting the underground bases. I am not saying that I agree with the some of the speculation of what is going on in some of these places, specifically the alien agenda and FEMA camps, although it wouldn't surprise me, but I was looking for evidence that underground bases exist, which I believe I found. So I asked myself, if there are all of these bases and tunnels underground, and specifically at Hawthorne, as John Lear suggests, isn't it possible that biological warfare is being created there as well? I believe so. Add to that, the fact that Nevada is the #1 state in the country with the most Federal Government owned land. The Federal Government owns a whopping 89.4% of all of Nevada.[51] It really makes you see the probability of it all being true.

Testing For Biological Warfare

After this last reading I was curious to see if there was a way to test the local dirt for biological warfare. I have some military friends, one in particular that is in the National Guard, who I will refer to as "G.I. Joe." He specialized in nuclear, chemical, and biological weapons. I thought I would pick his brain a little. I told him that I had my son with autism tested on a machine which looks for frequencies of substances energetically in a person's body and some very interesting things came up in the results. Things like anthrax, Lyme and other pathogens used in biological warfare were supposedly in his body. The frequencies matched. The practitioner mentioned that she thought some of it could be coming from the air.

I asked G.I. Joe if he knew of a way to test our dirt for biological agents and he said that they didn't have the equipment

[51]http://www.strangemaps.wordpress.com/2008/06/17/291-federal-lands-in-the-us/

to test it where he worked and added that a civilian can't just send dirt in to a military facility with the detection equipment and ask them to test it for anthrax and other biological warfare without raising eyebrows." There are machines you can buy, but they are very expensive, and sometimes only military personnel can obtain them.

I told him that I wanted to find out where this stuff was coming from, and that I felt it was military related. He said he wouldn't be surprised. He knew quite a few other guys in the Guard who had children with autism. I found a scary statistic that autism is diagnosed in military children at roughly double the rate that it is in the civilian world, a striking 1 out of 88, according to Department of Defense data.[52] At the time, the autism rate was 1 in 150 according to the CDC.

G.I. Joe added that the military keeps lots of things secret, adding that he was working in Las Vegas once and saw a UFO. He said that he knows all of the different kinds of military planes out there, and none of them can fly that way. Off topic, but

---

[52]http://www.usnews.com/articles/news/national/2008/12/21/military-parents-battle-the-syst...

interesting none the less. A few "alien" references came through in our readings, so it was probably no coincidence that he brought it up randomly. I ran into a dead end with testing for the "dust" but maybe it was for the best. They did say in an earlier reading that it was new technology and not detectible, so maybe nothing would have shown up anyway.

In my search for information on biological warfare detection equipment, I found a device online called the R.A.P.I.D. System, (Rugged Advanced Pathogen Identification Device) used by the U.S. Department of Defense for pathogen identification in both field and clinical settings. It is also used by the U.S. Environmental Protection Agency to assess drinking water for potential bioterror agents. It said that the system can test for the following: *Anthrax, Ricin, Smallpox, Plague, Listeria, E. coli 0157, Salmonella, Campylobacter, Cryptosporidium, Tularemia, Ebola, Brucella, Anthrax IVD, Avian Influenza, Botulism,* and *Marburg.*[53] Only people from a U.S. government agency can obtain one. Just the fact that this thing exists was of interest to me, and that these pathogens were admitted bioterror agents. It was obviously a big enough threat that our military has this type of

[53] http://www.idahotech.com/RAPID/index.html.

equipment. There are actually many different types of equipment available to detect the presence of bioterrorism agents. None of which I could randomly get access to. Maybe someone reading this has access to some type of detection equipment that can test for contamination in the air or soil.

The more I discovered, the more I believed. The explanation from the readings that biological warfare is part of what is causing the autism epidemic didn't seem so far fetched any more. It was a matter of connecting the dots. The information was falling at my feet, just as I was told it would.

***

Chapter Eight

MEDIUM: "OKAY, TODAY IS JUNE 26, 2008, AND WE ARE DOING ANOTHER SESSION FOR WHAT WE ARE REFERRING TO AS 'THE MUMMY' RIGHT NOW. OKAY, I'M GOING TO SAY A PRAYER AND THEN WE WILL GET STARTED. (SHE SAYS A PERSONAL PRAYER.) I ASK FOR THE HIGHEST AND BEST SPIRITS TO COME THROUGH NOW. I'M PICKING UP THAT THERE IS GOING TO BE A LOT OF CHANGE, A LOT OF CHANGE. OKAY, WE NEED INFORMATION FOR THE BOOK."

"I'M SEEING A MAN, AND HE'S WALKING IN A CIRCLE. IT'S LIKE IT'S ALREADY OUTLINED. IT'S A CIRCLE, AND IT'S OUTLINED, AND HE'S JUST WALKING AROUND AND AROUND AND AROUND. AND HE HAS SOMEBODY ELSE FOLLOWING HIM, AND THE ONE THAT'S FOLLOWING HIM IS A YOUNGER PERSON, AND THEY ARE FOLLOWING HIM AND GROWING. SO IT'S LIKE SOMEONE THAT IDOLIZES

SOMEBODY ELSE. SO, THEY ARE WALKING ON THE CIRCLE, AND HE'S BEING FOLLOWED. AND THEN HE GROWS TALLER THAN EVEN THAT PERSON WAS...AND THEN THERE'S TWO MORE...AND THOSE ARE THE ONES THAT ARE GOING TO BE WORKING WITH US, OKAY."

"I'M SEEING THE WORLD, I'M SEEING THE BLUE, AND THE WORLD...AND ONE OF THEM IS GOING TO BE HERE ON THE PHYSICAL, AND THE OTHER ONE IS GOING TO BE SICK, AND THE SICK ONE IS GOING TO BE ADVISING THE YOUNG ONE. BUT IT'S LIKE THOSE THAT HAVE WALKED THAT CIRCLE FROM EACH GENERATION. I AM SEEING THAT 'TOP SECRET" AND THEY JUST PUT A RIBBON AROUND IT. THAT'S WHAT HE IS SHOWING ME."

"OKAY, NOW I SEE THE WIRY ONE. 'YOU THOUGHT I WASN'T COMING, DID YOU?' IS WHAT I HEARD HIM SAY. YOU KNOW WHEN HE WAS HERE ON THE PHYSICAL, HE HAD ALL THESE THINGS GOING ON WITH HIM, BUT HE ENJOYED THE PUBLICITY. HE ENJOYED GOING OUT AND BEING AROUND PEOPLE. HE LIKED THE TEA STUFF, THE TEA PARTIES OR WHATEVER; YOU KNOW THE SOCIAL

GATHERINGS. HE LIKED ALL OF THAT. IN THE CONDITION THAT HE WAS, THE MENTAL STATE, HE ENJOYED THAT. BUT HE LIKED TO BE COACHED. HE LIKED TO BE COACHED."

"IT'S LIKE I'M HEARING A PERSON WITH A BAD MICROPHONE. YOU KNOW, REMEMBER BACK IN THE DAY WHEN THE MICROPHONES SOUNDED....WITH NO...NOW WE HAVE TREBLE AND ALL THAT STUFF. AND I SEE SOMEONE STANDING AT A PODIUM AND THEY'RE TALKING...AND IT'S GOT A BIG ROUND THING THERE (ON THE PODIUM). INSTEAD OF ALL THAT DESCRIPTION, I SHOULD HAVE TOLD YOU WHAT I WAS HEARING."

"'I ASSURE YOU THESE KIDS WILL BE HEALED!' IS WHAT HE WAS SAYING INTO THE MICROPHONE."

"THERE'S GOING TO BE A LOT OF CHANGE. THERE IS A LOT OF CHANGE GOING ON IN THE GOVERNMENT. PEOPLE ARE REBELLING. YOU WOULD THINK THAT THIS GAS THING WOULD BE ONE OF THE FIRST THAT YOU COULD CALL 'THE ONE' TO START IT, BUT IT'S NOT. IT'S NOT. THERE'S SOMETHING ELSE THAT'S GOING TO GO ON THAT HAS TO

DO WITH PEOPLE JUST REBUTTING THE GOVERNMENT. RIGHT NOW, LOGICALLY, JUST STANDING BACK AND LOOKING AT THAT WHOLE SITUATION, YOU WOULD THINK THAT IT WOULD BE THE GAS, BUT THAT'S NOT WHAT IS GOING TO REALLY STIR UP THE PEOPLE. THAT'S JUST TICKLING THEM. EVEN THOUGH RIGHT NOW IT DOESN'T FEEL LIKE A TICKLE TO MANY OF US BECAUSE OF THE COST."

(The gas prices were over $4 per gallon at the time of the readings, an all-time high.)

"IT'S MUCH BIGGER. IT'S WHEN THE DIFFERENT TYPE OF A CAR STARTS BEING BROUGHT IN. AND THAT'S WHEN THE PROBLEM IS GOING TO START...THAT THE GAS ISN'T GOING TO BE NEEDED. THEN, THAT'S WHEN IT'S GOING TO BE A BIG RUCCUS BECAUSE THEN IT'S DIPPING INTO THE FINANCIAL ARENA OF THESE PAST POLITICAL PEOPLE, BUT IT'S NOT GOING TO MATTER BECAUSE THEY ARE FROM THE PAST."

"THE PRESIDENTS...YOU KNOW BUSH, AND THE PREVIOUS BUSH...THE WAY THAT THIS BUSH CAME IN WAS THROUGH

FORCE FROM THE PREVIOUS BUSH. BECAUSE THEY NEEDED TO BE IN THAT POWER BECAUSE THERE WERE OTHER THINGS THAT THEY HAD TO FINISH UP FROM THE OTHER BUSH. SO IT'S NOT LIKE THIS BUSH JUST CAME IN AND SAID, 'I WANT TO BE PRESIDENT' AND IT'S FOR MY COUNTRY AND THAT KIND OF THING. IT'S ALMOST LIKE A HOUSE DECORATION; JUST SOMETHING THAT YOU PUT THERE. I DON'T SEE THAT IT CAME FROM THE HEART WITHIN HIM. IT HAD NOTHING TO DO WITH THAT."

"IT'S THE PREVIOUS BUSH GOING IN THE SECOND TIME AROUND WITH HIS ENTIRE GROUP. SO, IT'S NOT JUST A ONE-MAN-BAND, WE'RE TALKING A WHOLE GROUP OF PEOPLE. SO, THEY SAW AN OPPORTUNITY TO PUT THE SON IN THERE. BUT THE SON DIDN'T REALLY DO ANYTHING. THE PATH WAS ALREADY THERE. AND THERE WAS FEAR FROM THE OTHER PEOPLE THAT WERE RUNNING AGAINST HIM. AND PEOPLE JUST DIDN'T SEE IT, THEY WERE LOOKING FOR EXPERIENCE. BUT THEY DIDN'T KNOW THAT THEY WERE BRINGING IN THE SAME OLD, SAME OLD. AND THAT OTHER PRESIDENT DIDN'T GET ENOUGH TIME TO BE ABLE TO IMPLEMENT AND GET THINGS GOING EXACTLY

HOW HE WANTED BECAUSE THEN HIS TIME ENDED. SO THAT IS WHY THE SON CAME IN. SO IT'S BEEN UNDER THE SAME POWER FOR A LONG TIME. AND WE'RE SUPPOSED TO BE A NATION THAT DOESN'T HAVE KINGS AND QUEENS THAT JUST STAY IN POWER."

(TO LAURA) "AND THIS ISN'T THE FIRST GOVERNMENT PERSON YOU ARE GOING TO RUN INTO, LIKE THIS SENATOR YOU WERE TALKING ABOUT THAT YOU MET WITH THE LIMO, AND THAT WHOLE EXPERIENCE (THE MAN THAT LAURA MET WHO TOLD HER ABOUT BEING IN THE UNDERGROUND CITY IN HAWTHORNE). THERE ARE SOME OTHER PEOPLE THAT HAVE BEEN IN THE GOVERNMENT THAT ARE GOING TO CROSS YOUR PATH. AND THE REASON THAT THEY ARE SPILLING THEIR GUTS LIKE THIS LIKE THEY ARE, IS THAT THEY HAVE TO UNLOAD SOMEWHERE. CUZ THERE'S A LOT OF GUILT, THERE'S A LOT OF GUILT OF WHAT IT IS THAT THEY ARE DOING AND WHAT HAPPENED, AND WHAT THEY KNOW. AND THEY WANT TO GET IT OUT, BUT THEY DON'T WANT TO DO IT THEMSELVES."

"THE ONE THAT YOU WERE TALKING ABOUT, THE SENATOR, THE PREVIOUS SENATOR, HE WOULD NOT GET KILLED BECAUSE IT'S TOO LATE. IT'S TOO LATE. THE GUY IS...HE'S AT THE BOTTOM, AND HE'S BOUNCING UP AND DOWN. I JUST SEE HIM LIKE A BUBBLE, YOU KNOW ONE OF THOSE LAMPS, THOSE BUBBLE LAMPS, BUT I SEE HIM WAY DOWN LOW. HE DOESN'T CARE. HE ALREADY IS WHO HE WANTS TO BE, AND HAS NO MORE AMBITION. HE DOESN'T WANT TO BE A SENATOR OF ANOTHER PLACE OR ANYTHING. BECAUSE HE MORE OR LESS WASHES HIS HANDS OF A LOT OF STUFF THAT HE WAS INVOLVED IN. HE WOULD LIKE TO WASH HIS HANDS, BUT HOW DO YOU WASH THAT OFF? IT'S BLOOD. AND I JUST SEE HIS HANDS AND IT LOOKS LIKE THEY'VE BEEN DIPPED IN PAINT...RED PAINT. A LOT OF PEOPLE ARE LOOKING FOR THEIR GLORY."

(The fact that they brought up this information about the former Senator that I met was a validation that what he told me was true.)

"YOU HAVE SOME QUESTIONS, LAURA?"

Laura: "I do."

<u>MEDIUM:</u> "LET'S DO ONE."

<u>Laura:</u> "I am a little confused about the whole autism thing...how the kids get it. From what we've gathered so far, it sounds like there are multiple ways of getting it; the combination of the biological warfare and the MMR vaccine, or if the child has a fever and they are exposed to the biological warfare. Are there multiple ways of getting it or is there just a main...?"

<u>MEDIUM:</u> "THE MAIN THING IS A LOW IMMUNE SYSTEM AND WARFARE THAT DOES ALL OF THAT ATTACKING AT THE SAME TIME. ANYTHING THAT LOWERS THE IMMUNE SYSTEM. IT'S NOT ABOUT WHAT CAUSES IT, BUT WHAT ALLOWS IT TO ATTACK IS A LOWERED IMMUNE SYSTEM."
(This could possibly explain the children that haven't been vaccinated that have autism; when their immune system is lowered with fever and they are exposed to the biological warfare in the environment at a young age.)

"NOW IF PARENTS TOOK THE INITIATIVE TO SEPARATE SOME OF THOSE SHOTS. DON'T GO IN THERE AND GIVE

YOUR KID FOUR SHOTS ALL AT ONCE AND GO, 'OH, THEY'RE GOING TO GET OVER IT,' AND JUST LET THEM SUFFER IT OUT ALL AT ONCE INSTEAD OF LITTLE BY LITTLE. IT WOULD BE BETTER TO DO IT LITTLE BY LITTLE THAN IT IS TO JUST DOWN THEIR IMMUNE SYSTEM SO MUCH THAT THEY CAN'T FIGHT WHAT'S IN THE ENVIRONMENT."

"AND THAT'S WHERE THEY'VE GOTTEN SLOPPY. THE MEDICINES THEMSELVES DON'T INTERACT WITH EACH OTHER, BUT THEY'RE NOT CONSIDERING THE RECIEVER. AND THE RECEIVER IS THAT CHILD GETTING POKED ALL AT ONCE."

"AND IT SEEMS VERY EASY, BECAUSE YOU JUST SAY, 'OH JUST DRINK THAT,' AND IT TASTES SWEET, AND IT'S TAKEN FOR GRANTED WHAT IT IS. BECAUSE IT IS SO MASSED, IT'S LIKE, HERE'S YOUR BALLOON AND GO ON YOUR WAY. IT'S SO DECORATED. PEOPLE ARE NOT UNDERSTANDING THAT IT'S REAL. LOOK AT AN ECSTASY OR A MICRODOT, I MEAN IT IS SO SMALL, AND IT DOES SO MUCH."

"SO, YOU HAVE TO CONSIDER THAT YOU ARE THROWING ALL OF THIS INTO YOUR CHILD'S SYSTEM AND YOU SHUT THEM DOWN, AND THEN YOU WANT THEM TO WAKE UP AGAIN? IT'S LIKE YOU SHUT THEM DOWN, AND THEN SHOOT THEM. IT'S JUST TOO HARD ON THE BODY."

"AND THEIR BODY IS STILL IN DEVELOPMENT, THEIR BONES ARE STILL SOFT. HOW DO YOU THINK THEY GROW SO FAST? THEIR BONES ARE NOT MADE TO STAY AS THEY ARE, SO IT'S NOT LIKE THEY ARE GETTING STRONGER, AND YOU'RE THINKING, MY KID IS SO FLEXIBLE, THEY FALL, THEY DO THIS, THEY DO THAT...IT'S BECAUSE THEIR BONE STRUCTURE IS DIFFERENT THAN OURS. THEN A PERSON GETS OLDER AND THE BONES GET STRONGER AND STRONGER."

"BUT THE CHILD, IT CAN GET INTO A LOT OF DIFFERENT LEVELS OF THEIR LAYERS, VERSUS AN ADULT. BECAUSE AN ADULT IS ALREADY COMPLETE IN FORMING. THEN WHAT HAPPENS IN AN ADULT IS THEY START AGING BECAUSE THE BODY IS COMPLETELY BUILT. BUT THE PROCESS OF IT

BEING BUILT IS WHEN IT'S AT ITS MOST VULNERABLE STATE, AND PEOPLE ARE NOT LOOKING AT THAT."

"THE BODY IS MORE COMPLEX. IT'S VERY, VERY COMPLEX. WE ARE NOT MACHINES. WE ARE SELF-HEALING. WE'RE SOULS, WE'RE SPIRITS. AND IF YOU WANTED A WHOLE THIRD SET OF TEETH, YOU COULD GET IT; BECAUSE IT IS JUST YOUR MIND THAT DECIDES THAT YOU GET TWO. BUT YOU CAN HAVE THREE. AND YOU CAN LIVE LONGER AND NOT EVEN LOOK THE AGE THAT YOU GUYS HAVE DECIDED THAT YOU'RE SUPPOSED TO LOOK."

"BUT THE FIRST NINE YEARS OF DEVELOPMENT IS GOING TO BE THE CHARACTER AND THE FOUNDATION OF THE PERSON. AND THEN THE TENTH TO THE TWELFTH, IT'S THE BODY GROWING INTO THAT, TRYING TO SEE IF THE GLOVE FITS. TRYING TO MAKE ITSELF WHAT IT'S GOING TO BE, AND THEN AFTER THAT, IT'S JUST APPLYING WHAT THE BODY HAS ALREADY STAGED OUT. BUT THE BONES STAY SOFT AND THEY CONTINUE TO GROW IN SOME AND IN OTHERS THEY DON'T. THEY ARE FULL GROWN. SO, IN MANY, IT CAPS OFF AT THIRTEEN. AND THEN SOME GO THROUGH

NINETEEN. AND THAT'S WHAT IS BEING FOOLED AROUND WITH. THIS IS THE AREA THAT'S BEING FOOLED AROUND WITH. AND THEN YOU WIND UP WITH A 28-YEAR-OLD AND THEY HAVE PROBLEMS, AND THEN YOU WONDER WHY. YOU HAVE TO TAKE CARE OF YOUR KIDS."

<u>Laura:</u> "What do we do about the vaccine schedule? How do we prevent it?"

<u>MEDIUM:</u> "TAKE IT INTO YOUR OWN HANDS. DON'T ALLOW THE IMMUNE SYSTEM TO EVER BE KNOCKED DOWN THAT MUCH. AND STAY OUT OF THE ENVIRONMENT THAT IS HARMFUL FOR TWO DAYS."

"AND...THERE'S A LOT OF CLEAN-UP GOING ON. THERE IS A LOT OF CLEAN-UP GOING ON RIGHT NOW. BUT IT'S NOT GOOD ENOUGH; IT'S NOT ENOUGH, BECAUSE THERE IS WAY TOO MUCH GARBAGE OUT THERE. TOO MUCH ALREADY THERE. AND THE CLEAN-UP THAT THEY ARE DOING, IT DOESN'T ALL FIT UNDER THE BED. IT'S SLOPPY, IT'S JUST VERY SLOPPY. IT'S BECAUSE THE PRESIDENTS ARE CHANGING AND SO THEY'VE GOT TO GET ALL THAT STUFF

OUT AND THEY ARE IN A HURRY. SO A LOT OF THAT IS GOING ON RIGHT NOW. AND I SEE DOLLARS. A LOT OF IT HAS TO DO WITH DOLLARS."

"OBAMA IS VERY FEMALE, HE HAS FEMALE ENERGY. HE HAS A LOT OF SUPPORT TOO. THERE ARE PEOPLE THAT GIVE HIM A LOT OF ENCOURAGEMENT. WHENEVER HE GETS DOWN AND SAYS NO, I DON'T WANT TO DO THIS, BECAUSE THERE HAS BEEN A LOT OF NEGATIVITY WITHIN HIMSELF. YOU ARE GOING TO SEE HIM DIFFERENTLY. IT IS REALLY HARD FOR HIM TO STAY ON, READING HIS MATERIAL. THAT'S WHY HE MESSES UP AND OFFENDS PEOPLE, BECAUSE IT IS REALLY HARD. BUSH IS REALLY GOOD AT READING HIS MATERIAL. HE WILL NOT GO UP THERE COLD. HE WILL NOT GO UP THERE AND JUST SAY, 'I THINK THIS,' AND 'THIS IS WHAT WE ARE GOING TO DO,' AND THAT HE HAS IT IN HIS MIND, BECAUSE IT IS NOT THERE. OBAMA DOESN'T STAY FOCUSSED BECAUSE HE IS NOT BEING RUN. NOT THAT HE WOULD BE THE BEST PRESIDENT THAT WE COULD GET, BUT THERE IS A LOT OF FEMALE ENERGY WITH HIM."

"AND I SEE A LOT OF MUDSLINGING; HILLARY AND HIM; A LOT OF MUDSLINGING."

(This was before Barack Obama was running against Hillary Clinton for the Democratic nomination for President, and their campaigns both contained lots of mudslinging.)

"THERE IS ANOTHER WOMAN THAT SHOULD HAVE RUN THIS TIME AND SHE DIDN'T, SHE HELD BACK. SHE IS A BRUNETTE AND HER HAIR IS SHOULDER LENGTH, KIND OF FULL. SHE'S BEEN IN POLITICS FOR A LONG TIME, AND HER NAME STARTS WITH AN 'L.' SO SHE'LL COME INTO THE PICTURE AT SOME POINT."

(MEDIUM'S WORDS) "OH MY GOD...SHOW IT TO ME AGAIN BEFORE I SAY IT."

"I SAW OBABMA GET SHOT...AND I ASKED HIM TO SHOW ME AGAIN, AND I SAW IT AGAIN."

"ANGER, ANGER, ANGER. I SEE ANGER, SOMEBODY ANGRY."

Laura: "Is he the President, and then gets shot?"

<u>MEDIUM:</u> "I DON'T KNOW...I JUST SEE FLAGS WHEN YOU SAID THAT, I SAW A UNITED STATES FLAG WAVING BEHIND HIM. THEY SHOOT THE...I JUST SEE THE HEAD PART, THAT HE GETS SHOT. AND IT MAY BE BECAUSE, YOU KNOW HOW PEOPLE ARE ALL AROUND YOU AND THEN THAT'S ALL THAT STICKS UP, OR THAT'S A MARK OR SOMETHING."

"AT FIRST, I SAW SOMEONE VERY ANGRY, AND THAT'S WHY ALL THAT IS HAPPENING. BUT THEN I SEE A PERSON PUT EVERYTHING UP IN A SUITCASE, GET UP AND WALK AWAY. SO IT IS A PROFESSIONAL HIT. IT'S NOT A...SOME CRAZY...UNLESS THIS CRAZY IS A PROFESSIONAL. BUT I SEE A LOT OF ANGER, CUZ HE WAS LIKE, 'AAAGGGHHH!' AND THEN HE TRACKS HIM."

<u>Laura</u>: "Oh my God."

(This reading was before the election in 2008, where Obama was elected President.)

"AAH, I SAW LIKE A 'J', LIKE A 'J.'" (THE MEDIUM GETS UP OUT OF HER CHAIR AND DRAWS A LETTER 'J' ON THE CHALKBOARD).

(VIDEO CAMERA TURNS ON AND LAURA VIDEOTAPES IT AS THE MEDIUM DRAWS A LOT MORE NUMBERS AND SYMBOLS ON THE CHALKBOARD).

<u>MEDIUM:</u> "HE JUST SAID, 'PUT IT DOWN.' PUT IT DOWN AND WOW! (LOOKS AT WHAT SHE JUST DREW). PUT IT DOWN AND I JUST...ARE YOU THERE? I HEAR HIM LAUGHING... (VIDEO CAMERA TURNS OFF). I HEAR A CHUCKLE, LIKE A HMM, HMM, HMM, LIKE THAT, LIKE A CHUCKLE. SO, HE'S KIND OF JUST CHUCKLING AND..."

"THE WIRY ONE SAYS HE DOESN'T LIKE TO BE BY HIMSELF. HE NEVER LIKED BEING BY HIMSELF, AND SO HE USED HIS TIME THINKING, AND PUTTING IT OUT THERE TRYING TO HELP THE WORLD, AND HE WANTS TO HELP THE WORLD AGAIN."

"THE WORLD IS NOT GOING TO END IN 2012. THERE ARE GOING TO BE SOME CHANGES AND SOME REALIZATION. THE MINDS ARE JUST BECOMING MORE POWERFUL. YOU KNOW HOW YOU GROW UP, AND THE BODY GROWS? IT'S JUST GOING TO BE GROWING DIFFERENTLY. AND THE MINDS ARE GOING TO BE MORE POWERFUL, BUT IT'S ALL OF YOU THAT HAVE EXTENDED YOURSELF TO THE SPIRITUAL REALMS THAT WILL BE THE ONES WITH GROWTH. AND THEN YOU'LL BE CATEGORIZING THE ONES THAT DIDN'T TAKE THE SPIRITUAL GROWTH AS 'RETARDED,' OR 'SLOW,' OR 'WITH PROBLEMS.' SO THAT'S WHAT 2012 IS ABOUT."

Laura: "Okay."

MEDIUM: "I'M GOING TO NEED THOSE, IS WHAT HE'S SAYING. SO, YOU'RE RIGHT ABOUT THE CHALKBOARDS (LAURA BROUGHT TWO MORE CHALKBOARDS TO THIS SESSION, BUT THE MEDIUM TOLD HER NOT TO OPEN THEM YET). BECAUSE WHAT GOES ON THEM IS GOING TO BE INTERCHANGEABLE FOR UNDERSTANDING. THESE WON'T BE NEEDED FOR THREE SESSIONS. HE'S TELLING ME THAT

HE WAS TALKING THROUGH ME WITH THE INSTRUCTION NOT TO OPEN THEM. SO HE SAYS THERE MIGHT HAVE BEEN A CHANGE OF CHARACTER, OR TONE OR VOICE OR PERSONALITY THAT YOU MIGHT HAVE NOTICED BECAUSE I DON'T THINK THAT WAS ME, (THE MEDIUM); IT WASN'T ME THAT TOLD YOU, 'DON'T OPEN THEM.' OKAY, ON THIS, (THE CHALKBOARD WE WERE USING), SOME OF THE PIECES ARE OVER THERE (A TRAY THAT FITS UNDERNEATH). AND I DON'T EVEN KNOW, I THINK I HAVE EVERYTHING...BUT ON THESE, WE ARE GOING TO USE THE PIECES A LITTLE DIFFERENT THAN HOW WE USED THIS...THIS ONE IS JUST PROPPED UP LIKE THAT. HE SAYS I HAD THE RIGHT IDEA, BECAUSE I WANTED TO PUT CHALKBOARDS ACROSS THAT (A STANDING METAL CABINET), BECAUSE IT LOOKS SO UGLY, AND JUST PUT PERMANENT CHALKBOARDS ACROSS THERE. SO, I HAD THE RIGHT IDEA, BUT THAT'S TOO BIG. I AM ASKING HIM, 'WHAT DO YOU MEAN?' AND HE SAID, 'YOU'LL FIND OUT, YOU'LL KNOW.'"

Laura: "Should I get a bigger one?"

MEDIUM: "WE ARE NOT TO GET A BIGGER ONE, BECAUSE IF WE GET A BIGGER ONE, WE CAN'T TRANSPORT IT. THESE ARE GOING TO WIND UP ON AN AIRPLANE. AND IF WE HAVE A BIG BOARD, WE CAN'T EASILY LOAD IT. LIKE THESE, CAN GO IN A SUITCASE. AND THE REASON YOU HAVE BEEN SEEING LAQUER OR A FILM OVER THEM, IS BECAUSE THAT'S WHAT IS GOING TO HAPPEN TO THEM AT THE END. (THE MEDIUM SUGGESTED TO LAURA THAT THEY LAQUER THE BOARD SO IT COULDN'T BE ERASED). BUT THEY NEED TO BE THE SMALL ONE, NOT A BIG CHALKBOARD. PRESENTATION, PRESENTATION."

"SO THIS WHOLE THING, THE BOOK THAT HAS TO DO WITH AUTISM, IS GOING TO BE TARGETED FOR PARENTS THAT HAVE CHILDREN THAT THEY ARE HAVING TO...AND THE WORDS...I CAN'T EVEN PICK ONE...HE'S JUST PUTTING SO MANY...BURDEN...THAT'S JUST ONE OF THEM, IT'S JUST LIKE ALL OF A SUDDEN, I JUST HAD A THOUSAND WORDS THAT JUST CAME, AND THEY ALL MEANT THE SAME THING. AND SO IT'S JUST SO PROFOUND, AND SO MANY WORDS, THAT IT'S JUST HARD TO EVEN GET ONE. IT WAS JUST

OVERLOAD, WAS HOW I FELT. IT'S JUST ALL THESE WORDS THAT HE SENT AND THEY ALL MEAN THE SAME."

"AND SO IN PRESENTATION, THERE WILL BE THE SCIENTIFIC PART. THERE ARE GOING TO BE DIFFERENT TYPES OF PERSONALITIES, DIFFERENT TYPES OF INDIVIDUALS THAT ARE GOING TO BE INTERESTED IN THIS MATERIAL. THERE ARE GOING TO BE PEOPLE INVOLVED WITH THE BOOK THAT HAVE TO DO WITH THE FACT THAT THEY ARE IN IT, TRYING TO SEE WHAT'S GOING ON, LOOKING FOR A SOLUTION. THERE ARE GOING TO BE SCIENTISTS THAT ARE GOING TO BE TRYING TO FIND AND CREATE THE CONCLUDED UNDERSTANDING OF WHAT HE'S SENDING. AND THEN THERE ARE GOING TO BE THE PEOPLE THAT ARE JUST TRYING TO GET INTO THE LOOP, AND THEY ARE JUST SEEKING HOW THEY CAN JUST SEEP THEMSELVES INTO THAT WHOLE SITUATION SAYING, 'OH, I THINK I WAS IN THAT AREA, AND THEY ARE IN THE DARK, AND THEY ARE FEELING AROUND TRYING TO SEEP INTO THAT...'OH, I THINK I WAS RIGHT THERE.' THOSE ARE THE THREE MAIN GROUPS OF PEOPLE THAT WE'RE GOING TO BE APPROACHED BY, BUT WE NEED TO

DECIPHER WHICH IS THE FAMILY THAT NEEDS HELP, VERSUS THE SCIENTIST THAT IS GOING TO BE OF HELP THAT NEEDS TO BE TALKED TO, VERSUS A DISTINGUISHMENT OF THEIR WANTING TO JUST JUMP ON AND HOLD ONTO YOUR COAT."

"AND THE ONES THAT ARE GOING TO BE CONFUSED ARE THE SCIENTISTS AND THE...SO IF THEY START TO SAY THAT THEY ARE AN AUTHOR OR A SCIENTIST, AND A LAWYER, AND A DOCTOR AND A THIS, AND A THAT, WE NEED TO SAY 'LET ME SEE THE DEGREE.' AND THAT'S THE THING YOU NEED TO BE LOOKING FOR WHEN YOU'RE GOING INTO SOMEONE'S OFFICE AND TALKING TO THEM, BECAUSE THEY ARE GOING TO PUT THEM UP. THEY ARE NOT GOING TO WORK ALL THOSE YEARS FOR THOSE CREDENTIALS, AND NOT POST THEM. AND IF THEY ARE WHO THEY SAY THEY ARE, AND THERE ARE NO CREDENTIALS THERE, IT'S BECAUSE THEY PROBABLY ARE NOT. AND SO INSTEAD OF JUST TAKING THEIR WORD FOR IT, LOOK FOR THAT, AND WALK AWAY. BECAUSE THE ONES THAT ARE TRYING TO PULL THE WOOL OVER YOUR EYES ARE THE ONES THAT DO NOT HAVE THE CREDENTIALS,

THEY ARE JUST GOING TO LIE. SO BE PREPARED FOR THAT...FOR NOT TRUTH."

"OH MY GOD...THE WIRY ONE JUST ALMOST RIPPED HIS HAIR OUT! HE DOESN'T LIKE LIARS. IT'S LIKE; THEY HAVE NO PLACE, THEY HAVE NO PLACE. NOT THAT HE WAS GOING TO RIP HIS HAIR OUT, I FEEL LIKE HE PLAYS WITH HIS HAIR A LOT. THAT'S PROBABLY WHY IT'S ALWAYS SO MESSED UP. HE ALSO LIKED TO MASSAGE HIS HEAD. HE DID A LOT OF MASSAGING, SO HIS HAIR WAS A BIG MESS. BUT HE JUST, I SAW HIM REALLY GO AT HIS HEAD AND HIS HAIR WHEN HE...VERY UPSETTING WITH PEOPLE THAT LIE."

"THE KIDS OF THE WORLD ARE GOING TO BE ALRIGHT IN THIS SITUATION! THERE IS A LOT OF OTHER THINGS THAT ARE HAPPENING AROUND THE WORLD. BUT WHAT'S HAPPENING RIGHT NOW; THE THING THAT WE ARE WORKING ON IS A SCIENTIFIC FACT AND SOLUTION. BUT IT IS JUST ONE MORE TIME, ONE MORE TIME THAT I WANT TO HELP. BUT THIS IS ONE OF MY ENDEAVORS ON A SPIRITUAL LEVEL."

"AND YES, I HAVE CHOSEN YOU."

Laura: "I told you!" (Laura had told the medium the day before that The Wiry One had chosen them for this.)

MEDIUM: "AND JUST KEEP IT ZIPPED UP."

"HE'S TELLING ME THAT WE NEED TO START TIMELY (WE CHATTED A LOT BEFORE STARTING THIS SESSION, AND BEGAN ABOUT 30 MINUTES PAST OUR SCHEDULED START TIME). BUT WE NEED TO START TIMELY. AND HE'S SHOWING ME A CHALK BOARD, AND MADE A BIG CIRCLE ON IT. (A CLOCK) AND HE'S CONFIRMING OUR NEXT APPOINTMENT. 'WE'LL SEE YOU NEXT TIME' IS WHAT HE'S SAYING. I WAS ASKING ABOUT THOSE OTHER PEOPLE, AND HE SAID DON'T WORRY ABOUT IT."

Laura: "What people?"

MEDIUM: "THE OTHER PEOPLE COMING THROUGH, LIKE THE PRESIDENT AND ALL OF THOSE PEOPLE. OR SOME OF THE

OTHER PEOPLE THAT ARE (STARTS TO SAY 'SUPPOSED TO' THEN STOPS) THAT ARE GOING TO COME THROUGH. NOTHING IS SUPPOSED TO HAPPEN, IT WILL. BECAUSE IT IS NOW, IT IS REAL; IT IS ALL THE SAME...THERE IS NO 'SUPPOSED TO.' (SHE ASKS HIM,) 'ARE YOU GOING TO STOP?' HIS ENERGY JUST WENT AWAY."

(CD ends)

***

Later Discoveries

Biohazard Suit

I received this last bit of information just as I finished this book. This was the icing on the cake for me. I had asked my friend who first told me about Hawthorne, NV to see if she could find out any more information about the underground base. She also has a child with autism and was very curious to see if the information I told her was true. Since she knew people who still worked at the military base, I asked her to see if she could get someone to tell her anything to validate the information from the readings. I said, just see if you can find anyone who is doing the kind of work they talked about, wearing the "beekeeper" uniforms or who would validate the underground facility. A few months later, we were at an autism training together and on the way out, she told me, "Remember what we talked about before? I have something for you."

She told me that she was at a social get-together and there was a group of military friends of hers there who worked at Hawthorne. Somehow the subject came up about the underground area of the base. One guy told my friend that his wife worked there recently and that she had to wear a biohazard suit at work and had to be hosed off before she left! My friend asked him what type of work she was doing, and he said she didn't know. She asked him if his wife was working underground and he wouldn't say either way. She said that even after a few drinks, nobody would admit if there was an underground base, but she understood from their conversation that there was, but that they couldn't talk about it.

I jumped up and down when she told me because it was just the validation I had been waiting for. Someone who has actually done the work described in the readings! My friend said that the way he described the biohazard suit was just as I described it to her from the readings, it looked like they were working with bees, with the protective suit and hood. And the added information that the guy's wife had to be hosed off before she left validated the information from the reading that the dust can penetrate the clothes and the skin.

Also, because he said that she didn't know what exactly she was doing describes the innocence of the military workers and the compartmentalization described in the readings. One person does something and doesn't know what came before or what happens after their job is done. They also said in the readings that a lot of women worked in the underground city, and this person doing the work was a woman. I am sure that the government will deny this or make up another reason for the use of the biohazard suit, but clearly something is going on there besides being an ammunition depot.

Closing Thoughts

I say closing thoughts because this was unfortunately our last reading. Even though I was told in the readings that it wasn't up to me to prove this, after discovering the previous information I feel much more confident that the cause of autism presented here is not only probable, but is in fact true. I feel that once this information is made available, the floodgates will open and people will come forward to validate it even further. The government is certainly not going to admit it outright; the truth will come from people whose families have been affected by this tragedy.

Isn't it the job of the military and our elected officials to protect the people that they govern? Against enemies foreign ***and*** domestic? Is this what our tax dollars are paying for? Debilitating our very own children? I am not anti-military by any stretch. My late father was a Marine, and I have many family members and friends in the Armed Forces and I honor their bravery and selflessness.

It is because of the military that we have freedom of the press and freedom of speech, which I am currently exercising. But don't our children deserve the right to life, liberty, and the pursuit of happiness? Not when it is taken from them in this manner. They are casualties of war. This is something that is happening without knowledge of the outcome. The truth needs to be exposed so that it can be corrected. What is happening to our innocent children is inhumane and inexcusable; it needs to be stopped!

The autism community will not stand for this; that much I know. I have seen them move mountains with their bare hands for their loved ones. They protest, they march on the nation's capital, they make things happen. They will not sit idly by, knowing that this injustice has been done to their children. They are the strongest Army on this planet and they fight for the right reasons; for the health, safety and future of their loved ones, our next generation. They have been the silent warriors fighting for the rights of their children with the school districts, the medical community, the insurance companies, and with service providers. This battle is far from over. Get your armor, warriors! There's a revolution coming!

***

EPILOGUE

A lot of things transpired in my personal life shortly after the last reading. Partly because of some of the information in these readings, namely that autism isn't genetic and that 95% of families split up and that they need to look at what they're doing and not run away from their families, I looked hard at my situation with my ex-husband, Matt. I had a lot more compassion and a lot less anger about our situation, knowing what I did now. I felt that not only was Trevor a victim, but that we were also victims in this whole scenario. We split up because we were so stressed and depressed and argued constantly about how to fix things, and we both gave up. Since we lived in Nevada, known for quickie marriages and divorces, we were divorced in a month and didn't give ourselves time to think about the consequences of splitting up. I think we both learned that the grass was not greener on the other side.

To make a long story short, we got back together in July of 2008, and then got remarried on our old wedding anniversary in

March 2009. We called the wedding: "I Do, Part Two." We also moved into a new home two weeks before the wedding. Getting back together was so healing for the whole family on so many levels. We did a lot of crying and forgiving and started fresh. It was as if we didn't skip a beat, even though we had been apart for 3 years. We were very happy, newlyweds again. Maybe we'll start a trend, who knows?

I was pretty busy getting my life back together, but I still tried to get together with the medium that channeled this information to finish it up. We were told that the formula for the cure for autism was going to be given to us, but the equation for the formula wasn't completed. I saw this happen right in front of me. I desperately wanted to get the rest of the information to help my son, but I couldn't do it without her.

I tried on numerous occasions to get together; I called her and left messages, e-mailed her, and sympathized with her, all to no avail. I don't want to personalize this too much, but I need to explain briefly what transpired. As I mentioned earlier, she was afraid that she would be killed if she put her name on it because of the political content. On the contrary, keeping this secret would kill me. Over a year had passed since our last session, and I had to make a decision on what to do. Her stalling was putting me in a very awkward position.

After one more failed attempt to get her to finish it, I finally decided that with or without her, I needed to get this part of the information out to the autism community. I couldn't allow this information to get buried. The cure was not going to be found until the real cause was known. I had no intention of letting this go. This was my son's life and future at stake. I wasn't about to let someone else's issues sabotage my son's future. I talked to a lawyer, told her my intentions, and I had to go it alone. Parents of children with autism, what would you have done if you were in my shoes and privy to this information? Sit on it and do nothing? Of course you wouldn't.

As a parent of a child with autism, I feel obligated to do the right thing and expose this information. Putting this book out on my own is either the bravest or the dumbest thing I have ever done; that remains to be seen. But if it gives our beautiful children with autism a chance of recovery, and saves families, it is worth the risk. I will know in my heart that I did my part. Now it is up to others to do theirs. This needs to be looked into at the very least. The numbers keep rising. Millions of dollars have been spent on the fruitless search for the cause of autism. What if this is it? Discuss.

To be continued...

UPDATE

I'm sure people will wonder what types of therapies I did with Trevor, so I will briefly discuss that here. He was in special classes at age three, but I didn't even start treating Trevor for his medical issues and deficiencies until he was five, which is considered late by today's early intervention standards. It wasn't until then that I started to figure out what was really going on with him and began trying different treatments. He was one of the earlier kids diagnosed with autism at the start of the epidemic, and I didn't really have a road map to follow, so I made my own. I became a detective and read everything I could and followed my instincts as to what therapies I felt would most benefit him.

I ditched Trevor's new pediatrician after he refused to refer us to a specialist to do allergy testing, and I took him to an integrated medicine doctor and we used homeopathy to detoxify him gently from fungus and yeast, metals, bacteria, and viruses. I educated myself in homeopathy and used this incredible system of medicine for almost all of our family's health care needs. I also did NAET (Nambudripad's Allergy Elimination Technique) with Trevor to eliminate his allergies with acupressure, dietary intervention (eliminated everything he was intolerant of), and added the essential supplements he needed such as multivitamins, digestive enzymes and probiotics. I didn't feel that blindly dumping a bunch of synthetic supplements into a body that couldn't assimilate them, as some autism protocols suggested, was the best choice for him.

I was open to just about anything safe and non-invasive. I also used the Far Infrared Sauna, AIT (Auditory Integration Training) and of course ABA (Applied Behavioral Analysis) for education. He has made steady improvements year after year. He can talk somewhat and is social in his own way, but he still has a way to go to be considered "normal." His healing process has been a marathon, and his improvements keep me going, always on the lookout for the next thing. I investigate everything thoroughly before trying it; I don't just follow the herd. I never gave up on him, and I never will.

After these readings, I tried to figure out a way to somehow test Trevor for biological warfare and to remove it from his body. It's not like I could go to a regular Western medicine doctor and ask them to test him for biological warfare, and get it out of his body, now could I? Disclaimer: this is not medical advice; it is just what I did.

I knew of an alternative method of testing and clearing the body that is similar to NAET, called BioSET™ and by chance found out that a friend of mine did it from her home. She was a retired baby nurse who quit her job because she could not continue to inject toxins into newborns with a clear conscience. Her husband was an MD, but she took a more alternative approach to healing. I asked my friend if she had the vials to test for pathogens that are used in biological warfare. She said yes. We set up an appointment for Trevor a few weeks later. I told her that I wanted to create our own protocol, and not use the autism protocol that they currently use in BioSET™. She was open to following my intuition.

BioSET™ (Bioenergetic Sensitivity and Enzyme Therapy) is a modern healing system and desensitization protocol that combines the ancient science of acupuncture (acupressure in kids) and the body's meridian system and 21st century electromagnetic technology and either computer software or muscle response testing (MRT) for the diagnosis of food and environmental allergies, chemical sensitivities, toxicity, and weakness of organ systems. It was created by Dr. Ellen Cutler, D.C. It is a non-invasive, safe, natural desensitization technique that often permanently eliminates food and environmental allergies and sensitivities.

Our first session was pretty incredible. I brought in a list of what items I wanted to test for, and she showed me boxes and boxes of other things she had. Basically, how this works is that there are Ergopathic vials which contain the energetic signature of any substance, food, virus, bacteria, etc., that are tested for in the patient using Applied Kinesiology (muscle response testing) and then cleared from the body using acupressure (on a child). A parent can be used as a "surrogate" for the child as long as the child is touching the parent. A weakness in the muscle indicates a blockage or sensitivity to the item being tested. You can use the arm or the fingers for muscle response testing.

A group of similar items is then put on a special tray and the patient is connected to an electromagnetic circuit and "cleared" by acupressure. After the session the patient is retested for the same items to make sure they cleared. Not only does the item get cleared, but also the organs and emotions that were affected, as well as the miasms (genetic predispositions to disease) that the person has inherited or acquired if needed. I know it sounds like "voodoo" for those who only know Western medicine, but it as been clinically tested and proven by thousands of patients using this system.

Are you still with me? We started testing for bacteria in the first session. The bacteria that we found in Trevor's system during the first session were: *Clostridium difficile* (lots of kids with autism have this; it causes diarrhea and other intestinal conditions), *Rickettsia rickettsii* (causes Rocky Mountain spotted fever, often a co-infection of Lyme), *Rickettsia prowazekii* (causes Typhus), *Mycoplasma bovis,* (from cows; all mycoplasmas lack a cell wall) *Mycoplasma neurolyticum, Mycoplasma pneumoniae,* (causes respiratory infections) *Mycoplasma synoviae,* (in chickens and turkey) *Borrelia burgdorferi* (causes Lyme disease), and *Bacillus anthracis* (anthrax). Adding to the bacterial burden, all bacteria give off waste products that further burden the body. She was shocked at our findings, but it was validating for me to know that I am not a raging lunatic. We decided we needed to get rid of the pathogenic burden first. Those things did not belong in his body. So, then we asked his body which ones he could clear that day, determined by muscle testing. We cleared the anthrax and the Lyme bacteria with acupressure.

We were also able to test which bug was the carrier of the Lyme, and it was not a tick, it was the Western Salt Marsh Mosquito. I had been reading a lot about Lyme since I thought he had it after our QXCI sessions. Most people with Lyme were never bitten by a tick. Mosquitoes and other flying insects can also be carriers. Look at *Malaria* and *West Nile virus*. The emotions he cleared in this session were panic, terror, worry, rage, helplessness, fear, confusion and frightfully overjoyed. She gave me a flower essence remedy for anger release.

Trevor's weak organs were corpus callosum (brain), gallbladder, hypothalamus, large intestine, small intestine, pituitary/pineal, skin, stomach and bladder. The clearing channels affected were: allergy, adrenal, corpus callosum, emotional, hypothalamus, gallbladder, large intestine, liver, lymphatic, nervous system, pituitary/pineal, sinuses, skin, small intestine, spleen, stomach, bladder, DNA, RNA. Helpers were parasites, viruses, bacteria, and Candida. Trevor's miasms (hereditary and acquired) for these items were Carcinosinum (cancer, my father died of this), Thuja occidentalis (brain, skin), Tuberculinum (tuberculosis, my great grandfather died of this), vaccinium (vaccines), Mercurius solubilis (mercury), virus, bacterium, allergy and mentalis (mental). I knew all about miasms from studying homeopathy. Trevor had taken some of these remedies in the past. This was not new or weird to me.

Then, after the acupressure treatment, a homeopathic remedy was prepared for Trevor to take daily for the next month which included the energies of the cleared items to further prompt the body to heal itself. These homeopathic remedies enhance detoxification and the drainage of toxins gently, without the uncomfortable side effects that often accompany other detoxification programs.

A month later, we had another session. We muscle tested to see if he cleared the first two pathogens, and he had. This session, we cleared the *Rickettsias*, the *Mycoplasmas*, and also found *Smallpox* (he didn't receive that vaccine), along with other vaccines he tested a weakness toward: MMR, DTP, and separately *Rubeola* (measles), *Diphtheria,* and *Mumps.* As the person gets stronger they can clear more things at once. Other vaccines he had a weakness for but we didn't clear this time were *Varicella* (chicken pox), *Rubella, Rabies, Typhoid fever,* and *Scarlet fever.*

Our third session, a month later, I had her test for a few more items that have been used in biological warfare: *Fusarium fungi* (makes the T2 toxin), and *Clostridium perfringens.* He showed a weakness for both of them. We also tested for more items and cleared the previous vaccines: *Varicella virus* (causes chicken pox), *Rubella*, *Rabies*, *Typhoid fever,* and *Scarlet fever,* along with *Aflatoxin,* (used in biological warfare), *Streptococcus, Borna virus* (common in horses), *Molluscum contagiosum* (a pox virus causing little bumps on cheeks and backs of arms), *Coxsackie virus B, Clostridium botulinum* (botulism), and *Clostridium difficile.* Then she made the homeopathic remedies for him to take for the month. One remedy contained the energetic signatures of the pathogens, another contained the vaccines. Homeopathy is based on the premise that like cures like. It gives the body the message to heal itself.

The scariest part of all of this was that from the listing of Pathogens and Toxins with Biological Weapons Potential,[54] Trevor had tested positive for (has been exposed to) the following forms of biological warfare: *Bacillus anthracis* (anthrax), *Clostridium botulinum* (botulism), *Clostridium perfringens* (foodborne pathogen), *Rickettsia prowasecki* (causes Typhus), *Rickettsia rickettsii* (Rocky Mountain spotted fever), *Dengue fever virus,* (Break-bone fever) *Lassa fever virus* (a hemorrhagic fever virus), *Monkeypox virus, Smallpox virus, and aflatoxins* (fungal mycotoxins). We cleared all of them.

Then in our fourth session, we checked for some more bacteria, and he tested positive for 29 of them! *Ehrlichia* and *Babesia* (more co-infections of Lyme) and also the following bacteria with Biological Weapons potential: *Bartonella quintana* (causes Trench fever), *Burkholderia mallei* (causes Glanders), *Burkholderia pseudomallei* (causes melioidosis), *Coxiella burnetti*

---

[54] http://cbwinfo.com/Biological/BWList.shtml

(causes Q fever), *Enterohaemorrhagic Escherichia coli* (E. coli), *Salmonella typhi* (Typhoid), *Vibrio cholerae* (Cholera), and *Yersinia pestis* (Plague).

Other bacteria he had were: *Bartonella henselae* (cat scratch disease), *Bordetella bronchiseptica* (kennel cough), *Camplyobacter coli* (intestinal bacteria), *Camplyobacter jejuni* (foodborne bacteria), *Heliobacter pylori* (causes stomach ulcers and inflammation), *Listeria monocytogenes* (foodborne pathogen), *Leptospira interrogens* (transmitted by dogs), *Porphyromonas gingivalis* (causes periodontal disease), *Salmonella enteritidis* (from eggs), *Salmonella typhimurium* (from peanuts), *Staphylococcus aureus* (nose and skin), *Staphlococcus epidermidis* (on skin), *Streptococcus pneumoniae* (causes pneumonia and ear infections), *Streptococcus agalactiae* (group B strep), *Streptococcus pyogenes* (group A strep), *Vibrio parahaemolyticus* (causes Cholera), *Vibrio vulnificus* (in seafood), *Yersinia enterocolitica* (in food and water), and finally *Yersinia pseudotuberculosis* (foodborne, mimics tuberculosis. This is the bacteria the Soviets inserted myelin toxin into in genetic modifications).

At Trevor's fifth BioSET™ appointment, all of the miasms had cleared. We checked for fungus, molds, and mycotoxins (byproducts of fungus and mold). There are only two fungal pathogens currently considered of significance as biological weapons against humans according to the aforementioned list. They are *Coccidioides immitis* (causes Valley Fever) and *Histoplasma capsulatum* (from bird and bat feces). Trevor tested positive for both of them, along with 32 different types of fungus/mold/yeast and six different mycotoxins including: *Aspergillus, Bipolaris spicifera* (from plants and soil), *Trichothecenes* (mycotoxins used in chemical warfare by Russia), *Trichophyton violaceum* (fungal parasite causes cracked toes and cradle cap), *Wangiella dermatitidis* (soil and plant fungus), *Stachybotrys* (black mold), *Cryptococcus neoformans* (from bird droppings), *Satratoxin-H* (mycotoxins of Stachybotrys), *Rhizopus oryzae* (sinonasal tract fungus), *Penicillium marneffei* (pathogenic penicillin fungus), *Mucor indicus* (fungus on plants and decaying fruits and vegetables), *Microsporum canis* (causes ringworm in dogs and cats), *Fusariotoxin* (mycotoxins from T-2 toxin). The good news was, no *Candida albicans,* which was responsible for the systemic fungal infection he had when he was younger. We cleared *Candida* years ago with probiotics and NAET.

Trevor also tested positive for Stress Induced Sympathetic Dominance, where his Sympathetic nervous system instead of his Parasympathetic nervous system is dominant, which shuts down the immune system, leaving it susceptible to viruses and bacteria. We cleared that as well.

Before Trevor's next appointment, a story came out that researchers at the Whittemore-Peterson Institute in at the University of Nevada, Reno found a retrovirus called XMRV in 67% of Chronic Fatigue patients. A retrovirus copies its genetic code into the DNA of its host but uses RNA- a working form of DNA to do so. Known formally as xenotropic murine leukemia virus-related virus, XMRV has also been found in some prostate tumors and is also known to cause leukemia and tumors in animals. A local autism group sent out an email to our group that stated that they also tested a small group of children with autism, and that 40% of them had the virus as well. The lead researcher said that the finding only shows a link between the virus and Chronic Fatigue Syndrome, and does not prove that the pathogen causes the disorder. Further research is needed to determine whether XMVR directly causes CFS, is just a passenger virus in the suppressed immune systems of suffers or a pathogen that acts in concert with other viruses that have been implicated in the disorder by previous research. (Like *Epstein- Barr virus*.)

So, I asked Trevor's practitioner if she could test him for XMRV using BioSET™ and she said yes. She ordered the vial of the energetic substance, and we did Muscle Response Testing, and there was a weakness. This means he has it or has been exposed to it, or they are allergic to it. I know this sounds crazy to someone who doesn't understand this type of thing. It is not black and white. Read Dr. Ellen Cutler's book *The Food Allergy Cure* and *Say Goodbye to Allergy-Related Autism with NAET* by Devi S. Nambudripad if you want to understand this process more. Sometimes you have to look outside the box for answers.

In addition to XMRV, we tested for other viruses, and found that Trevor has or has been exposed to many other viruses (which we cleared and treated) including *HHV-4 or Epstein-Barr virus* (associated with mononucleosis and Chronic Fatigue Syndrome), *Mad Cow prions* (have been used in biological warfare), three different *Coxsackie viruses*: B-4 variety (can cause type 1 diabetes and used in biological warfare), A-16 variety (causes Hand, Foot, and Mouth disease), and A-24 variety (causes acute hemorrhagic conjunctivitis), *Severe Acute Respiratory Syndrome* (SARS), *Human Respiratory Syncytial virus* (hRSV), *Rift Valley Fever virus* (common in Africa), *St. Louis Encephalitis virus, Japanese Encephalitis virus, Haemopilus influenza type b* (Hib, could be from the vaccine), *Influenza A virus, Human adenovirus f,* and *Kunijin virus* (related to West Nile Virus) as well as *SV-40* (the Simian, yes that means monkey, virus found in the Polio vaccine).

There is an interview you can watch online in which Maurice Hilleman, former chief of Merck's vaccine division admits that they knew about the *SV-40 virus* in the Polio vaccine, which was caused by culturing the vaccine on infected African Green Monkey kidneys.[55] *SV-40* is a known carcinogen, yet they let people get the vaccines anyway. This is another reason that the Polio vaccine is a problem; beside the fact, according to the readings, that it is causing MS in young women.

In our final appointment before this book was published, we found some very interesting things. The practitioner had received

---

[55]http://liveleak.com/view?i=377_1195303011

the actual Ergopathic vial of XMRV from the manufacturer to test Trevor, and he had a weakness for it. It was the same result as the test we did with just the name written down on paper. So, it was a good validation. It didn't clear with the paper only, so we used the vial to clear it this time. He also had a weakness for the *Oropouche virus* and for the bacteria *Cryptosporidium* (in water).

Here's where it gets interesting. I asked the practitioner if she had the vials for potatoes. She had a whole box of nightshades, which include potatoes. Trevor tested a weakness toward Russett potatoes. Then I asked if she had any local dirt in a vial. She did. She had two samples of actual dirt. One was from her yard and one of the dirt from the Reno Rodeo. She also had an Ergopathic vial of common dirt. Trevor tested weak for all three. Then I asked her to get out the vial of *Bacillus anthracis.* He muscle tested strong for it because he had cleared it previously. But when we put the *Bacillus anthracis* in combination with the dirt, he had a weakness. We tested another combination of another bacteria he was not weak toward with the dirt, and he tested strong. We put the dirt back with the *Bacillus anthracis* and he was weak. So, we cleared all of them; the dirt, the potatoes, and the anthrax again, along with the other items.

I also had her check him again for all of the gluten and wheat items and all the dairy items. He was still strong in all forms of it. Yeah! I wondered if he had become re-sensitized to them now that he was eating them again. He hadn't.

After this last session, we are going to move on to the actual BioSET™ autism protocol, which looks great. A lot of the allergy removal we have already done with NAET, but a lot of it is strengthening the body and immune system so it is not susceptible to re-infection. Also, testing for other environmental toxins, nutritional and other deficiencies and excesses, and testing the effectiveness and dosages of the supplements he's currently using. The practitioner was so encouraged by Trevor's fast progress, as well as shocked by our findings, that she said "We are going to have to share this, there are lots of families suffering." Hopefully other practitioners can use this as a guide for things to check for in our kids. This goes to the cause of the problem, not just the deficiencies that resulted from it.

So, now I must ask...how did all of this (insert expletive) get into my child? Some of it I understand, vaccines, the environment, but this is ridiculous! He's never been in a hospital except when he was born, never went out of the country, no one in the family is in the military and he has lived a typical existence, playing outside, running errands with me, mommy and me classes when he was younger.

I believe that because of the hit he took when he was exposed to the biological warfare in the environment and became "mummified," his immune system was so suppressed, that he was vulnerable to contracting anything and everything that came across his path. The proverbial canary in the coal mine. So, the presence of or exposure to all of these pathogens does not necessarily mean they are the "cause" of autism. Correlation does not equal causation. But I have to ask, how did he get exposed to all of these things? Are they in the air, the food, the water, or the vaccines he received? A little here, a little there?

I felt blessed that I found a treatment modality that could address these issues and get them out of his body. I know he still has a way to go with this protocol, but I wanted to include it because it gives a treatment option until the cure is discovered and implemented.

Progress

The question remains, have I seen any progress in Trevor? Yes, I have. After we began these BioSET™ treatments, he began to make lots of verbal gains, and every month he progresses more. The first month, he knocked on my bedroom door in the morning (very appropriately), climbed in bed next to me, and said, "Mommy, I want pancakes, please." He used to just barge in the room and say, "Pancakes, please." He also knew we were going fishing with his grandparents who were visiting one weekend, and he said spontaneously, "Ready to go fishing." I looked at him in disbelief, and smothered him with hugs and kisses and told everyone what he said. We were all proud of his accomplishment.

He also began labeling things and using the person's name to whom it belonged. For instance, "That's Grandma's lemonade." He used to just label the item with the word, "lemonade." He also began asking for me whenever I wasn't home. "I want mommy please." He also started talking in more complete sentences, for instance, he began saying "Be careful, that's very hot" while sitting near the stove. He also started answering "Wh" questions.

I can now ask him "What animal says 'moo, moo?' and he answers all animal noises correctly. He used to only tell you what sound a particular animal made, not which animal made it. I can ask him what he had for dinner, and he answers, 'I ate noodles,' or whatever it was that he ate. I can even ask what he ate at a certain meal, breakfast, lunch or dinner and he correctly answers me. He also answers the question "What are you watching?" with the correct name of the DVD he's watching.

He has also been saying spontaneous, unprompted things that surprise me all the time. For instance, he was taking a bath and he had been in there a while and he said on his own "Pull the plug, please." What? Where did he learn that? I give him his bath every night and he never hears me say that; I just unplug it when I think he's done and tell him it's time to get out. He also hands me the water container and says, "Wash hair please, mommy." He asks for people by name to do things with him, for instance, "Jump on the trampoline please, mommy please." He even asks to go see the practitioner who does his treatments by name. I think he knows it is helping him. He asks her for the click, clicks (acupressure tool) and always hugs her and tells her goodbye.

One day, shortly after our last session, Trevor's brother hit his head on the door when they were chasing each other and started crying. For the first time ever, Trevor showed some sympathy and asked him, "Damon, what's the matter?" Normally, he appears to be oblivious to other people's pain or feelings. This was another breakthrough for him. He also started teasing and imitating Damon when he's upset like a big brother would. It was very typical behavior, and very refreshing. He's also been joining Damon and I in our nightly dance party, having fun dancing and laughing with us. After his bath, he says, "Dancing, please." He's learning new moves and social skills.

On a physical level, the cracks between his toes that he's had for years finally started healing (from the fungus *Trichophyton violaceum*). Also the little white dots on his cheeks are clearing up (from *Molluscum contagiosum*). He stopped wetting his bed at night. His screaming has also diminished dramatically. He sometimes goes a whole day without a meltdown. Imagine that. He used to scream and cry for hours at a time sometimes for no apparent reason. I think I have permanent hearing loss because of it. No joke. As you can probably guess by this surge of progress, I plan to continue this protocol as long as necessary.

I have also been using some new supplements from Klaire Labs™, which is a division of Prothera, Inc.® I know a few company employees, as they are based in Reno, NV. They have incredible products specifically designed for children on the autism spectrum. Their products are dairy-free and gluten-free, hypoallergenic and vegetarian capsules. He uses their probiotic ABx Support, which includes *Saccharomyces boulardii* which supports against *Clostridium difficile* and other intestinal pathogens. He also takes their multivitamin/mineral supplement VitaSpectrum which includes all of the nutritional deficits common in Autism Spectrum Disorders. He takes their Vital-Zymes chewable digestive enzymes which assist in the breakdown of a wide range of proteins, peptides, fats, complex carbohydrates, sugars, and fibers. Serratia peptidase helps protect GI tissues against inflammation. Enzymes with DPP-IV activity and a full range of disaccharidases are included. He also takes one of their new products called Interfase Plus which has been documented to reduce the Biofilm activity of many of the pathogens that Trevor tested positive for including *E. coli, H. pylori, Staphylococcus aureus*, two *Streptococcus* varieties, as well as *Candida.* He also takes their Amino Acid Complete, as he tested deficient in many of them. But only a doctor or healthcare professional can order them. Visit their website, klaire.com.

So, since I heard the messages in these readings, I have made some changes in Trevor's protocol. I have removed potatoes and other root vegetables from his diet. I use distilled water for cooking his foods and drinking water. I started testing for and clearing biological warfare agents and other pathogens with BioSET™ and using homeopathic formulas that include the energetic signature of the cleared pathogens. I have added supplements that support the removal of harmful pathogens and give him the nutritional supports his body needs. Most of all, I give him lots of love. I understand what happened to him now, and don't blame him when he's having a bad day. I know that he will overcome this, and I will be with him every step of the way.

***

DISCUSSION

After reading all of the information presented in this book, one can't help but ask, "What do we do with this information?" All resources need to be utilized to complete the puzzle. Many things need to be done; including but not limited to the following...

1. First and foremost, is this information true? Without evidence, one can only speculate. Hard scientific proof needs to be found proving that our children with autism have what is suggested in this book; a form of biological warfare that "mummified" them. Because the readings said that this is new technology and potentially undetectable, that may prove to be a challenge.

2. Proof of what is going on in Hawthorne. Is there an underground city producing biological warfare? We need military personnel and scientists who worked on this that are willing to come forward and break their oaths to tell the truth.

3. Testing of the soil. I don't have the resources personally, but I am sure someone in the autism or scientific community does. If the topsoil is so contaminated in certain areas that we shouldn't be growing food on it, it needs to be tested. If people are being contaminated by potatoes and other root vegetables as the readings suggest, it is a health issue for all of us. Again, detection may be an issue.

4. Environmental clean-up. If the topsoil and water that we drink are contaminated with biological warfare, it needs to be not only tested, but cleaned up.

5. The food problem. It was mentioned in the readings that we need to be growing food in salt water because of the contaminated topsoil. Large hydroponic gardens will need to be started. Animals need to be on high ground and eat uncontaminated grass and food themselves.

6. A new label for our children. The children with regressive "autism" who are actually contaminated should not have

the label of "autism." It is inaccurate and they will not be tested and treated appropriately in the future with the wrong label. Also, when children with "autism" who begin to improve, they should not just be downgraded to another inappropriate label such as ADHD. It is also inaccurate. The school districts, doctors, and diagnosing agencies will need to take a look at this.

7. Who are the various people mentioned in the reading? If anyone recognizes any of them, please contact me. Who is the man currently working on the cure with the temper? Who is John Pecan (spelling may be wrong)? The man with the theory who can help with the cure. The younger man following in the footsteps of the older man who can help with this? Who is the group in Washington/Oregon area that was mentioned? Maybe this information will be a jump start and we won't have to wait 30 years for the cure.

8. Reparations. If this information is true, families deserve to be compensated for the financial and personal losses they suffered as a result of war. Not to mention the children themselves; they should be taken care of for life

if necessary. Most families of children with autism had to finance most, if not all, of their child's treatments. They are excluded from health insurance because of their label, which is a separate issue. If the government caused this, they should be liable.

9. Starting the Big Brothers and Big Sisters-type program for autism that was mentioned in the readings in different cities. If you want to help out in this manner, contact me by email or the website in the contact section. Maybe this can be affiliated with an existing autism organization. I don't want to reinvent the wheel, maybe just add another spoke.

10. Part of the Big Brothers and Big Sisters-type program included using gifted mediums and psychics. They can help parents develop their telepathy and other types of phenomenon that were mentioned in the book as ways that our "crystal children" can communicate with us. Again, if you can help in this manner, contact me; I will be setting all of this up.

11. Arms control. If advanced biological weapons are being created in the U.S., other countries, and even rogue nations, it needs to stop! Clearly, the BWC treaty is not being followed or enforced. Things need to be done on a Governmental level to keep this situation from getting worse.

12. People and organizations with the financial resources for testing and development of the cure. So many of things take money. This is a medical issue, with a medical solution. Scientists, physicists, mathematicians, brainiacs; this is your chance to use that gift!

13. Getting this information out there. I am only one person. I published this book myself to get it out as quickly as possible instead of going the traditional publishing route. I don't have the time or resources for extensive marketing. If anyone has any ideas to get the message out, I'm open to suggestions.

14. Help setting up the website. Volunteers?

CONTACT

This book is the foundation, yet there is much more to discover. If this book is going to do what it is intended to do, put a stop to and find the cure for autism, it is going to take people to come forward who want to make a difference. So, if anyone reading this has any information that they can share to validate any of the information from the messages in this book, or that can help in any way, please contact me through the email address below. I can't do this alone.

I am putting a call out there to all scientists who can understand this and want to help, to anyone who has inside information or knowledge that they are willing to share, and especially to military people who can validate the underground facility and activity. For the sake of the children, please come forward. We need to stop this tragedy!

I've set up a website at www.foundationofdiscovery.com. If the email is not set up yet, or is full, I can be also be reached by email at foundationofdiscovery@yahoo.com. To be clear, all shared information becomes my property to do with as I see fit, without any obligation or compensation to the sender. I may decide to use it in a future publication, for instance, an updated version of this book. If you choose to remain anonymous, say so, and I will absolutely respect your wishes.

***

ABOUT THE AUTHOR

Laura Hirsch was born and raised in Wisconsin and graduated from the University of Wisconsin-Whitewater with a Bachelor of Arts degree in Speech Communications. She is the author of *Widowed Too Soon: A Young Widow's Journey through Grief, Healing, and Spiritual Transformation;* an autobiography about her experience of being a young widow which led to her investigation of mediumship as a therapeutic avenue for grief. She is also a contributing author of a short story called *Trevor* about Auditory Integration Training in the book *Sound of Falling Snow.*

Laura met her second husband, Matt, and moved to his home state of California in 1995, where they had two beautiful sons, Trevor and Damon, before moving to Reno, NV in 2002. While living in California, their older son Trevor was diagnosed with autism. Laura knew that her son was not born that way, which set her on a quest for answers to bring her son back. Her devotion to her son led her back to mediumship to find the answer to the question, what happened to my child?

Laura is active in the autism community as a volunteer Rescue Angel for Generation Rescue. She is also involved with many autism groups including FEAT (Families for Effective Autism Treatment of Northern Nevada), TACA (Talk About Curing Autism) and ACON (Autism Coalition of Nevada). She volunteers and participates in local autism fund-raisers. Her passion is to be a voice for children with autism, whose voices were taken away.

***